Stories Find You, Places Know

Stories Find You, Places Know

YUP'IK NARRATIVES OF A SENTIENT WORLD

Holly Cusack-McVeigh

THE UNIVERSITY OF UTAH PRESS
Salt Lake City

The Defiance House Man colophon is a registered trademark of The University of Utah Press. It is based on a four-foot-tall Ancient Puebloan pictograph (late PIII) near Glen Canyon, Utah.

Printed and bound in the United States of America.

Library of Congress Cataloging-in-Publication Data

Names: Cusack-McVeigh, Holly, author.
Title: Stories find you, places know : Yup'ik narratives of a sentient world / Holly Cusack-McVeigh.
Description: Salt Lake City : University of Utah Press, [2017] | Includes bibliographical references and index. |
Identifiers: LCCN 2017021796 (print) | LCCN 2017028118 (ebook) | ISBN 9781607815839 () | ISBN 9781607815822 (pbk.)
Subjects: LCSH: Yupik Eskimos—Alaska—Yukon-Kuskokwim Delta—Folklore. | Ethnology—Alaska—Yukon-Kuskokwim Delta. | Discourse analysis, Narrative—Alaska—Yukon-Kuskokwim Delta. | Oral tradition—Alaska—Yukon-Kuskokwim Delta. | Storytelling—Alaska—Yukon-Kuskokwim Delta. | Folklore—Performance—Alaska—Yukon-Kuskokwim Delta. | Yupik Eskimos—Alaska—Yukon-Kuskokwim Delta—Religion. | Shamans—Alaska—Yukon-Kuskokwim Delta.
Classification: LCC E99.E7 (ebook) | LCC E99.E7 C87 2017 (print) | DDC 398.20897/140798—dc23

LC record available at https://lccn.loc.gov/2017021796

for *Cugmir*

CONTENTS

LIST OF FIGURES

ACKNOWLEDGMENTS

Quyana caqneq to my friends and collaborators in Hooper Bay for sharing their stories and understandings of place, but also for opening their homes and hearts to me. I cherish memories of jigging for smelts on the sea ice, catching tomcods on the riverbank, hunting for mouse food on the tundra, collecting wood on the beach, listening to stories in the steam bath, and, yes, "cutting" (okay, mutilating) my first fish at fish camp. A special word of thanks to the Hooper Bay elders who shared their knowledge and will always be among my most important teachers. I will "go back and follow" your words.

I wish to acknowledge the current and former members of the Hooper Bay Traditional Council and the city of Hooper Bay for giving me their trust and willingly including me in many projects, and the village of Chevak for their invitation to participate in the mapping initiative. Through these collaborations I gained a deeper understanding of the power of place.

A very special word of thanks to former Hooper Bay Traditional Council president Bosco Olson, friend and collaborator. I have never known a person who demonstrated a greater capacity for leadership. Thank you for sharing the knowledge of your elders, your understandings of place, and, yes, even your *iluraat* (teasing cousins)!

This book would not have reached completion without the continual encouragement and guidance of my mentor and dear friend Phyllis Morrow, whose thoughtful reading of multiple drafts and invaluable insights helped this work take meaningful shape. Understanding intimately the challenges of doing truly collaborative work that results in relevant scholarship (sometimes "shaky ground"), she is an important role model and continued source of inspiration.

I owe a debt of gratitude to my friends and generous colleagues who have influenced my thinking and encouraged this work in so many different ways: Yvonne L. Parsons, for her unfailing encouragement throughout the writing of this book—Miigwech Niidj; Karen Evanoff, for sharing the wisdom of her own elders—Chinaan; Kenneth Austin—Gunalcheesh Te Shaa Kee; Chase Hensel, for teaching me the importance of food and subsistence activities in southwestern Alaska, an understanding that allowed me to fit in so genuinely; William Schneider, whose work reminds me that it is not enough to simply create an oral record for future generations, but that we must also struggle to share our understanding and the richness of our experience; Barre Toelken, a leader in our field who always shows a genuine interest in the work of emerging scholars; Megan Musgrave, my colleague and friend, for holding me accountable to our weekly writing dates; Elsie Mather, whose written words have guided me; Eliza Cingarkaq Orr, for her excellent work on the transcription and translations of the recorded narratives; Sue Mitchell of Inkworks, for both her friendship and professional editing of this manuscript at various stages; Dorothy Lippert of the Smithsonian Institution, National Museum of Natural History Repatriation Office; Indiana University–Purdue University of Indianapolis' (IUPUI) colleagues Larry J. Zimmerman, Paul Mullins, Sue Hyatt, and Elee Wood, for providing invaluable feedback of my written work; Stephen Towne in Special Collections at IUPUI Library; Edith Millikan and Mary Cox, for their assistance with grant writing during the final phases of this research; my graduate student research assistant, Rebecca Jacobs; Lawrence Kaplan at the Alaska Native Language Center for permission to incorporate previously published material; Aldona Jonitis and Angela Linn at the University of Alaska Museum of the North; the staff at the Alaska and Polar Regions Collections & Archives; George Nicholas, Julie Hallowell, and my many colleagues at the Intellectual Property Issues in Cultural Heritage project (IPinCH) at Simon Fraser University; David Kingma at the Gonzaga University Archives and Special Collections for always making the archival collections accessible to me while I worked in Alaska, and later, at IUPUI. Thanks also to the Mellick family, Julie Cruikshank, William A. Fox, Patricia Partnow, Mary C. Pete, Robin Barker, Carol Zane Jolles, Ann Fienup-Riordan, Alice Rearden, Marie Meade, Anthony Woodbury, Walkie Charles, Stephen Jacobson, Robert Drozda, Louann Rank, Susan Hansen, and James Barker. I am grateful to John Alley, editor in chief at the University of Utah Press, for his belief in this project, and the anonymous peer reviewers whose constructive criticism helped me move this work forward.

Several of the chapters in this book were delivered as professional papers at annual conferences, benefitting greatly from the comments and questions of my peers. For these opportunities, I thank the Alaska Anthropological Association, the American Anthropological Association, the American Folklore Society, the American Society for Ethnohistory, and the Oral History Association.

I wish to acknowledge the Alaska Humanities Forum for their belief in our community-based projects; the Office of the Vice Chancellor for Research at IUPUI for support through the Release Time for Research (RTR) award; the staff in the IUPUI School of Liberal Arts dean's office; my colleagues in the Department of Anthropology at the University of Alaska Fairbanks; my colleagues in the Anthropology Department of Indiana University School of Liberal Arts at IUPUI and the Museum Studies Program at IUPUI.

This publication would not have been possible without the continual love and support of my family. To my husband, Darren J. McVeigh, my son, Shane, and my daughter, Kayla (Cugmi): thank you for always playing an important part in my work. To my parents, Dennis E. Cusack and Nancy M. Cusack, and my mother-in-law, Adele McVeigh, three incredibly loving grandparents who helped when I was away doing fieldwork, and in memory of my grandmothers, Jessie M. Becker and Wanda F. Cusack, whose own stories vividly colored my world.

PREFACE

My First Day in Hooper

A Cautionary Tale for the Anthropologist

On the evening in 1996 when I first arrived in Hooper Bay, Alaska, summer was in full swing on the Bering Sea coast. The tundra was alive with activity. The return of waterfowl and long days had signaled the beginning of a very busy time in the village. The beauty of this place struck me before the plane ever touched the runway. As we made our approach, I suddenly recalled the words of a *kass'aq* man I had met in the Bethel airport (the regional hub) earlier that same morning. The Yup'ik Eskimo word *kass'aq* translates to "white person" or "outsider." When I told him where I was going, he simply replied, "Oh, you will love the beach." It struck me then, as it does now, a strange comment to make about a community. His words left a lasting impression. It is true that this is a beautiful place, but this outsider's statement felt strangely incomplete. What about the people in this place? That kass'aq wasn't wrong, I *did* love the beach, but I also came to have many close, lasting friendships in the community.

The gravel airstrip is bordered on one side by a vast expanse of grass-covered sand dunes and flat, dark sandy beach that extends as far up and down the coast as the eye can see. Towards the village there is a stretch of grassy tundra interspersed with hundreds of tiny ponds and Napareayak Slough, a winding river that flows to the Bering Sea. Farther inland from the village is another wide expanse of open, grassy tundra that stretches away from the coast toward the Askinuk Mountains.

Shortly before the plane touched the gravel airstrip, several people gathered down below, coming by four-wheelers to greet family members or to claim mail-order groceries and supplies. I got off the plane, clutching the large foam-board poster that proudly displayed a sampling of the archival black and white photographs I hoped to "visually repatriate" to the community. The wind whipped at the poster as I awkwardly looked around for my ride. A woman finally approached me, "Holly?" I nodded as she smiled and said to me, "Welcome to Hooper Bay."

In an instant I was sitting on the back of her four-wheeler (all-terrain vehicle), racing down the long stretch of gravel road that leads from the airstrip to the village. I was holding on to the four-wheeler, my luggage, and the project poster with everything I had. The poster board was almost torn from my hands as it flung wildly from side to side. I thought about the numerous flights I had taken that day to get here and how I had insisted on carefully hand-carrying the item. I laughed to myself as I imagined the irony of losing it somewhere on the tundra in those last few miles of my journey.

When we reached the Sea Lion Hotel, an ATCO unit (modular building) owned by the Sea Lion Native Corporation and situated at the edge of town, she shut off the engine of her four-wheeler and helped me carry my bags to the weathered, wooden boardwalk. She sat with me for a few moments and we visited. I told her that I was a graduate student in Fairbanks. We talked briefly about our families and my reason for coming to Hooper Bay. Before long she was telling me a story about a kass'aq woman who had come to Hooper Bay to work on a similar project. She told me that this woman "drove the elders crazy" with her insistent questioning.

Soon after that, we parted company, she on her four-wheeler and me still sitting on that boardwalk pondering her words. She had directed the story about the kass'aq woman who "drove the elders crazy with questions" at me. Her tale was a cautionary one and it would serve me well in the weeks, months, and even years to follow. Her message was simple: there is a right way and a wrong way to learn from the elders; find the right way!

It does not escape this author that I've opened with the well-worn trope of an anthropologist entering "the field," but my first impressions of this place and the ways in which stories began to find me are important in terms of framing this book.

Most of the stories and personal narratives in this work were shared with me in the context of daily life and, only later, were some recorded. Stories found me sitting on the riverbank fishing, around the table sipping tea after dinner, in a steam bath with friends, or busily collecting driftwood on the beach.

These stories—of place and in places—are an active part of day-to-day living in Hooper Bay. Experiencing them allowed me to understand something about a lived sense of story and place, an approach that follows in the footsteps of other scholars like Julie Cruikshank, Phyllis Morrow, and Bill Schneider.

I have adopted a style of writing that reflects the way these narratives came to me personally as a listener and learner, on more than one occasion over several years. I am telling a story myself. My story reflects the nature of the information people conveyed and the manner in which I learned it. This style allows me to show readers how I have learned particular narratives. As anthropologist Carol Zane Jolles reminds us, "Native experts and non-Native researchers interweave their life histories and storied lives in the course of field research" (Jolles 1994, 86). I cannot offer an emic analysis (inside perspective) of the stories that have been shared with me over the years. I can, however, offer explanations and raise questions that are informed by an emic understanding of Yup'ik places as expressed through story and personal narratives.

Many of the stories were recorded only after a friend or community member had shared the story with me in a personal context. For example, I simply asked tellers, "Do you remember that story you told me about the giant footprints? Could we sit down with a recorder so that I could get your words to paper exactly as you told the story to me?" Sometimes people declined to retell their story with a recorder running. But more often than not, I already had rapport with the tellers and they accommodated the request in spite of their discomfort, teasing me about my lack of memory and insistent habit of "getting it right." Some of the stories presented here were originally recorded as part of my doctoral dissertation research at the University of Alaska Fairbanks.

When we sat down to record, I presented a consent form. While community elders were often reluctant to sign something that signifies a "transfer of title, interest, and copyright," given a well-grounded historical distrust of "outsiders," we were always able to work through these tensions. One Hooper Bay community elder, when I asked him to sign a release, teasingly stated that if I didn't have his permission I wouldn't be sitting in his kitchen having tea and listening to stories! Similarly, Pomo elder Mabel McKay told author Greg Sarris to write her story but not to record her words. She trusted him, her friend, not the recording machine, to tell her story (Sarris 1994). Many tellers did prefer to remain anonymous. For one reason, many Yupiit do not wish to go on record as some kind of "cultural expert" (Mather 1985; Hensel 1992). People freely share stories but are often reluctant to claim the knowledge as somehow individually "owned." They are also concerned about making mistakes. Although I would like to acknowledge each teller by name, I have honored each individual's decision.

Like people everywhere, Yupiit imbue places with story. But for Yupiit, places—and the land in general—also respond to people. This experience and the strong feelings it evokes are consonant with long-held understandings. But beyond their general connections with Yup'ik cosmology/worldview, physical changes in certain places are, in a more specific sense, a barometer of social and personal wellbeing. And, as I will demonstrate in the final chapters, the stories associated with human-made places are a barometer of intergroup social relations and the resultant tensions.

One of the greatest honors bestowed on me over the years has been the opportunity to visit and work with elders at Hooper Bay. It is they who have helped me to understand these relationships between stories and particular kinds of places. I use the term "elder" to refer to those community leaders who are respected for their knowledge and life experience. Through various projects, we have shared happy and sad times. I consider them my teachers and hope that my deep respect is clearly felt throughout this work. The knowledge freely shared with me not only informs this book, but, more importantly, it has guided me to "live right."

I am writing with two intended, overlapping audiences in mind. This work is largely grounded in anthropological and folkloric theory and, as such, I write for an academic audience. I draw upon a body of established literature. I have, however, another intended audience. With each line I write I ask myself how a Yup'ik audience will see and respond to my words. While anthropologists used to assume that their "informants" would almost never read what was written about them, I both hope and expect that Yupiit will.

I also aspire to produce a book that gives all my readers, Yup'ik and non-Yup'ik, academic and nonacademic, food for thought. Perhaps it will stimulate dialogue between audiences and lead to a better understanding of how people relate to places—and places to people. My greatest hope is that my deep respect for Yup'ik culture and worldview is strongly felt by all of my readers and that the way I have interpreted and presented Yup'ik narrative is viewed not as distant analysis, but rather as a heartfelt struggle to better understand what people have shared with me and why.

In July of 2015, the Hooper Bay Traditional Council asked me to give a community presentation at a Native Village of Hooper Bay and City of Hooper Bay joint public meeting on some of the past cultural heritage projects the council and I had collaborated on over the years. Among the projects discussed was the long, hard journey of returning Hooper Bay ancestors and their funerary objects from the Smithsonian Institution's National Museum of Natural History. At the completion of the presentation, and to my great astonishment, the tribal chief announced that they had decided to make me an honorary tribal member of the Native Village of Hooper Bay. No greater honor could be bestowed upon me. With this status comes even greater responsibility to make a difference in the community by continuing to give back. I have a responsibility to share my knowledge and understanding with the generations to come and I take that role very seriously.

As I have worked over the years to understand these teachings and shape this book for publication, one very important audience has remained on my mind and in my heart: the youth of Hooper Bay. These young people are the knowledge bearers for generations yet to come. Having worked with Hooper Bay youth on several projects over the years, I am inspired by their resilience and resolve. It is another small way to "put back" into the community that has given so much, but all royalties from the sale of this publication will go directly to the Hooper Bay Youth and Elder group.

Yup'ik storytellers at Nunivak Island employed a particular phrase when concluding their tales. They ended their stories by saying, "May all my small mistakes go into their places and make little noise" (Himmelheber 1993, 84). This understanding is especially relevant when one considers the potential power that words possess, a power that is considered especially strong for Yupiit. As the author of this book, I am cognizant of this responsibility as I put words to the page. I've done my best to convey what I have learned and it is my hope, above all else, that my deep respect is abundantly evident and that my own mistakes will go into their places.

A note to the reader concerning archival sources: When I began my archival research, I was accessing the material on microfilm. The microfilming of the Alaska Mission Collection followed the organization of the Oregon Province Archives and contained 730 manuscripts (49,816 pages) written by Jesuit missionaries in Alaska from 1886 to 1955. Documents were separated into mission stations (reels 1–25) and biographical material on the missionaries (reels 26–42). In 2014, Gale Cengage Learning launched *Indigenous Peoples: North America*, an online database sourced from both American and Canadian institutions. The collection consists of thousands of archival records including the Alaska Mission Collection. The online materials for the Alaska Mission Collection do not follow the original ordering of the microfilm rolls and thus, I cite them differently and include the last access date. In-text citations labeled "AM Collection" were accessed on microfilm, while citations labeled by the specific names of the mission or missionary (i.e., John P. Fox Collection or the Hooper Bay Collection) refer to Alaska Mission Collections that were accessed through the Gale Cengage Learning online database.

1

Introduction

This work is grounded in existing understandings of Yup'ik folklore, cosmology, and worldview. It builds on the contributions of various scholars, including Fienup-Riordan, Hensel, Mather, Morrow, and Pete, but is unique in centering on how a Yup'ik community uses their stories of place within the context of social life. Moving beyond a general discussion of sense of place, my work explores the ways that people relate to each other through places and the lore associated with those places. The tales also demonstrate the ways that community members relate to specific kinds of places and how those particular places relate to people.

By showing how community members interact with different types of places, both features on the land and human-made structures, and how places interact with community members, I also hope to make a unique contribution to the literature on place. One compelling aspect of my work is the understanding that for Yupiit, places are not only imbued with story and expressive of moral principles (as Basso 1996 demonstrated), but are in essence actors themselves that react to human actions and states of being. People learn about people through encounters on the land, but places also learn about people through such encounters.

Different groups and academic fields variously treat the term *sense of place* as the way people feel about or perceive a place, be it a community, a landmark, a space, or a region. The phrase is often used in relation to those characteristics that make a place special or unique, as well as to those that foster a sense of authentic human attachment and belonging. Others, such as geographer Yi-Fu Tuan (1980), have pointed to senses of place that are not inherently "positive," such as fear. The term is also increasingly used in urban and rural studies in relation to place-making and place-attachment of communities to their environment, homeland, or even a neighborhood.

Anthropologist Leslie Main Johnson's discussion of Kaska ethnoecology prompted me to think about "kinds of place," how people discern meaning (Johnson and Hunn 2010, 203), and how that process applies to the specific types of stories and narratives that have been shared with me. While I did not set out to record an ethnogeography (or ethnoecology) of the landscape, Johnson's perspective has led me to examine distinctions in Yup'ik conceptions of place.

This is not, however, a systematic effort to collect stories[1] or create a typology of Yup'ik story and place. Such an attempt could perhaps be approached by bringing people to different places and eliciting the stories that they associate with those places. Elicitation, however, misses the natural environment of storytelling, and with it, much of the meaning to the people who make sense with stories and the places with which they connect. *None* of the recorded/published "collections" of Yup'ik stories include *any* told and alluded to spontaneously in the course of ordinary interactions. All of them have been elicited in some way. The researchers and educators who recorded them began with "tell me stories about X" or "what stories do you remember hearing as a child," or "do you know any Raven stories," etc. Such elicited tellings often happen in comparatively formal settings (an elder's conference, classroom, land claims documentation) divorced from day-to-day activities. While I, too, include some stories recorded in such contexts, my focus is entirely different.

This book is, instead, a contextualized treatment of narratives that emerged naturally as I moved from place to place along with the tellers, and whoever else was along, as they went about their daily activities. It is thus, in a sense, an ethnography of narrative and narration in and around a single community. It is, if you will, a natural sampling. And this natural sample suggests that while a basic emphasis on the importance of awareness (and consequences of the lack thereof) underpin Yup'ik stories, different narrative elements are indeed associated with different types of places, some human-made and others not. Corresponding to these differences, the stories variously reveal ideas about relationships among human groups and relationships between humans and nonhumans. This hints at a systematic correlation between places and particular narrative elements that I integrate into my overall argument, one not previously explored by anthropologists or folklorists.

Finally, readers will note that the chapters are loosely ordered from places that are general features on the land in areas beyond the village to human-made structures in the village and out on the tundra. There is also a rough chronology in their order. Thinking about the narrative elements associated with different types of places reinforces this order, as I progressively reveal the relationship between stories and the places with which they are associated. This allows me to end with some discussion of the significance, in narratives, of what happens to people in preexisting land features (volcano, hill); features that are not exactly "human-made" but result from human behavior (giant footprints); bodies of water; and human-made structures of different types (graves, abandoned houses, a church).

It was the fall of 1995, while working in the Alaska and Polar Regions Archives at the University of Alaska Fairbanks, when I first came across the large collection of black-and-white photographs taken at Hooper Bay by Disney that I later set out to visually repatriate. These images taken by Alfred and Elma Milotte in 1946 (figure 1.1), along with personal letters, travel journals, and other documents, had only recently been donated to the Alaska and Polar Regions Department. The photographs and related documents had not yet been fully processed or assigned accession numbers, and most of the images lacked any kind of contextual information.

Walt Disney himself hired the Milottes because he was interested in capturing images of Eskimo[2] people for his *People and Places* film series. The images became the basis of a short film entitled *Alaskan Eskimo*. Disney's goal was to achieve "complete photographic honesty, without bias, and to study people as they have been influenced in nature and custom by environment" (Fienup-Riordan 1995, 140). But the twenty-six-and-a-half-minute film, although it won awards for Disney, is fraught with stereotypic images of Eskimo peoples, reflecting many of the misconceptions that people have about cultures of the North.[3]

FIGURE 1.1. Disney photographer at Hooper Bay, 1946. Alaska & Polar Regions Collections & Archives, University of Alaska Fairbanks

Several authors have written about the stereotypes of Eskimo people, noting that twentieth-century literature and films produced by Hollywood in the 1920s and 1930s, such as Robert Flaherty's 1922 silent film *Nanook of the North*, cast Eskimo peoples as passive, peaceful characters set against a harsh climate (Brody 1987; Cusack-McVeigh 2015; Fienup-Riordan 1990). Canadian Arctic researcher Hugh Brody traces pre-Hollywood images of "the Eskimo" to the journals and ship logs of early 1800s explorers who were in search of a Northwest Passage. The Parry Expeditions of 1819, 1821, and 1824, for example, brought a familiarity with Inuit peoples of the central Canadian Arctic. Thus,

Westerners soon associated all Eskimo peoples with igloos, and this "became the Eskimo of our imagination" (Brody 1987, 19).

From the early drawings of the famed 1824 Lyon Expedition comes the stereotypic image of an eternally jovial people. "The Eskimo makes his and her appearance with a smile" (Brody 1987, 19). For a more in-depth discussion of Eskimo stereotypes and how they are perpetuated in contemporary settings, see my discussion on the Intellectual Property Issues in Cultural Heritage (IPinCH) blog page titled Appropriation(?) of the Month: "The Eskimo of Our Imagination" (Cusack-McVeigh 2015).

In March of 1953, *The Hollywood Reporter* proclaimed that this film would have broad public appeal, stating that *Alaskan Eskimo* was a "fascinating pic." The review stated that "of particular fascination is the industriousness, enterprise and resourcefulness of the Eskimos in coping with their raw and largely barren surroundings, the way they live in absolute freedom and in harmony with each other" (APRD, Milotte Collection, 31).

While the stereotypes perpetuated by Disney annoy listeners today, they also are met with a sense of humor in Hooper Bay. At one point the film shows a Hooper Bay family sharing *akutaq* (also known in English as "Eskimo ice cream"). The Disney narrator boldly and authoritatively mispronounces the Yup'ik word as "ack-you-tack" rather than akutaq (correctly pronounced, roughly, "uh-goo-duck"). This became a standing joke among people working on the project, who poked fun at the seriously flawed pronunciation of a common Yup'ik word.

Akutaq, "literally a 'mixture,' most frequently a mixture of whipped shortening, sugar, and berries" (Hensel 1996, 20), has always been an important food for Yupiit. This dish has played an important role in Yup'ik ceremonial life. "*Akutaq* (the tallow, seal oil, and berry mixture) . . . was a particularly valuable item for a woman to contribute" to ceremonial occasions held in the *qasgiq* [4] (a traditional semisubterranean men's house and place of ceremonial gatherings), (Morrow 1984, 116). In 1913, Hawkes described this dish as an important part of Yup'ik Eskimo ceremonialism and gifting, describing akutaq as "a concoction of reindeer tallow, blueberries, and chunks of whitefish kneaded in the snow until it is frozen" (Hawkes 1913, 9).

Akutaq remains a valued food among Yupiit and is often made for family gatherings and community celebrations. Eliza Cingarkaq Orr and Ben Orr write that akutaq is "an important dessert, feast and gift food made of a mixture of berries and fat" (Orr and Orr 1995, xiii). The women who have taught me to make akutaq, in Hooper Bay and in other Yup'ik villages, take great pride in their particular recipes. One woman I know in Hooper Bay always uses Crisco and *aatunaq* or sourdock (*Rumex arcticus*) with whatever berries are in season. Collected from the local tundra, this plant is valued for its high nutritional value of vitamin C. Sometimes the secret ingredient is *anlleq* or "mouse food" [seeds and roots gathered from vole caches on the tundra] or a certain kind of whitefish; other times it is the addition of "Betty Crocker's instant mashed potatoes."

Most importantly, people make and share akutaq because of its continued importance as a mark of cultural identity and pride. The discourse surrounding such an identity marker is also very significant for Yupiit. Anthropologist Chase Hensel writes, "In the same way that turkey is obligatory for Euro-American Thanksgiving, *akutaq* [Eskimo ice cream] is required for feasts" (Hensel 1996, 66).

More than once that first year I was asked if I would "like some ack-you-tack," followed by much laughter. This Disney narrator's mistake is marked and met with humor because it is so characteristic of the often authoritative and yet ignorant stance of outsiders. If akutaq is a strong identity marker[5] for Yupiit, then this flawed pronunciation is a clear marker of the outsiders' ignorance.

There were other instances of ignorance and stereotyping in the collection. I recall stumbling upon a letter written by Walt Disney in which he informs the film makers, Alfred and Elma Milotte, that the Yup'ik Eskimo drumming music they had recorded in Hooper Bay would not make the final cut. Walt Disney, in a letter to the Milottes, wrote that this music, recorded in either Hooper Bay or Kashunuk for the documentary soundtrack, was too far from what his audience would expect (APRD, Milotte Collection, 31). Instead, Disney settled upon a studio-generated soundtrack reminiscent of the old "Indian drum beat" music popularized by Western "cowboy and Indian" films. Apparently the Yup'ik music of Hooper Bay was just *too* Eskimo for Disney.

The black-and-white still shots, lacking narration, do depict a wide range of community activities. Some were clearly posed, but others appear to be more candid in nature. Like many archival collections, the images had little in the way of identification. There was no real contextual information to accompany the images. A few handwritten notations were made, but most naively identified the people in superficial ways. One image, which showed a group of Hooper Bay children playing in the snow, simply read "Our little Eskimo friends." It is important to understand these early stereotypic images and how they emerged. Understanding these stereotypes helps us to understand the misconceptions and ongoing tensions that exist between Yupiit and non-Yupiit. This is a central point and will be addressed several times throughout this work, where we see how such contrasts emerge in daily discourse and narrative.

A Visual Repatriation: From Stereotypes to a Legacy

As I worked with these images, I wondered whether the people pictured in these photographs had ever seen them. Did they have copies in the community? Was the community aware that these photographs existed? Every person pictured, after all, was somebody's sister, daughter, father, mother, or grandfather. I realized that some of the older people pictured in these images probably were not still alive and that, perhaps, these were the only extant images of these community members. Others, who had been just children at the time of the Disney visit, would now be parents and grandparents themselves. Perhaps they would be able to identify people and contextualize these images.

I decided to write to the Hooper Bay Traditional Council and inform them of this collection. They were very interested. Together, we applied for, and received, a grant from the Alaska Humanities Forum in order to repatriate these images. By producing high-quality photocopies we were able to "visually repatriate" the collection. "Bringing Images Home" was the first in a series of successful collaborative grants in which we have worked to gather and contextualize materials related to Hooper Bay's rich cultural heritage.

The *Tundra Drums* newspaper ran a story on this project that was published in both the Yup'ik Eskimo and English languages (Bingham 1996). Along with the text they published many of the black-and-white images. This article stirred excitement in villages throughout southwestern Alaska as people recognized the individuals and places pictured. That following spring *Alaska Magazine* ran a short article in their "Ketchikan to Barrow" section, furthering the project's exposure (Marsh 1997). A man in Pennsylvania, for example, read the magazine article and decided to send back another original black-and-white photograph that he had taken while visiting Hooper Bay in the 1930s. Many projects, some ongoing as of 2016, have grown from this initial collaboration.

A Place Called Askinuk

Russian naval lieutenant L. A. Zagoskin was the first to document the people of the Hooper Bay region in his travels between July of 1842 and August of 1844. Zagoskin made reference to these people, who occupied the coast from the Kashunuk River to the Black River, as the Magmyut (Pratt 1984). The Magmyut (Magemiut), according to Zagoskin, were "those who lived on the level tundra places" (Michael 1967, 210). Zagoskin's early grouping of the Magmyut encompassed "the villages of Kashunuk and Askinuk [*Naparear* [*sic*], or Hooper Bay], the entire area of Cape Romanzof, the village of Kutmiut [Old Scammon Bay], and the stretch of coast from Kutmiut north to the Black River" (Pratt 1984, 51).

During Edward W. Nelson's 1878 visit, Hooper Bay was known as "*Askinuk*." Nelson was an American naturalist who traveled throughout the region collecting natural history specimens and material culture for the Smithsonian Institution. His detailed descriptions of the *Magemut* people and their cultures remain an indispensable tool for understanding the past (Nelson 1983 [1899]). The village was also recorded as "*Askinaghamiut*."

According to Pratt, however, there are some discrepancies between Zagoskin's early accounts and those of Nelson. Pratt explains:

> An interesting problem associated with Nelson's *Magemut*/*Kaialigamut* boundary is that people living north of Kashunuk (village) and south of Cape Romanzof are not clearly identified as members of either of these two groups. This apparent "grey area" included the large, important village of Askinuk (Hooper

> Bay), which was one of the villages Nelson visited during his 1878–1879 sledge journey through the delta region. (Pratt 1984, 51)

The 1890 census reported 138 persons living in fourteen homes (Alaska Department of Community and Economic Development 2002). Few outsiders had come to this part of the Yukon-Kuskokwim Delta before Nelson's arrival. Nelson wrote that

> Askinuk, south of Cape Romanzof, is built on the top of an earthen mound which rises about 15 feet above the level of the surrounding country. The present village covers nearly the entire top of this mound. The inhabitants say that this elevation has accumulated from the long occupancy of the spot by their people, and its present appearance would seem to justify the assertion. (Nelson 1983 [1899], 249)

Following Nelson's own account at Askinuk, James VanStone writes:

> The delta of the Yukon, however, remained almost completely unknown and unvisited by outsiders until well into the American period; even today it is one of the most isolated areas of Alaska. When Edward W. Nelson, an American naturalist and collector of ethnographic materials for the Smithsonian Institution, visited Hooper Bay in December of 1878 he noted that the people appeared to have seen few, if any, White men. (Damas 1984, 235–37)

A Contemporary Setting: The Village of Hooper Bay

Much has changed in Hooper Bay since Nelson's first visit in 1878. At this point I will fast forward to the present, but I will return later to some of the intervening history, which lives in the community memory and shows up in local stories. The present-day village of Hooper Bay is one of the largest villages in the state of Alaska. Hooper Bay is located between the mouths of the Yukon and Kuskokwim Rivers. The region is often referred to as the Big Lake District. The Yup'ik Eskimo name for the village is "Naparyarmiut" which literally translates to "stake village people" (Alaska Department of Community and Economic Development 2002). Linguist Steve Jacobson lists the words "Naparyaraq" or "Naparyaar" for the Yup'ik name of this village (1984a, 250). *Napartaq* means pole, post, or stake in the Yup'ik language (Jacobson 1995, 497). A Hooper Bay community description says that the present Yup'ik name *Naparyarmiut* means "people from the Naparyaraq Slough" (Stockburger 2000).

In the late 1940s, Hooper Bay received the new nickname "Windmill City" from neighboring villagers. This new nickname resulted from the many windmills that sprang up around the village and could be seen at some distance. During this period, Hooper Bay was experimenting with the use of coastal winds to provide electricity for community members (Oswalt 1951). The contemporary community is made up of several areas or neighborhoods. These areas represent different periods of housing development in the village. The oldest part of the contemporary village, which is heavily built up, is often locally called "town site."

Hooper Bay lies twenty miles south of Cape Romanzof in the Yukon-Kuskokwim Delta region. The climate in Hooper Bay is maritime and has a mean annual snowfall of 75 inches, with a total precipitation of 16 inches. Temperatures range between −25 and 79 degrees F. The Bering Sea is ice-free from late June through October, but winter ice pack and winds do create severe conditions (Alaska Department of Community Economic Development 2002).

According to the 2010 Census, Hooper Bay has a population of 1,093 people, with 95.8 percent of that population of Alaska Native heritage (Alaska Department of Commerce, and Economic Development, Community and Regional Affairs 2016). Commercial fishing and subsistence activities are important economic activities in Hooper Bay. Most employment, as in villages throughout the state, is seasonal. Coastal Villages Seafood, Inc., processes halibut and salmon in Hooper Bay. The Bureau of Land Management (BLM) also offers seasonal firefighting opportunities. Additional income is generated through the production of Yup'ik grass baskets and ivory carvings. There has been some interest in developing a local arts-and-crafts cooperative to support the growth of these valued activities. Many families supplement their income with subsistence activities (Alaska Department of Community and Economic Development 2002).

A city government was officially incorporated in 1966. The tribe is federally recognized as "The Native Village of Hooper Bay," its government often known locally as the Hooper TC (traditional council). Residents depend heavily on water and air transportation. The air strip, a stretch of gravel that runs parallel to the Bering Sea shore, is owned and operated by the state. Barge lines continue to be of primary importance for the delivery of fuel and essential bulk supplies. Skiffs and four-wheelers are widely used for summer transportation. Snow-machine travel is the norm during the winter months. Winter trails are established between Hooper Bay and the neighboring villages, Scammon Bay (thirty-two miles to the north) and Chevak (twenty miles to the south). Like their ancestors before them, Yupiit spend a great deal of time traveling from place to place. Narratives in Hooper Bay often refer to these modes of transportation and places encountered along the way.

The Nature of Discourse and Narrative: An Ethnographic Approach

My anthropological training has given me the lenses through which I view the world. I have come to this work with a strong background in folklore theory, particularly influenced by a performance-centered approach. Long before I first went to Hooper Bay, I had been asking the question of *why* people were telling me the stories that they did. A linguistic-anthropological background has also encouraged me to look at discourse that centered in real, day-to-day cultural contexts. Daily discourse and narrative have long interested me, because they are seldom isolated from one another in actual settings.

The term "discourse" encompasses a multitude of verbal expressions found in a given culture. Scholars have examined such forms of discourse as stories, metaphor, song lyrics, laments, gossip, ceremonial speech, and other related forms of verbal expression (Bascom 1965, 1977, 1984; Bauman and Sherzer 1989; Ben-Amos 1972, 1976; Goffmann 1976; Gumperz and Hymes 1972; Paredes and Bauman 1972). Contemporary anthropological treatment of discourse is far-reaching and diverse. Several forms of discourse, including narratives, have been shown to be a persistent source of personal and group empowerment. In Hooper Bay, narratives convey meanings that extend well beyond "the moral of the story." As I will later demonstrate, words have the potential for initiating action in the Yup'ik region. Narrative and other forms of discourse, then, are to be spoken with an air of caution.

The Power of Words: Discourse as Action

The concept of discourse as a particular form of *action* is key to understanding Yup'ik narrative in relation to sense of place in southwestern Alaska. In the community of Hooper Bay words have the potential to actuate the ideas they express. This can be either a positive or a negative. Helen Oswalt, who visited Hooper Bay when a University of Alaska Fairbanks student, wrote that "words made these [Yupiit] people safe" (Oswalt 1951, 14). Words must be carefully weighed for they have the power to come true, to bring about action, sometimes unwanted (Fienup-Riordan 1990; Morrow 1990). Similar notions of discourse have been noted in other Alaska Native cultural groups as well.

Kenneth Austin, who was both a respected colleague and a dear friend, spoke and wrote about the power of words from a Tlingit perspective. Ken often recalled living with his granduncle when six years old and the warnings he received in relation to words and their power. He shared the following narrative with me on many occasions. This excerpt, which comes from his master's thesis, reinforces this notion that words are, indeed, very powerful:

> During a rest period from stacking firewood, he told me to sit down, for he had something important to tell me. He told me to listen closely, for he would tell me only once. He said, metaphorically, we all carry an invisible spear and that we should be careful how we handle it. That is, we should not unnecessarily jab people with it. This spear can be used to hurt people, keep them at bay, move them around, and control them. But we have to be careful with it. Later, I asked my parents, grandparents, and uncles as to what my grand uncle meant by the invisible spear. They told me that since it was imparted to me in a

> metaphorical vein, I had to unravel it myself. I was about thirty years old when I finally learned what *Kaa Ji.aas* [his uncle] tried to impart. The invisible spear is the potential power of speech. (Austin 1999, 91–92)

Yupiit often avoid explicit discourse (Morrow 1990). This is both consciously understood and respected. The avoidance of explicit statements enables one to avoid situations where definitive statements and judgments might otherwise cause offense or conflict, or be construed as telling someone what to do. Yupiit recognize that cultural meanings are "contested, temporal and emergent" (Clifford 1986, 19). Elsie Mather said that "Yupiit know and feel that the world is experienced in different levels" (Morrow 1995, 27). They also avoid discourse that might actuate events. To talk about poor hunting prospects, for example, may lead to the presence of fewer game animals. To speak of illness might bring about sickness in your own community or family.

In Hooper Bay there is a cautious awareness about how and when to speak. Certain things are not discussed because, perhaps, this "talk" will bring about an undesired consequence. In the case of suicide, for example, one would not want to "invite" such pain and suffering into their own home. Thus, it proves safer to not verbalize such tragic events, at least not explicitly. Indirection is a salient feature of Inuit/Eskimo cultures and well documented by other researchers (Brody 1987; Fienup-Riordan 1990; Mather 1995; Morrow 1995; Morrow and Hensel 1992). For Yupiit in general, allusion, metaphoric speech, and narrative discourse allow for expression in situations where direct speech is considered dangerous.

Anthropologist and folklorist Phyllis Morrow has also noted this discourse pattern among the Yupiit of southwestern Alaska (Morrow 1984, 1990). Morrow writes that "one danger of words is that they can actualize events" (Morrow 1990, 151). In their article on hidden dissension, Morrow and Hensel state: "The idea that one's speech can 'make things happen' is well-attested in Yup'ik society" (1992, 43).

A Yup'ik colleague once reminded me that a mistyped word was almost as bad as a misspoken word (generally the opposite view is held in Euro-American circles). Thus, he was cautioning me about the powerful nature of words both spoken and otherwise. Inaccurate information is recognized as potentially harmful, but accurate information can also, in the wrong hands (mouths), cause harm to others. Morrow states that such information may violate "the protective boundary between insider and outsider" and that "in the past, outsiders had done a lot of harm with what they had learned, suppressing a variety of customs" (Morrow 1995, 45). This suppression of customs ultimately led to much of the pain and suffering that is an ongoing fact of life in Alaska villages today. I will argue that this aspect of cross-cultural communication has, in fact, strengthened and perhaps changed the way that certain narratives are utilized in daily life.

Tensions Between Orality and Literacy: A History of Privilege

There is a long-standing, Euro-American assumption that written knowledge is somehow more credible and accurate than oral forms of knowledge. This privileging of written forms of knowledge has been an integral part of colonization and missionization throughout the world. For several centuries European cultures have tended to "lay stress on the idea of literacy and written tradition" (Finnegan 1970, 1). Greg Sarris reminds us that literacy has long been used as a tool of domination, "an effective colonizing device" (Sarris 1993, 189). Any written work that takes oral discourse as its subject must do so with this awareness.

A comparison to orality in South Africa also demonstrates that the oral narrative, which includes historical narratives, constitutes a true literary form. This literary form is one that should enjoy the same "privilege" as written history. Finnegan argues that there exists "no essential chasm between this type of literature (oral literature) and the more familiar written forms" (Finnegan 1970, 25). Written history has enjoyed a privileged position in South Africa as a "literate society" exerted control over "non-literate societies" (Finnegan 1976; Hofmeyr 1993). While the historic tendency has been to privilege the written text, folklorist and anthropologist William Schneider notes how "they [South Africa] view a whole field of study focused on 'the oral information systems,' that is how people orally communicate" (pers. comm. November 11, 2001).[6]

With growing emphasis on orality, scholars are now paying closer attention to the spoken word in the context of everyday life. Hofmeyr's work, for example, demonstrates the fluid nature of the oral tradition and gives readers a strong sense of how oral performance is "crafted" for a particular audience. She also reminds us that oral performance cannot be teased apart from the historical "underpinnings of time and place" (Hofmeyr 1993). This recognition is extremely relevant in terms of understanding how narratives are lived in the Yup'ik region. Several of the Hooper Bay narratives, especially those in the second half of this work, can only be understood within a historical framework that takes into account these underpinnings.[7]

Greg Sarris, in his biography with Pomo elder Mabel McKay (Sarris 1991, 1994), has shown how orality serves to maintain the dynamic nature of storytelling and discourse.[8] The orality of Mabel McKay's stories presents a challenge for the scholar or audience member who wishes to analyze her tales (or discourse) as "objects." Sarris states, "Mabel's talk impeded these specific literate tendencies for closure by continually opening the world in which oral exchange takes place" (Sarris 1991, 174). Sarris extends his argument, warning readers that "the context of orality—or, if you want, literacy or any combination thereof—is vast" and that "essential distinctions become debatable" (1991, 127).[9] Julie Cruikshank, working with Yukon elders, has similarly noted that "the issue of transforming oral tradition into written text is a complex one." She further notes that these concerns are not new to our discipline: Franz Boas, the father of anthropology himself, struggled over this "inevitable loss in style and form" (Cruikshank 1990, 16). Schneider expresses this same concern, stating that "for too long we have collected and interpreted just text and lost track of these other expressions of meaning" (Schneider 1995, 202).

Recognition of these tensions between the oral and the written word has also come to light in southwestern Alaska. Yupiit know well the historical influences that led to a privileging of the written text. Many Yupiit recognize that the orality and fluidity ("these other expressions of meaning") of their narratives is lost when written down, but also feel an urgency to preserve this part of their cultural heritage. This creates a tension because of the historical emphasis on literacy. It also creates a tension for those who record and write down these narratives because, once on paper, the fluidity is lost. Yup'ik scholar and educator Elsie Mather has referred to literacy as a "necessary monster" in relation to the recording of her own elders' oral traditions. "Necessary," because her own Yup'ik tradition bearers are passing away and taking their knowledge with them. A "monster because of the distance it puts between us and our sources" (Mather 1995, 20). When I write down Yup'ik narratives, I am keenly aware of the problems of distortion and the privileging of the written word. I am also encouraged by the positive potential of getting it right and the legacy that can be realized.

Any attempt to capture the spoken word involves a complicated set of choices. There is no satisfactory way to convey oral performance in writing without reducing the complexity of setting, tone of voice, listener interaction, and so on. A transcriber's choices reflect the purposes of the transcription. Among other things, such choices relate to theoretical interests, because different methods yield different kinds of information and draw a reader's attention to different aspects of a story.

My own choices are relatively simple as compared to transcription methods used for Yup'ik narratives by some other scholars (e.g., Woodbury 1987; Morrow and Mather in Swann 1994). For sociolinguistic analysis, in particular, it is critical to transcribe and represent narratives in a rigidly consistent format, often using a system of line breaks to highlight prosody. I have chosen a generally simple prose format for my own purposes.[10] Brackets indicate anything I added to the original speech to provide context or clarification. A pause, for example, is often as significant as the spoken word. Words that the speaker has emphasized are <u>underlined</u>. In my transcriptions, I have omitted words where the speaker repeats in a halting manner or cuts off a projected word, but I have chosen to retain repetition where it suggests the teller's emphasis on a particular element of a tale. Where I have incorporated the transcripts of previously published stories, I maintain the format of that translation.

Because I am less concerned with what can be learned from sociolinguisitic analysis than with the larger social context of stories, most of the stories and personal narratives in this work were not recorded when they were first shared with me in the context of daily life. The narratives were told to me on multiple occasions over several years. It is through these informal, personal experiences of living and working in the region that I came to understand how the stories themselves are actors in social life. This ethnographic immersion allowed me to understand the life of stories in actual practice. This is not possible in an artificial setting where the tape recorder is running. Thus, I intentionally did not record all the narratives—and one effect of this choice is also to preclude the possibility of technical transcription. It should be further noted that, although I formally studied Yup'ik Eskimo language at the University of Alaska Fairbanks, I do not speak Yup'ik fluently. Most of the people I worked with in Hooper Bay are bilingual, and when I conversed with them one-on-one they spoke English for my benefit. When working with community elders who preferred to speak Yup'ik, I worked with an interpreter. These recordings were later transcribed and translated by a Yup'ik speaker.

Looking to Ethnohistorical Accounts: A Word of Caution

Early accounts, such as the ones discussed in this book, are fascinating and at times read like a great novel. It is tempting for the researcher to accept these accounts as fact, rather than partial truth, but use of these sources warrants a serious set of cautionary measures. Scholars of arctic studies do continue to rely upon early historical accounts to reconstruct a picture of Eskimo peoples as they lived in the past, and in the following, I make use of them as well. Often historical accounts are coupled with archaeological evidence in order to present such a "reconstruction." But cultural anthropologists have, in general, cautioned against the uncritical use of historical accounts, which are certainly flawed in ways that we probably can't fully conceive. Products of their time, these works are shaped by their authors' biases, both socially (including gendered) and ideologically.

Barber and Berdan address this issue with their "reality-mediation model," which places an emphasis on the "complex interplay between the author and reality," noting that such ethnohistorical accounts are "reflections shaped by the author's experiences, convictions, and desires" (Barber and Berdan 1998, 33). This is particularly relevant to using early accounts about and from the community of Hooper Bay, many of which were written by Catholic Jesuit priests whose religious perspective and gender bias shaped their understanding.

Researchers have long acknowledged that early traders, missionaries, collectors, and explorers all journeyed to Inuit/Eskimo lands with an agenda. Their written records are often tainted with an obvious bias. This bias, no doubt a product of the time, reflects a paternalistic attitude towards the indigenous peoples being described. Another important factor in using and evaluating this material is that the female voice is often downplayed or dismissed altogether. This is due in large part to the fact that most early historical works were produced by men, many of whom had little or no interest in (or access to) the world of Inuit women.

Another related issue involves the long-standing relationship between the missionaries who generated many of these written records and the anthropologists who use such documents to reconstruct the past. This past, and often present, relationship between anthropologists and missionaries is one characterized by conflict and tension. Traditionally, anthropologists cast the missionary as a destructive force and condemn them for their actions. Much of the anthropological literature casts anthropologists against missionaries in an attempt to "salvage" cultures throughout the world (Marcus and Fisher 1986). Anthropologist Ann Fienup-Riordan writes of this conflict, stating:

> The rift between anthropologists and missionaries is long standing. Within anthropological literature, missionaries are a much-maligned group subject to both ambivalence and outright antipathy, as they have come to represent the "quintessential colonial figure" and "an essential part of empire." They are alternately presented as ineffectual blunderers and all-too-effective destroyers of the cultural integrity of the native populations they set out to convert. (Fienup-Riordan 1991, 3)

By the 1960s, anthropologists, in a "crisis of representation," began to take a harder look at their own role and the impact of an anthropological presence on "the other." It was during this time that anthropology began the "questioning of the discipline's relationship to colonialism" (Marcus and Fisher 1986, 34). More recently there has been a trend within the field that recognizes indigenous agency in the colonial process. Anthropologists have brought to light the many complexities that existed between Alaska Native groups and the missionaries who sought to convert them. Fienup-Riordan, for example, writing about the Moravian influence, states that "the Kilbucks' mission had an undeniable impact, but ultimately the Yup'ik people dictated the terms of their success" (Fienup-Riordan 1991). Sergei Kan has made a similar case in various works relating to Tlingit culture and missionization in southeast Alaska (Kan 1985, 1987, 1991).

While there is always a case to be made for mutuality between any two groups, there are various histories that were played out in Alaska. Some cultural groups experienced less impact than others. Hooper Bay history is characterized by a particularly contentious past. Hooper Bay community members were no less agents in the process of historical change, but I suggest that some villages contended with greater hardships than others in the face of domination and conversion. This will become evident as I employ Hooper Bay church records and documents. It will become even more obvious in light of the narratives of place that are circulated in the community.

Narrative Discourse as Political Empowerment: Ethnographic Examples

There is an increased awareness that discourse is central in understanding social settings and the political forces that shape them. I will argue that it is also crucial for identifying and understanding complex processes of adaptation and resistance in the face of domination. Such cultural strategies are often born out of, and maintained in, narratives and day-to-day discourse. At the group level there is a sense of political empowerment that is achieved and maintained through the regular use of narrative discourse. Certain forms of narrative discourse allow community members a venue for maintaining a sense of political power and control over external forces (i.e., government agencies and policies). This sense of empowerment is dynamic and especially vital where there is a long history of domination and control by external forces.

It seems particularly pronounced in places where there are continued political tensions surrounding issues of subsistence rights, land and resource use rights, control over local education, and local government. The community of Hooper Bay, like Native villages throughout Alaska, has experienced colonial and postcolonial interference and control. Moreover, many decisions made in the present day continue to be imposed from the outside, rather than generated from within. To Yupiit, government rules and regulations often seem ridiculous, or misguided at best (Hensel 1996). These tensions are deeply rooted in the historical relationship that Yup'ik communities have had with *kass'aqs*, and they continue to be expressed in the folklore.

While the groups described are dramatically distinct from Yup'ik examples and one another, contemporary ethnographers have documented numerous settings in which discourse and narrative serve to empower cultural groups (vis-à-vis their neighbors or states) and subgroups (e.g., local minority communities, women, etc.). Understanding something about this varied literature will help readers better understand the complexity of narrative and other forms of discourse in the Yup'ik Eskimo community of Hooper Bay. Michael Herzfeld, for example, examines the notion of "owning history" in the Cretan village of Rethemnos, Greece. Here the local population feels hostile towards a bureaucracy that insists on defining an official sense of conservation and identity. Modernity, identity, and historical ownership are negotiated through discourse. Discourse that makes reference to the state as a *listriko* (bandit) allows for a form of expression and empowerment among a people who are otherwise powerless in the face of sweeping change (Herzfeld 1991).

Nadia Seremetakis, working in her mother's homeland with her own relatives, demonstrates that lament empowers women of Inner Mani, Greece. Her emic account of death rituals and associated discourse provides readers with a sense of the strategies employed by women in order to temporarily elevate their position in a male-dominated society. Seremetakis highlights the "stratification of discourse by gender." Dream discourse, for example, falls into the realm of the woman. Dream-related discourse allows for "a weakening of masculine power, a momentary surrender of authority to the woman" (Seremetakis 1991, 56).

Anthropologist Elizabeth Povinelli challenges traditional notions of male-dominated hunter-gatherer societies as she seeks to understand the complexities of work in an indigenous Australian community. Povinelli examines the values and motivations underlying labor in the Belyuen community of northern Australia. Her ethnography demonstrates the ways in which discourse, specifically talk about work, has fostered a "transformation of power over time" (Povinelli 1993, 13). She reminds us that any meaningful discussion of indigenous "labor-action" and power must consider "local discourses of action and the apparatuses of power that accompany their assessments" (Povinelli 1993, 14).

"Blundering Fools"

Jokes and stories about outsiders may define social boundaries and reinforce the types of relationships that characterize interactions between insiders and outsiders. Keith Basso explores jokes that portray white men as "blundering fools" (Basso 1979). In Hooper Bay, such stories are used to exclude outsiders by explicitly casting them as the "other" and, through the narrative, exposing their ignorance of Yup'ik cultural ways. I argue, and will demonstrate with several direct examples, that kass'aqs are routinely cast as figures who don't understand the cultural rules and/or don't respect the warnings of Yup'ik community members and pay a price for their ignorance.

Anthropologist Patricia Partnow has also noted this phenomenon in the oral tradition of the Alutiiq region. Her analysis of Alutiiq tales demonstrates the ways that Alutiiq ethnicity is reinforced by contrasting it with the inappropriate behavior of the nonnative (Partnow 1995).

These types of narratives from Hooper Bay, as well as from other villages in the Yup'ik region, demonstrate how kass'aqs are excluded: they are the direct target of such narratives (tales are told *about* them, not *to* them) and, more subtly, they are not expected to "get" the narratives when they do hear them. This fact is often explicitly stated by the teller. Yup'ik elder Madina Flynn stated that when "some people [kass'aqs] are told about these things [ghosts] they do not believe them or scoff at them, those are the ones who see ghosts" (Orr and Orr 1995, 205).

Stories that cast insiders (the indigenous community) as more knowledgeable than outsiders are empowering to the group members who know and retell them. Group identity is reinforced through their shared understanding, but it also reinforces the teller's individual role in society. In this way, narratives not only empower the group, but also serve to empower people on an individual level.

"Now Do You See Why We Tell These Stories?"

Stories say other things about the relationship between Yupiit and kass'aqs, too. One day I sat drinking tea with a dear friend in another small Yup'ik river village. We recalled with laughter the previous evening in which we had attended a small family gathering, a birthday celebration. During and after dinner the family had entertained me with comical stories about their childhood memories. In particular, there were several stories about their first memories of interactions with white people. One story, for example, retold the day a barge with white men arrived in the village. According to these tellers, women now in their seventies and eighties, they wanted to "look like the white women in the Sears Roebuck catalogue." They described with great hilarity how they had placed round iron rods in the fire so that they could curl their straight hair. They continued the story, laughing all the way through the telling, as they explained that the rods had gotten too hot in the fire and they had managed to singe off their hair entirely.

Our conversation of the night's celebration faded to my friend's sad recollection of a tragic time in which two of her young sons had died within only a few months of each other. The night of this family celebration, she informed me, was also the same day on which one of the two boys had died. Sadly, she turned to the window and looked up at the crosses where the two were buried. The comical stories of the previous night had allowed family members to mask the painful memory of this tragic anniversary. There is a complex irony here worth noting. The Sears Roebuck story not only distracted the family from the painful anniversary of the boy's death, but it also "plays" with the tensions and pain of young Yupiit who feel the terrible imposition of Western standards of beauty and the costs of that. We wanted to be kass'aqs and we couldn't be, the story says, and when we tried we damaged ourselves. Words now failed her, but she managed to ask of me, "Now do you see why we tell these stories?"

These stories allow people to make sense out of a world that is not always ordered and it helps individuals to maintain a sense of meaning and direction in the face of internal and external strife. Various types of stories are employed for this purpose. Like the humorous narratives told to ease the tensions at the birthday party, Hooper Bay narratives are also an outlet for the fears and frustrations of individuals. The act of telling is directed at the pain and feelings of helplessness.

People find a way of individual expression without the risk of painful, explicit, and often dangerous statements about the world.

"She Drove the Elders Crazy"

That story I was told about how an outsider "drove the elders crazy" with her persistent questioning and her tape recorder was related more than once that first year by multiple tellers, not just on my first night in Hooper Bay. This short, cautionary tale about the behavior of another kass'aq woman was delivered with intent. Each time, the tellers shaped their telling with me in mind. Tellers used this narrative discourse to inform, instruct, and warn me about appropriate and inappropriate behavior. It would, over time, prove to be an invaluable lesson. This lesson is one that I continue to reflect upon and one that continues to guide and direct my behavior some twenty years later, especially in the presence of community elders.

Yupiit employ narratives in other purposeful ways that may bring about action. In this sense narratives can be seen not only to define appropriate and inappropriate behavior but to encourage appropriate actions and discourage or limit inappropriate ones. They may also highlight the fact that insiders possess such knowledge, which is empowering in the face of outsiders' dominance in so many institutional spheres.

In Hooper Bay, as elsewhere, people tell stories for various reasons (see, e.g., Bauman 1986; Ben-Amos and Goldstein 1975; Cruikshank 1995). Yupiit tell stories to entertain, to inform, to instruct, to enlighten, to offer criticism, and to caution listeners. More than one purpose may be achieved in a single telling. Some stories can connect people in meaningful ways, while others establish and maintain boundaries between groups. The tellers often intentionally "shape" a narrative with one or more purposes in mind, depending on their intended audience, and of course, listeners may put stories to different purposes than those envisioned by the teller as well. In Hooper Bay, as in other parts of the Yup'ik region, we shall see that there are marked differences between tales told to other Yupiit and tales told to, or about, outsiders (kass'aqs).

The Yupiit of Hooper Bay also use stories in everyday discourse to instruct others about dangerous situations and to make statements indirectly about events that are otherwise unspoken for fear that such discourse may "make bad things happen." In short, stories are not only expressions of, or reflections of, something else, but are active in social life. In particular, narratives about place in Hooper Bay are powerful, direct indicators of the health (or illness) of the community and the world.

Learning Through Stories: A Yup'ik Way of Learning

This work represents several years of experience and understanding on my part. This understanding is constantly growing and shifting. During my time of living and working in Hooper Bay in the mid-nineties, then a graduate student, one Yup'ik elder teasingly reminded me that even after the completion of my degree I would still be a student of life. Many, many stories have been shared with me over the years. My first year of fieldwork taught me that my greatest tool for understanding the role of stories was my heart, and secondly, my ears. I would learn to be a very good listener. One friend commented that I was "more like a Yup'ik" now (as compared to who I was when I first arrived in the village). I did learn to become a better listener and consider this remark a great compliment. Among the Yupiit, a person is expected to learn through direct observation and first-hand experience. This kind of learning is an integral part of everyday living, which served me particularly well as I lived and worked in southwestern Alaska. One does not learn by insistent questioning, nor does one acquire all of his or her knowledge through the study of books.

My first experience with this understanding came as I sat fishing with a group of Yup'ik women on the bank of the Naparyaraq River, a slough that runs from the inland Askinuk Mountains to the Bering Sea. I did not have a clue how to catch a fish at the mouth of the Bering Sea, but by then I luckily knew enough to sit quietly and watch. I sat down next to an elder as she baited her hook and cast it into the murky river. (Locals call this way to catch tomcods "hooking"). She knew I was watching, but tolerated my quiet observation. By the end of the day I was proudly contributing to the pile of tomcods and devilfish that was growing on the riverbank. This harvest was then divided and distributed among many families. Recording is often impractical when one is learning by watching and doing. I learned much more from situations where I found it necessary to leave my recorder, pen, and paper at home than I would have if I'd interrupted activities to record or asked for information in a "controlled" setting. What I soon discovered is that when you stop "looking" for stories, stories find you.

Lessons from Sleetmute

This lesson on Yup'ik ways of learning and acquiring knowledge is one that I would experience many times, in many places over the years. It is a salient feature of Yup'ik culture and something I, as an outsider, would better understand over time. This way of learning is not unique to the peoples of the Bering Sea Coast but rather part of a broader cultural pattern among Yupiit throughout the region. In the winter of 1998, for example, under a grant from the University of Alaska Museum, I made a return trip to the small village of Sleetmute, Alaska, the farthest inland Yup'ik community. The purpose of this grant was to index and contextualize a large and valuable collection of images owned by Nick Mellick Jr. and his family. I had already been working in Hooper Bay, but looked to this opportunity as a chance to experience Yup'ik language and culture in a very different setting.

One cold winter day I hatched a plan to make a trip up the frozen river to Lime Village, a neighboring Athabascan village. Nick and I had wanted to get these images back in order to identify people and places captured in the still shots. It was too cold to fly, so I decided that I would ask someone to pull me in a dog sled by snow machine. This "plan" was met with much laughter as Nick informed me that there was no way I could safely make the trip and that nobody was crazy enough to take me. It had been so cold all that week that planes were not coming or going. It had been 45 to 55 degrees below zero and besides, I *was* six months pregnant at the time. Nick never did stop teasing me about this half-brained idea. He would laugh and say "imagine that story about some crazy white woman lost somewhere upriver!" He was, of course, looking out for my best interest and absolutely correct. I tell this story because of the understandings that came from this event.

Later that day I was sitting with a Yup'ik woman sharing a cup of tea. She had heard from others of my idea of traveling up to Lime and began, without any introduction, to tell me story after story about pregnant women who had not observed the Yup'ik knowledge surrounding pregnancy and birth. Specifically, these stories emphasized the importance of getting up early. The narratives highlighted how a lack of respect for these beliefs has resulted in difficulty during birth or afterwards. Fienup-Riordan reports that "the reproductive capacity of the women's house was explicit. In certain contexts, its interior was likened to the womb from which children would be produced and, concurrently, from which the spirits of the dead would be reborn in human form as they reentered the world of the living. Elena, a Yup'ik woman being interviewed, remembers the pregnancy taboos that required her to quickly exit through the doorway so that her unborn child would emerge in a similar manner from her body. The baby ultimately finds the door and exits" (Fienup-Riordan 1990, 61).

She never overtly told me to get up and out the door as soon as I was awake, but I realized that I was being instructed to do so. From that day on I made sure that I was up early, dressed quickly, and through the doorway without hesitation. This understanding was transmitted to me out of concern and it was done in the indirect way that is characteristic of Yup'ik discourse. Her narratives of what her own elders had taught her and her stories of other women's experiences had an immediate effect on my behavior.

It is also noteworthy to mention that this knowledge was shared with me only after it was deemed necessary. The necessity arose out of my demonstration of ignorance, in this case the plan to journey and bump my way up the frozen river in a dogsled. So, had I not been pregnant (and demonstrated ignorance) I probably never would have heard these particular narratives that instructed me about proper conduct during pregnancy. This is a crucial point in understanding narratives and Yup'ik ways of transmitting knowledge. Stories are told to those who need to hear them! In contrast, Wendall Oswalt, for example, working and writing in this same Yup'ik region, reported that "customarily a young woman made no obvious preparations for the birth" (Oswalt 1990, 32).

Perhaps "preparations" would have been more obvious had he been a pregnant female during his stay in the region. Other female researchers in the Yup'ik region have also noted this knowledge surrounding pregnancy and birth (Fienup-Riordan 1990; Morrow 2002). This understanding, that one learns many important teachings through stories told at the time they matter, was something I would continue to develop as I spent more time in other Yup'ik villages, especially in Hooper Bay.

"I Go Back Again and Follow Their Words"

William Schneider reminds us that "to experience oral tradition is first and foremost to meet and know elders, to learn how to listen, and to come to know what they mean over many tellings" (Schneider 1995, 202). In 2003 I had the opportunity to record the stories of a Hooper Bay community elder who, on various occasions, had shared stories with me. He began his stories and personal narratives by explaining to me how he obtained his knowledge. It was important to him that I understand that his education had come from the stories of his father and grandfather. Knowing that I was a university graduate student, he explained to me that his grandfather was his "principal and teacher," and that his father was also his "teacher." In this case, I was recording.

Elder: That's where I learn more and more and I [pause] graduate, like in school.
Holly: Right.
Elder: Graduate from my [pause] principal and from my daddy.
Holly: And in your education [pause] there were stories, yeah?
Elder: *Ii-i* [yes]. That's the way I was educated.
Holly: *Ii-i*, a knowledge that you can't get at school.
Elder: I learned from my dad and my grandpa [long pause].
Any questions? [we laugh]
Holly: Do you remember, um, the kind of stories that they would tell to children, stories that they would (use) to teach children?
Elder: Always. They always do it, they did do it (have these

life experiences) themselves, before we do it. And, uh, that's what they told us about, not to do this and that.

Holly: Yeah.

Elder: Sometimes I, uh, I don't know what to do and I, I finally remember my grandpa told me to do this. It's the right way to do. Just like going on a . . . path. The road.

Holly: Yeah.

Elder: Sometimes, when I do something like a, from doing mistakes, that's what I mostly learn. Learn by [pause] learn by hard way, by doing mistakes. Cause right way, sometimes my grandpa tell me what to do. . . . Getting words. What he told me about. I'm off the road. I go back again and follow their words.

Stories are often used to teach listeners proper behavior in a given situation and to show the consequences of inappropriate behavior. They might tell, for example, how to behave if one encounters a ghost or spirit. These brief, aphorized instructions, collectively known as "teachings" in English, are called *alerquutet* or *inerquutet* in the Yup'ik language. These are defined as instruction, advice, warnings, or prohibitions (Jacobson 1984a, 56 and 169). Morrow says these teachings are "a body of information upon which people can rely when they encounter various situations in life, ranging from falling through the ice to bearing a child" (Morrow 2002, 337). Paul John, a respected Yup'ik elder of Toksook Bay, talks about the importance of learning life lessons and teachings through story and personal narrative (John 2003). Paul John, as a young boy, lived in a *qasgiq* where these teachings were routinely passed on to younger generations. He now works to perpetuate this knowledge by handing it down to his young Yup'ik audiences.

Yup'ik elder Marie Nichols reminds listeners that "if a person has none of the teachings, he will be like someone lost in a blizzard. But the person who has the teachings will derive strength from them and use them like a walking stick to prevent himself from getting hurt" (Tennant and Bitar 1981, 109; Morrow 2002, 338). Such "teachings" routinely accompany and reinforce such stories. People in Hooper Bay also talk about the teachings of their elders in relation to a walking stick. I have been told to "use your walking stick like a partner" when going out on the land. I have always suspected that Hooper Bay elders were using this discourse about "a walking stick" both literally and figuratively. The advice given is to take a stick as a guide, and to take "our words" (teachings) as a guide as well. Before he began to share stories, this Hooper Bay elder referred to these narratives and accompanying teachings together: "Always. They always do it, they did do it [have these life experiences] themselves, before we do it. And, uh, that's what they told us about, not to do this and that." He again reinforces how, in recalling his own elders' stories, he is able to think and act appropriately.

"I go back again and follow their words" is a strong metaphor. Stories are active. You follow them and they take you somewhere. Learning through story, then, is like traveling upon a path. This journey can be uncertain. There are places to stop, ways to become lost, and decisions to make about which way to turn next, but there is assurance in knowing that if you are lost, you can always "go back again and follow their words." Many times this speaker has related to me how he recalled the stories of his grandfather and father and how they led him safely home. Stories guide people and allow them to live well in their place.

This discourse eloquently illustrates the importance placed on Yup'ik knowledge and the sense that stories are active. Stories convey others' knowledge and experience as you experience something similar. This is a theme that will weave in and out of the various narratives presented in the following chapters. It is a central theme among the Yupiit of southwestern Alaska, one that is often deemphasized, misunderstood, or altogether dismissed by non-Native outsiders (health care providers, clergy, teachers, government agency personnel) working in the region. A non-Yup'ik audience often misses the significance of stories and narrative, even when they are accompanied by more or less explicit instruction. This fact has contributed to a history of social and political tensions in the region.

A Painterly Image: Contrasting Images of the Land

The imagery of pathfinding and carrying a walking stick, both literally and figuratively, is fundamentally based on a sense of land and landscape. Rather than viewing the land (landscape) as a surface to measure or manage, a Yup'ik sense of place is a storied place.

Understandings of the land reflect a permeable place where worlds overlap in the existence of time and space. A Yup'ik "theory of place," then, is shaped by a deeper cultural knowledge of the beings, often unseen, who inhabit and share their world. A hill, for example, is often much more than a geographic feature or landform. It may be a dwelling place or a doorway to other worlds.

To understand these complexities of Yup'ik beliefs about the land, readers most familiar with a Western, Euro-American worldview must consider how their own views of the land have been shaped. For Yup'ik readers this will be a discussion about how the "other" sees the land and why it differs so greatly from their own perceptions. I do not wish to enter here the current theoretical debate surrounding landscape, but rather draw out some themes that inform Western thinking about the land. I hope that this brief discussion will stimulate, for my readers, some thoughts about their own ideas of the land and how these were formed. I refer, herein, to the "land" and "landscape" in the broadest sense of the terms, and for my purposes I employ them.

Concepts of the "land" and "landscape" are a part of particular cultural processes. These differences are expressed in myriad ways, but looking to language provides important clues. In the Yup'ik Eskimo language, the postbase *miu* means "people of" or "belonging to" a particular place. *Kuigmiut* means people "of the river" and *Kuigpagmiut* translates as people "of the big river" in reference to those who live along the Yukon River (Jacobson 1995, 51). This concept of "belonging to the land" extends to other Eskimo-speaking peoples in the north. *Nuna*, for example, means land, in both the Yup'ik and Inupiaq Eskimo languages. The Inupiaq people who live in Alaska's northwestern interior call themselves *Nunmiut*, which translates to "people of the land." In contrast, Westerners routinely name places in the possessive (e.g., Browns Ridge, Greenstown, McMasters Landing), or name them for the particular family or individual who "founded or settled" that place (e.g., Adamsville is said to have been named for John Adams, the "first citizen" to settle on Old Telegraph Road).

The concept of landscape is difficult to define and approaches vary greatly from one discipline to the next (Thomas 1993). An anthropological approach to landscape, we are reminded, takes into account that the mindscape forms the landscape (Hirsch and O'Hanlon 1997). For people with Western European cultural roots, the term is closely linked to the concept of nature and these two are also used interchangeably. These two terms "have had a long and somewhat parallel lexical development within the Germanic (landscape) and Romance (nature) languages respectively" (Olwig 1993, 309).

The term *landscape* and cognates of the word *scape* have been employed in a variety of linguistic contexts. These variations can be traced over time and place in the Germanic languages. According to Olwig, "the most common spellings still in use in modern English are 'ship,' as in the word 'township' and, as a verb, 'shape,' in the sense of creating by shaping, or, more precisely, 'carving out.' Another permutation of the suffix is 'shaft,' a word which can be applied in various Germanic languages . . . to objects with a shape which is suitable for carving something out" (Olwig 1993, 310).

Hirsch and O'Hanlon (1997) trace the origin of the English word "landscape" to a term used by painters of the sixteenth century. The Dutch word *Landschap* was transformed to *landskip* in the English language. Olwig notes that in a Germanic language such as Danish, the term *land* refers to an "open space" or the "parts of the surface of the earth which have been taken into use by people; particularly to the surface of the earth used for . . . agriculture" (Olwig 1993, 311). Hirsch and O'Hanlon further note that this notion of the land "reminded the viewer of a painted landscape" (Hirsch and O'Hanlon 1997, 2). This "painterly" image of the land has continued, throughout the centuries, to pervade Western thought about land. It casts the land, in Western thinking, as a fixed, permanent object upon which actors act out their social lives.

"Landscape," then, is a concept that has emerged in a Western, capitalist world. Such Western notions "evoke a particular set of elite experiences—a particular 'way of seeing'" a place (Bender 1993).[11] The Western appreciation of or focus on landscape grew throughout Europe from the sixteenth to the nineteenth centuries (Lovejoy 1964; Hirsch and O'Hanlon 1997), during which time anthropology traces its own origins as a discipline. "Anthropology draws on the same common intellectual background which led to the emergence of an explicit idea of landscape" (Hirsch and O'Hanlon 1997, 1).

These Western images of the land have long had an impact on the way that outsiders see and portray the homelands of the Yupiit.

Southwestern Alaska, in descriptive writings and imagery, is cast in a somewhat misleading way. Hensel, in a discussion of "wilderness" and its associations, remarks:

> Flying over the delta, or examining it on a map, Euro-Americans often assume that the land is "wilderness," that is, unoccupied, unproductive, and uncontrolled . . . [but] it has been occupied for thousands of years, its resources are known intimately, and there are travel routes appropriate to each season. Straight lines through brush or grass and wear marks on the tundra give evidence of snow-machine routes, and clumps of taller grasses and greens mark sites of old villages and middens, as do graves. (Hensel 1996, 51–52)

Outsiders' images of Yup'ik landscape were largely negative and that negativity is described in vivid terms, like "a mud hole." The Westerners' "painterly image" of landscape is one key to understanding this perception. Visually the tundra landscape has few of the qualities that mark natural beauty to those looking for dramatic topographic features such as snow-peaked mountains and luxuriant vegetation. Jacobson states that for non-Yupiit the land is "seemingly devoid of topographical reference points of the kind appreciated by Europeans and Euro-Americans" (Jacobson 1984b, 185–86).[12] Written works produced by outsiders (travel journals, church diaries, and personal letters) exported largely negative descriptions of the land in part because they lacked such dramatic or valued qualities.

A distinct boundary between human beings and the land (an embedded assumption in Western science) simply does not exist in the worldview of the Yupiit and other indigenous groups. Anthropologist Julie Cruikshank has noted the ways in which indigenous images of the land differ from Western notions. Her study of the Yukon landscape, climate, and ecology highlights contrasts between Western "scientific" models of explanation and those of the Yukon elders (see Cruikshank 1991, 23–43). The way that people view the land is an inseparable part of this understanding. Anthropologist Thomas Thornton also emphasizes this stating "for Tlingits, and perhaps all indigenous peoples, place is not only a cultural system but *the* cultural system on which all key cultural structures are built" (Thornton 2008, 4). Similarly, Robert Drozda's experiences working with Yup'ik elders to document important place names, cemeteries, and other historic sites highlights these important contrasts (Drozda 1995). His work illuminates the important beliefs and feelings that Yupiit share in terms of the land and its varied features.

In the village of Hooper Bay, narrative and metaphoric speech about place serve to empower people. Daily discourse and narratives of the land illustrate that Yup'ik notions of the land (landscape) extend well beyond surface. Yupiit, of course, also hold an appreciation for the visual aspects of the land such as the many waterways, subtle colors of the tundra floor, and dramatic skies. These forms of discourse make strong statements about people and their place in the world. To truly understand these forms of expression we must understand the way that Yupiit perceive the world.

The land, in Western terms, is viewed as an inanimate object. That's not to say that these Euro-Americans don't have feelings for the land and attachments to it—people everywhere typically form emotional ties to their place—but rather that their relationship is one based on their own notions of a landscape. It is a tangible object of study, it is invested with meaning and sentiment, but it is certainly not an actor in a social setting. As Susanne Küchler has written, "In our consideration of landscape we are imprisoned by long-standing assumption[s] about its nature as a record of, or stage for, significant human actions. The landscape of the western tradition is an inscribed surface which can be measured, described, and depicted" (1993, 85). As we will see in subsequent chapters, Yup'ik concepts of the land and the water turn this notion on its head.

2

Metaphor and Allusion

DISCOURSE AND METAPHORS FROM THE LAND

"There Used to Be a Lot More Flowers Here on the Tundra"

In the previous chapter I laid out some of the important distinctions between a general sense of place and a more specific, storied sense of particular places. Stories and day-to-day discourse about particular places on the land help us to understand how people relate to each other and the nonhuman world through those places. The Yup'ik tundra, seemingly "vacant" to outsiders, is never void of beings. Places on the land and the nonhuman world are ever-present and aware. Watching and listening. This understanding informs peoples' behavior and shapes the words they speak.

The wind was blowing gently across the tundra as I walked behind a friend who was busily collecting driftwood. As we made our way down the beach, she methodically selected certain pieces, discarding others. This driftwood is an invaluable resource that keeps her family warm at night. I tried to contribute, but soon found that many of the pieces I selected were plucked out of the small trailer and tossed back onto the beach. Too big for the small stove, I wondered, or maybe too wet to burn without filling the house with unwanted smoke? I didn't ask, but continued on with the group.

Her small daughter and two sons trailed behind as we followed the sand dunes southward along the shore. As we worked we began to discuss the recent and tragic loss of yet another local youth to suicide.

The conversation quickly became an uneasy exchange. As quickly as the direct talk had begun, it ended with my companion turning to look at the tundra and the mountains beyond. She was silent for a moment before making a seemingly abrupt shift in which she began to speak of the land.

She said that when she was a child "the ponds had much more water in them." She described how the children used to swim in the surrounding tundra ponds for hours on end. She told me they don't do that as much anymore. She continued her observations by telling me, "There aren't as many birds here anymore." After a brief silence she said to me, "There used to be a lot more flowers here on the tundra." The purpose of her words was clear to me. She was indirectly expressing her own fears and sorrow, but by shifting the topic she was also instructing me not to continue this explicit conversation. Her words held another purpose and that message was directed at a sentient world. She knew that direct talk could bring about unwanted outcomes. Our talk was dangerous. Her metaphoric speech was purposefully intended to restore balance by redirecting a dangerous discourse that could have potentially brought about similar tragic events in her own life.

Understanding a teller's purpose helps us understand how narratives can be viewed as action or a stimulus for action. This is true among the Western Apache and, as I will argue throughout, it is true for the Yupiit of southwest Alaska. The Western Apache narratives reflect a natural landscape that "makes people live right" (Basso 1986, 95). Tellers use narratives to "guide" people (their intended audience), and the physical landscape will, in essence, "take over and perpetuate" the intended message and/or lessons. Stories associated with a place are recalled whenever one is there. As I will show in subsequent chapters, natural features and human-made features alike are places that recall story and anchor memory.

A sense of place involves the relationship that people hold with a particular place and how that relationship is expressed through "feelingful" speech (Kahn in Feld and Basso 1996). In Hooper Bay, the land itself instructs people because it directly responds to the actions of individuals. The land guides people who are observant by reacting to danger, pain, and suffering, thereby reminding them to act appropriately. In the case of my friend who spoke of fewer tundra flowers and dried-up ponds, she was also getting a message *from* the land about the health and well-being of the community.

This reminder serves to minimize those ill effects on the people and to minimize them on the land as well. The land is, in essence, a being among beings, and a particularly powerful and sensitive one. It is, I would argue, a distinct cultural feature of Yup'ik communication that sets them apart from "the other."

The Abundance of Eel Grass: Musqueam Well-Being

In the fall of 2014 I was in Vancouver, British Columbia, to attend "Weaving Us Together," the IPinCH (Intellectual Property Issues in Cultural Heritage) final team gathering held on Musqueam territory. Team members gathered to share their research findings and to reflect on the successes and challenges of the IPinCH seven-year project. Following several days of meetings and presentations, participants were offered a tour of the Musqueam Reserve led by a local community member. The Musqueam are part of a larger language group known as the Coast Salish which encompasses many tribal cultures and languages.

Our guide shared many stories of this place. Among those tales was one connected to the significance of eelgrass. I was struck by the similarity between this Musqueam place-based tale and some of the metaphoric speech I had come to know in the community of Hooper Bay. He explained that the river grass, or flowering eelgrass, is a significant part of the Frazier River's fragile estuary, but it also seems to be a reflection of community wellness. He commented to his listeners that there was less in the area today. That when subsistence foods were more plentiful and people were well, the eel grass was abundant. He turned toward the river and said in a low voice, "There is not very much of that grass out there today." The tribe's website also offers a similar explanation.

> The Musqueam people have lived in our present location for thousands of years. Our traditional territory occupies what is now Vancouver and surrounding areas. The name Musqueam relates back to the River Grass, the name of the grass is məθkʷəy̓. There is a story that has been passed on from generation to generation that explains how we became known as the

> xʷməθkʷəy̓əm (Musqueam)—People of the River Grass. "It was noted that in some periods the məθkʷəy̓ grass flourished, and in some periods it could scarcely be found. It was also noted that in some periods our people would flourish and in some periods the population would dwindle, perhaps by plague or war. It was in this way that we became known as Musqueam." (Musqueam Indian Band 2015)

This parallels the way in which the land and natural world are responsive to the well-being of community members at Hooper Bay.

Similarly, Julie Cruikshank, in her discussion of glaciers, states that for the Athapaskan (Athabascan) and Tlingit peoples,

> glaciers take action and respond to their surroundings. They are sensitive to smells and they listen. They make moral judgments and they punish infractions. Some elders who know them well describe them as both animate (endowed with life) and as animating (giving life to) landscapes they inhabit. (Cruikshank 2005, 3)

Similarly, we must consider the unique ways in which Yupiit, as Feld and Basso write, "encounter places, perceive them, and invest them with significance" (1996, 8). They do so through metaphor and allusion. One example is the shaman's grave.

The Shaman's Grave

I had only been back in Hooper Bay a few hours when a friend called to see if I had arrived safely. Just a few minutes had passed as we shared news and accomplishments of our children when the conversation took an abrupt turn. She flatly stated that she had gone to check out "that grave." She went on to say:

> I went to check out that grave yesterday [long pause]. Still about the same I would say [another long pause]. There's no more fish. The birds are dying off.
>
> That's the start of starvation right there!

Five years earlier she had first explained to me that this grave holds great significance and that "it is getting lower." Her mother had always told her that when the shaman's raised grave is level with the ground "the world will end." Prior to missionary influence, the dead were placed in above-ground grave boxes (Nelson 1983 [1899]). This teller believes that, when the grave is level with the tundra, it will signal a time when famine will return to Hooper Bay. Starvation is something people have faced many times before. "The people are terribly hungry and the mission has little left to help with," wrote a sister at the Hooper Bay mission in March of 1933 (AM Collection 14, 593). My friend ended by telling me that she was not able to "put up a lot of fish this year" and that she was unable to buy diapers this week, all signs that things are not well.

One year later this woman and I were traveling back from a visit in the neighboring community of Chevak. She had recently suffered the loss of a very close family member. My friend was suffering and although I sensed that she wanted to talk about this tragic loss, she never did. A trip to Chevak seemed like a good thing for her to do, and our visits from house to house were great fun. On our return trip, just as we got close enough to see Hooper Bay off in the distance, she suddenly turned the snow machine and headed out towards the frozen tundra and open sea. I was puzzled and did not understand this diversion until the snow machine stopped. There we were, at the shaman's grave.

Recent offerings of what appeared to be seal oil in a glass jar were sticking up through the snow. I realized that this was a place of significance for other community members as well. I asked if I could get off the snow machine, but respectfully remained back and did not approach the grave. It is situated on high ground looking out towards the Bering Sea. My thoughts turned to an old publication that had contained stories about "medicine men" at Hooper Bay. One narrative described the death and burial of a village shaman. The author wrote that "he was buried on a little hill where he could look out toward the sea and watch for seals" (Gillham 1955, 10). I wondered if this was the same spot. A few moments passed before she restarted the snow machine. I climbed on and we headed back to town without exchanging a word. We never spoke directly about this visit to the grave, but later, in the course of conversation, both agreed that the grave was indeed very low.

FIGURE 2.1. The Yup'ik landscape—a sentient world. Courtesy of James H. Barker 2004

My friend found a way to express her pain and suffering through the use of metaphor and allusion to this place on the land. Her brief statement that "it is getting lower" allowed her to express painful realities that were otherwise unbearable. The shaman's grave became a very tangible symbol for her individual fears and suffering. Few words were needed as the land spoke for her. These are issues that she wanted me to understand and feel as a friend. Over the years and up until the time of her tragic death, the shaman's grave continued to weave in and out of our daily discourse, suggesting the enduring impact of the allusion.

Scholars working elsewhere have noted the importance of place as expressed through specific forms of discourse. The work of Keith Basso notes the significance of knowing and "speaking" Apache place names. Basso demonstrates that in order to understand the meaning of the narratives linked to those names and places, one must incorporate the names themselves into daily discourse. Basso, in his discussion of this kind of discourse, remarks that "Apaches enjoy using them" (Basso 1986, 101). This understanding of place extends well beyond the Apache world. Yup'ik "talk" about place is also relevant in terms of exploring sense of place in southwest Alaska, and it is a central feature of everyday life and storytelling.

Other researchers in the Yup'ik region have also noted the significance of place and its centrality in Yup'ik discourse. Robert Drozda writes that the Yup'ik elders with whom he collaborated "talked of the land and water with much respect as though they were referring to another human being" (Drozda 1995, 119). The land is not an inanimate object as it is thought of and spoken of in Western terms.

Ellam Yua: Perceptions of the Land, Perceptions of the Universe

There are marked differences in the way that Western thinkers speak about "landscape" and the way that the Yupiit speak about the universe. From Yup'ik perspectives, to talk about "geography" without consideration of the spiritual dimensions of the world is to talk about the land in a superficial way.[1]

The Yupiit of Hooper Bay see beyond the "landscape." Their sense of the land includes land features, rock formations, the plants, the animals, and other beings who inhabit the tundra. The earth, as has been explained to me many times, was once much thinner than it is today, allowing for more frequent interactions with the nonhuman realm. Spirit beings have the ability to appear in different forms: sometimes they make themselves known to the living in the form of an animal or a bird. These beings may not always be seen by the living, but they are often sensed by those who are aware (see also Carpenter 1973, 106). When the earth was thinner, the spirit world was nearer that of the living. The notion that *nuna* (the earth/land) is now "thicker" is an essential concept to understanding Yup'ik perceptions of the land in Hooper Bay.

The idea that the world is aware is clear in its Yup'ik personifications. Yupiit refer to *Ellam Yua* ("the world's [Ella's] person") and *Ellam Pania* ("the world's [Ella's] daughter"). *Ella* is a complex and multifaceted concept. It is alternately defined as "world; outdoors; weather; universe; awareness, sense" (Jacobson 1984a, 140). *Yua* [its person] is said to exist in many things that Westerners would consider nonliving, inanimate objects (Fitzhugh and Kaplan 1982; Fienup-Riordan 1990, 1996; Hensel 1996; Meade 1996; Morrow 1984). Although such dichotomies are often imposed by non-Yupiit, Yupiit do not make hard distinctions between the natural/spirit world and the human/human-made world.

Ellam Yua is further defined in the *Yup'ik Eskimo Dictionary* (Jacobson 1984a) as "the Spirit of the Universe." Jacobson notes that the more recent term, *Agayun*, is widely used for "God." He further notes that Ellam Yua probably predates the arrival of missionaries to the Yukon Kuskokwim region (Jacobson 1984a, 415). Interestingly, Birket-Smith recorded a story among the Chugach Eskimo in 1953 that makes reference to *nunam-yua* (the land's person; Birket-Smith 1953, 121–22; Fienup-Riordan 1996, 181). A sleeping hunter awakes to find "a spirit-woman standing by his feet." "She added that it was difficult for any people to see her and that she was *nunam-yua* (the land's person), but where she came from she would not tell him" (Birket-Smith 1953, 121–22; Fienup-Riordan 1996, 181). In contrast, Jacobson lists *nunam yui* as "the people of the earth" (Jacobson 1984a, 269), while the connotative force of nunam-yua is that of a nonhuman being. It is unclear as to whether or not there was ever a belief about a particular "spirit" of the earth, but it does warrant further investigation. What is clear is that the land is aware.

"Things Kinda Know": Yup'ik Notions of Awareness

A wonderful, contemporary example of how ellam yua is understood in everyday living comes from a story told by Robin Barker, a non-Native teacher who had arrived in the Yup'ik region in the 1980s. She observed a young boy who was annoying his mother by smacking the window with ice balls. The kass'aq woman was, at first, surprised to see that the Yup'ik mother did nothing about the behavior. When the boy finally mustered the courage to come into the house, his mother was busy popping popcorn for the children.

> He stayed away all afternoon until his hungry stomach brought him in during the early evening, just as Irene was putting a bag of popcorn into the microwave for Jana. She asked Kyle whether he would like one too, and, with his assent, she added a second. When the bell rang, the two expectant children hurried to the table where Irene placed one puffed up bag and one flat

> one. She said to Kyle in a regretful tone, "If you had been good, yours would [have popped]. Jana has been good all day. Things kinda know." (Barker 1994, 98)

The boy's popcorn didn't pop because of his earlier actions in a world that is always watching. His mother simply responded, "things kinda know," and in doing so imparted a lesson about appropriate behavior as well as important understandings about the sentient world in which they live (Barker 1994).

This story demonstrates that individuals don't always have to act or intervene because things are often taken care of by a universe that is watching and aware of human action. Barker's example well illustrates that "the idea that children are being watched extends from strangers to supernatural beings and even to inanimate objects" (Barker 1994, 97).

Connected to the notion of ellam yua is this pervasive belief that things have a way of "equalizing" themselves and that bad thoughts, bad attitudes, or bad actions will cause bad things to happen to oneself and others. While this expression is seemingly counter to the notion that narratives stimulate action, I argue that they are actually interconnected in a complex belief system that resists simple definition or explanation.

A similar understanding was shared with me some years ago in an Athabascan village on the Yup'ik Eskimo–Dena'ina Athabascan border. It was June of 1995 and I found myself bouncing along in a skiff as I made my way up Lake Clarke with a group of Nondalton (an Athabascan community that borders the Yup'ik region) community members. We were heading to their ancestral village known as Kijik. Long before we stepped ashore, I had been told that it is a place known for its "power," a place where one must demonstrate respect. As we worked to pull the skiff up on the beach well above the lapping waves, one elder told me that "many Dena'ina ancestors are buried at this place." She went on to say that, over the years, outsiders had tried to claim this ancestral land, including a white homesteader who built his cabin and other structures over the graves. Legal attempts to remove him ended in frustration, but where the government had failed the ghosts of their ancestors had prevailed.

She was explicit in detailing how and why he had suddenly had a change of heart, stating that one night he "suddenly up and left." He was apparently in such a hurry that he left many of his personal effects behind in two cabins and an outbuilding. Turning to me and nodding she quietly said, "Our ancestors take care of themselves" (pers. comm., June 1995). She was making a strong statement about her community's stand to protect their ancestors, but through this retelling she was also reasserting the power exercised by the ghosts of her ancestors.

Just as in the case of the Dena'ina ancestors taking matters into their own hands and causing the trespassers to leave, similarly the young Yup'ik boy's naughty action of throwing snowballs did not go unnoticed by a sentient world where awareness exists in all things (Fienup-Riordan 1990; Morrow 1996). Yupiit stress that an individual must keep a positive disposition in order to maintain his/her own "awareness" (Fienup-Riordan 1994; Morrow 1996). I have been explicitly warned on many occasions to keep a positive outlook and not to verbally express my fears and concerns in a negative manner. Morrow has written, "Yupiit typically understand mind as active" (1996, 415), seeing "action as inseparable from the power of the mind" (1996, 417). Yupiit also recognize the need for human response to inappropriate or offensive behavior but know things also have a way of balancing out in a world that is aware. Human *action* and *agency*, then, must be understood within a complex of culture-specific beliefs.

An examination of place in an Icelandic community suggests some interesting parallels between Iceland and the Yup'ik southwest. Kirsten Hastrup's work has shifted the anthropological focus on *place* and *memory* as "an objective, fixed, and measurable surface" to one that extends to landscape. She argues that the relationship between a landscape and community memory does not have to be captured in "architecture, monuments, or other visual landmarks" (Hastrup 1998, 111). In Iceland then, the land "is not simply a surface or a stage upon which people play their social roles; it is part of the social space" (Hastrup 1998, 111).

This is an essential aspect of place in the Yup'ik world as well. However, I would extend this argument by stating that the land of the Yupiit is not only a part of the social space, but is in fact an actor itself in the social world. The land is not simply being acted upon, it is reacting to the actions of those in the human world. In his work on landscape, Tilley summarized what, to Yupiit, might seem obvious when he said, "People and environment are constitutive components of the *same* world" (Tilley 1994, 23). While this is a thought-provoking observation for most Euro-Americans, it would be obvious for Yupiit. The land is both a vehicle for expression and a social actor that responds to human action.

Narrative Discourse and Painful Realities

> Scenting the air with its rancid nature, a spirit of suicide and alcohol and drug abuse seemed to walk freely among the members of a small Alaska river community. It had just claimed two more victims and was looking for more. (Alakanuk Community Planning Group 2009, 1)

Alaska has one of the highest rates of suicide per capita in the country. I have struggled for years to find a way to write respectfully and meaningfully about this issue. I often feel that I have no right to put my feelings and thoughts to paper, yet as someone who has lost so many people close to me, I feel compelled to address it. I have chosen to write about this issue for personal reasons, but also because it is so strongly part of people's lives and consciousness. I do not presume to know the devastating pain they live with every day. I address this topic with the deepest respect for my friends and collaborators and continue to struggle with how to write about it. In this book, I have chosen not to include personal experiences and individual stories of loss.

It may be difficult for outsiders to truly understand the impact that suicide and alcohol-related deaths have had on Alaska Native communities (Shinkwin and Pete 1982; Alakanuk Community Planning Group 2009).[2] Alutiiq author Gordon Pullar writes, "In the case of Alaska's Native groups, there have been many major disruptions since the first European contact. . . . Few realize that these events, while having taken place generations ago, affect the way we live today" (Pullar 1992, 185).[3]

In February of 2003, the Hooper Bay Traditional Council agreed to share this horrible pain with the outside world. The *Anchorage Daily News* interviewed community members and ran a story about the recent tragedies that had so greatly impacted the community once more. One man who grew up in the community told the reporter, "Our children no longer see hope" (Gay 2003). This quote reminded me of a friend's words in reference to the despair of Hooper Bay youth: "You have to have a dream."

I asked a friend in Hooper Bay how people in the community felt about the front-page article. She simply said it was part of the "healing that needed to take place." Another man would later remark that perhaps other villages were looking to his community (Hooper Bay) as a place of "healing." When this news story appeared outsiders who knew that I had ties to the community expressed shock and disbelief. Most told me that they had "no idea" what was happening in the village. Like so many of my close friends in the community, I could not respond to their expressions of shock with either words or tears.

Both of my friends' use of metaphoric expression and allusion to story allowed them to convey something to me that they could not otherwise convey: Fewer flowers and birds on the tundra, less water in the ponds, a grave that is getting lower—and young people going away. Metaphoric expression and allusion to stories connect people to the land and the rest of the world, which shares their pain. The land is *alive* and *aware* in much the same way that a person is *alive* and *aware*. The alarmingly high rate of suicides and accidental deaths among young people in Hooper Bay have not only been felt, and reacted to, by individual community members. The pain is felt by the natural world as well.

In short, places on the land not only remind people about proper behavior, but also react directly to the social, emotional, and mental well-being of people in the community. Pain is visible to everyone and felt by all things. In stories about places and narrative references to these particular places, as with the shaman's grave, the land's response to human tragedies and moral failure is evident.

3

The Rivers, the Mountains, the Tundra, and the Sea

Beyond the Mapping of a Landscape

"Learn your landmarks!" Yupiit have often told me. Over time I grew to understand that "learning landmarks" also meant learning the narratives and stories associated with particular places. Beyond that I learned important concepts, feeling or sensing the ways that ellam yua influences daily life and the world around us. There are many places that, at first glance, just appear to be natural features. As I will illustrate in this and subsequent chapters, stories of human encounters with places often explain why a particular feature exists, but they also embody and reinforce lessons, including instructing listeners in appropriate behavior.

Early on, my Yup'ik teachers told me that such understandings were not achieved overnight. I came to view the land around me differently as I learned the stories and began to realize that, in talking about the land, people were often talking about other things. With such metaphors and allusions, people begin to find ways to deal with and express their individual and collective fears, pain, and suffering. Much of that pain is rooted in historical relationships and events.

The records of early explorers, missionaries, and teachers reflect and highlight dramatic differences between Yupiit and outsiders, and not only in the way that the land is perceived and understood. The contrast in views is key to understanding both past and present in Hooper Bay.

"Lord, Lord! What a Place to Live!"

Captain Cook, who explored the Bering Sea coast in 1778, was apparently infuriated by the unique challenges of navigating the Bering Sea region and Kuskokwim Bay. Twelve-foot tides presented a formidable challenge to the English, who considered themselves extremely competent seamen. One mariner wrote that this was "a damn'd unhappy part of the world" (Oswalt 1990, 6).

Such views have persisted over the centuries. A missionary at Kashunuk in 1928, later stationed at Hooper Bay, wrote, "Lord, Lord! What a place to live! Akulurak was bad enough. But Kashunuk! No fuel, poor water, hardly any sunshine" (AM Collection 30, 72). Another Hooper Bay priest wrote in the 1940s, "The place itself is a mud-hole during the summer and wind swept tundra during the winter" (AM Collection 13, 498–515). The aforementioned *Hollywood Reporter* review of the 1953 Disney film told potential audiences that the film "shows the family and their fellow citizens [Hooper Bay community] at work and at play, fighting the rugged elements of their bleak surroundings" (APRD, Milotte Collection 31). Anthropologist Wendell Oswalt's negative description of the delta is typical of an outsider's perspective even in the 1990s:

> The watershed nearest the river mouth at Eek Island is characterized by a monotonous panorama. The flatness of the landscape is broken only by the river channel with its low, eroded banks. Where ice lenses in the banks are exposed, the summer melt produces oozing sections of muddy shoreline. Beyond the riverbanks, peat ridges provide minimal relief. The landscape is of a type called wet tundra. . . . The land is poorly drained, and countless ponds and lakes make it difficult to walk very far in a straight line during summer. (Oswalt 1990, 7–8)

Yukhpuk Lived in the Askinuk Mountains

Yupiit, in contrast, portray the land, the waters, and other features on the tundra as alive with story, memory, and the creative actions of beings. The following early description, from Edward Nelson, is identified as a narrative from the Lower Yukon. Entitled (by Nelson)

"The Strong Man," this tale is a good example. It describes by name the Askinuk Mountains, which rise some 2,300 feet above the tundra (Oswalt 1952), just north of the present-day village of Hooper Bay.

> In ancient times a very strong man (Yukhpuk) [Yugpak, in contemporary spellings, literally, "Big Man"] lived in the Askinuk mountains, near the Yukon river. One day he picked up a part of these mountains and, placing them on his shoulders, carried them out upon the level country, where he threw them down. In this way he made the Kuslevak mountains. When the mountain was thrown from the man's shoulders, the effort caused his feet to sink into the ground so that two deep pits were left, which filled with water, making two small lakes, which now lie at the base of this mountain. From there he traveled up the Yukon, giving names to all the places he passed. (Nelson 1983 [1899], 499)

In 2001 I partnered with the Hooper Bay Traditional Council on a project funded by the Alaska Humanities Forum. The purpose was to record local oral histories and document place names in and around the village.[1]

One phase of this project involved spreading a large U.S. Geological Survey map out on the floor of the traditional council office building. Throughout the day, community members stopped in to see what we were doing. We began to repair this huge area map with tape, restoring the torn edges as best we could. Before we had even finished this task several people, mostly men, began to study the map and identify Yup'ik names for the places shown.

As we laid down new strips of tape, running our hands over the map to smooth out the creases, tales of hunting, fishing, and trapping were already being exchanged. We all sat on the floor with recording equipment, paper, and pencils spread out across the mapped landscape before us. Some studied the map in silence for a long time before speaking, alternating between Yup'ik and English. It did not take long for these Yup'ik men, many of them community elders, to transform the map into something much more than words on paper. The map came to life as they recalled their experiences on the land and water.

One man used his finger as he followed rivers to his favorite fishing places. Another spoke about a place that had confused him and turned him around many times in the past and how he had almost lost his way. He studied the map for a long time and then added "left turn!" Touching a place with his index finger, one community elder explained to me how he and a companion were so surprised when they had come across a polar bear, rare in these parts, at that spot back in the 1970s. "Must have come down on an ice floe," he told me as he shook his head and stared down at the map spread out before him.

I recalled that, when Helen Oswalt visited Hooper Bay in 1950, a community member told her that a Hooper Bay "medicine man" "long ago said he would come back and speak through [a] polar bear if no one [is] afraid." According to Oswalt, "One [Hooper Bay] man wasn't afraid and talked to him" (Oswalt 1951).[2] Was this, I wondered, what the elder was referring to when he pointed out that place where he and his hunting companion had encountered a polar bear? Polar bears are considered particularly powerful creatures and are often associated with shamans in the lore. A Point Hope narrative, for example, makes this connection between polar bears and shamans. In this Inupiaq Eskimo tale, a boy becomes lost on the ice and is rescued by his uncle who is a shaman. "'Stop crying, nephew, and get on.' . . . And what Maguan saw was a polar bear" (Lowenstein 1992, 52). Perhaps these associations were in the Hooper Bay man's mind as he described his encounter with the bear.

Another community member got up and walked across the large map. Sitting down again he pointed to a place almost directly across from Hooper Bay. Smiling, he said to me, "This is where we go to berry camp!" As the others looked on, everyone became more serious. Very quickly, they began to share with each other the many places that should be avoided. One man pointed to a place on the Kashunuk River and said, "You don't want to camp here!" Two others silently nodded in agreement. He went on to say that this place is an old site and a dangerous place. Yupiit have similar concerns to those of the Koyukon Athabascan as described by Richard Nelson. He recorded the existence of sites known to hold potential dangers for people and described the presence of a "threatening spirit power" that is associated with "many places on the land." "Places imbued with it [power that is dangerous to people] are avoided at night. This is true especially for places where spirits emerge to lurk after dark—old village sites, for instance" (Nelson 1983, 35).

In October of 2001, those of us conducting the Hooper Bay oral history project received an invitation to participate in a session that explored "The Power of Alaskan Places" at the American Folklore Society Meetings held in Anchorage, Alaska. The theme of the conference was "partners in knowledge." A reporter from the *Anchorage Daily News* interviewed us about the mapping project and our contribution to the the Power of Place symposium. I told her that "as people began to fill the pages with more than just a place name but memory . . . it became a very emotional thing" (Gerjevic 2001). There were places that were identified for their powerful associations with the spirit world. Some were places of positive experience and some were known for their potentially dangerous power. The story I heard of that place on the Kashunuk River, for example, was one I heard more than once. Three years later I recorded more narratives about this powerful and dangerous place, to which I will return in a subsequent chapter.

Qemirrluar: A Place of High Winds

In the summer of 1988, Robert Drozda and Vernon Chimegalrea interviewed George Moses Sr., an elder from the Yup'ik village of Akiachak, as part of a Bureau of Indian Affairs Alaska Native Claims Settlement Act (ANCSA) historical place and cemetery site documentation project.[3] Moses was asked about a place known as Qemirrluar (translated as "a bit of a broad hill"). This site is located near Russian Mission between the Yukon and Kuskokwim Rivers, north of Akiachak. The transcript (see appendix for the full transcript as it appears in both Yup'ik and English) begins with the translator asking Moses if "there [is] a story or anything unusual that happened" at Qemirrluar. Moses replies, "This huge lake here acts in unusual ways" (Moses 1988).

Moses describes this place as somehow "unusual" from other places. He indicates that crossing this body of water can be dangerous for the living when "a fierce wind will come up on him." There is a sense that these high winds are something other than a natural occurrence. He goes on to describe this place as an old site and "former place for catching fish." He says that "it was their place of survival, those ancestors of ours, through our mothers' fathers. That one was also their place of survival."

Moses's description of this place as a "place of survival" indicates that this has long been an important place, one that the ancestors also knew well. Drozda (the interviewer) then asks Moses (through the interpreter) if there is anything that people do when such winds are encountered at this place. He asks, "In an instance like that where a storm or something would arise that would signify that something bad is going to happen, were there any rules for behavior, was there anything that they could do?" Moses responds that "if it happens . . . they discourage us from hunting fearsome animals, because that one [creature] would not leave us alone."

Moses, like so many Yup'ik elders, concludes his telling by making a strong statement about the persistence and value of Yup'ik beliefs. Moses says that "[this cultural knowledge] started with our ancestors, which started in the distant past, it did not die, that it will not die whatsoever, but that it will be alive for us." This is more than a general statement; Moses is asserting the reality and relevance of these truths grounded in his life experiences. He wants to be certain that his audience does not view or treat these stories as mere superstition. One interesting aspect of this narrative, although not explicit, is the mention of a "fearsome animal."[4] It is not clear if this creature is a water creature, but that possibility seems plausible in consideration of the fact that he is describing the dangers of "crossing" at this place. He warns of the potential danger to a family who might attempt to portage at this place and indicates that, perhaps, it might be safer to go by land, around the lake. Moses is warning his listeners to approach this place with both awareness and respect. As I will demonstrate in chapter 4, places of water often conceal unseen dangers, especially for those who lack appropriate awareness of the sentient world.

The Power of Place

Another phase of our 2001 community-based project was to conduct one-on-one interviews with community elders in order to record place names and life histories. Many of these one-on-one interviews were recorded by young people in the community; others were recorded by those of us involved in the grant. Most of these life histories were recorded in the Yup'ik language and were later transcribed and translated into English. The translations were also done by community members.

Once again, we sat on the floor of the Traditional Council office with that giant tattered map of the region, so large that we were actually sitting on parts of it as we listened to elders talk about places and their life stories (figure 3.1). One elder was on his hands and knees, an index finger moving across the map and pausing at remembered places. The names on the map were all in English, but he would say the Yup'ik name of each one. He did not start with his birthplace or early childhood but instead traced routes across the map, perhaps ones that he had often traveled. As he recalled his encounters in a place—the seals he caught, the fish camp he returned to each year—it was as if he were revisiting each one. He would turn to another elder and talk about the animals found here or something his family did there. There were long silences. And as his life story emerged—nonchronologically—I began to see how inseparable his story was from the stories of these places. This turned out to be the case for many of the elders in Hooper Bay.

The Giant Footprints

One of the first stories I ever heard in Hooper Bay is tied to a place on the tundra near the old village site. During my first visit back in 1996, at the urging of their grandmother, a group of young people had invited me to go with them to set nets in the mouth of the river across the bay. It was a wonderful day and we all enjoyed being "out on the land." We set several nets, walked the beaches where we discovered the carcass of a large whale, and took turns at target practice with a .22 rifle. We even pursued a seal that presented itself in the bay, but we gave up when it led us out into the choppier waters of the open sea. We agreed that it really was a good day to be out as the winds were low and had allowed for a smooth crossing inside the bay. Upon our return to the village shore they asked, now knowing that I had a particular interest in stories, "Have you seen the giant footprints?"

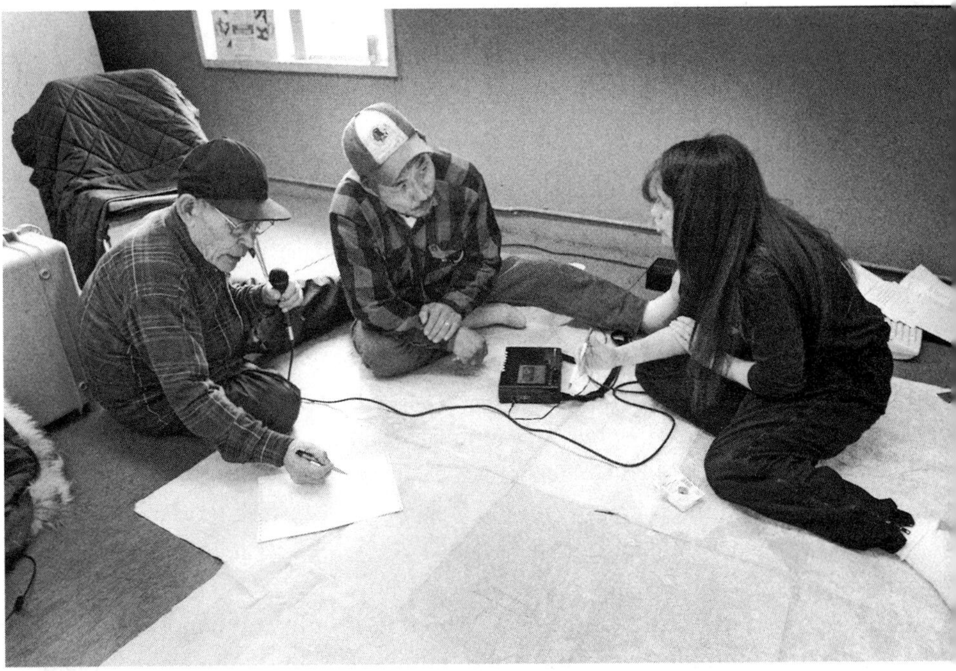

FIGURE 3.1. Mapping place names and narratives. Courtesy of James H. Barker 2001

When I replied that I had not, they quickly offered to take me to this place on the tundra.

As we approached by four-wheeler I could easily see from a distance the large, deep impressions left in the tundra. I was anxious to get down and examine them more closely, but I was teasingly warned by these young people not to step directly into these footprints. I cautiously and respectfully walked around them but never stepped into them. It would be years before I truly understood why.

Every version that I have been told of "The Giant Footprints" is similar in content. The narrative involves two or three young girls who have just begun puberty. The tellers often stop to explain to me that, in Yup'ik Eskimo belief, girls should not go out in public or dance during their time of menstruation. They are to stay somewhat isolated from the rest of their community. It was customary for girls to remain indoors and away from the rest of the family and community members during this time. Edward Nelson wrote that "a particular atmosphere is supposed to surround her at this time, and if a young man should come near enough for it to touch him it would render him visible to every animal he might hunt, so that his own success as a hunter would be gone" (Nelson 1983 [1899], 291). Nelson, however, also goes on to describe menstruating girls to be "considered unclean" (Nelson 1983 [1899], 291).

A Jesuit missionary in Hooper Bay who learned something of Yup'ik customs surrounding menstruation wrote about these observations and other "Eskimo Superstitions" in the Catholic Parish Publications newsletter. According to him:

> A girl after her first monthly sickness can't pick salmon berries, but only blackberries. If she would eat salmon berries they would rot her teeth, and if she would eat fresh food of any kind it would turn into sickness. While menstruation is going on she is not allowed to leave the house but has to hide herself in one corner of the igloo. And if the family just happens to have to move camp while she is in this condition she has to be laid in the sled and covered up so that she can not see anything, nor touch the ground. If she would touch the ground hunters would have bad luck, and spirits would likely take her soul away. (AM Collection 30, 1127)

While the writer simply dismisses these "superstitions," several contemporary researchers working in the Yup'ik region substantiate the above descriptions. Fienup-Riordan writes that "at puberty they were themselves confined to the house, their social invisibility approximating a fetus's hidden state" (Fienup-Riordan 1990, 62). Phyllis Morrow also acknowledges "a long list of prohibitions surrounding menstruation in Yup'ik Eskimo society," but she warns us to not assume a culture-bound notion that these behaviors simply repress females (Morrow 2002, 335).

Morrow argues that Yup'ik behaviors surrounding menstruation were not (are not) restrictions "experienced as rigidly inhibiting" (Morrow 2002, 345) but rather part of broader social rules that applied to all members of society. "Menstrual rules do not seem particularly harsh and do not seem to have restricted women more than other categories of persons" among the Yupiit (Morrow 2002, 339). Yup'ik men, for example, "who had lost a relative were not allowed to hunt" (Morrow 2002, 338). A Yup'ik man was restricted during both his wife's puberty seclusion (in the case of marriages arranged before puberty) and her menses (Fienup-Riordan 1994; Lantis 1960; Morrow 2002).

A parallel case is found among the Anishinaabe (Ojibwa and Odawa) people of the Canadian Shield region. Like Yup'ik women, Anishinaabe women were portrayed by early explorers and missionaries as repressed by cultural practices such as menstrual observances (women isolated from family quarters and village ceremonies). Research has clearly demonstrated that Anishinaabe men followed (and continue to follow) several cultural observances surrounding menstruation, pregnancy, and birth (Cusack-McVeigh 1993; Ross 1992) as well. One Anishinaabe elder told me in relation to menstruation, "It's something you might not want to believe. . . . They put a little shack just a distance from where they live, where they can watch them until after the period is over." He went on to explain that "when a woman gets pregnant . . . they say that the man was pregnant also. Once they found out that the woman was pregnant, the man was not allowed to hunt anymore, or to fish, or to do anything else except to go to cut wood, you know, to keep the fire going" (Cusack-McVeigh 1993, 27).

I have often heard women in Yup'ik villages talk about observations surrounding menstruation. This talk often comes when we are sitting in the steam bath. This, obviously, would be an appropriate time to discuss such matters since men and boys were excluded from this space. Young girls, who would have just begun to accompany their mothers in "steam," would have the opportunity to listen and learn these important cultural menstruation observations. I recall some laughter as I commented on the fact that I wished such a custom had been observed in my own culture, thus allowing for a time away from the regular routine of life. Because everyone is familiar with restrictions, when a story concerning menstruating girls is told, Yup'ik listeners know what is at stake if the girls ignore the menstrual prescriptions.

Passing through the Doorway

The story of "The Giant Footprints" tells of how the people were holding a feast and dancing down at the old village site of Askinuk.

Askinuk, as previously mentioned, was the name used for Hooper Bay when Edward Nelson first visited and documented this place. It is very near the Bering Sea coast, and the old dwellings at this site are still visible today. Before Zagoskin set foot in this region, his Eskimo guide informed him that the people at Askinuk "dig their houses in the ground and climb down into them through the smoke hole" (Michael 1967, 210). This early description gives the impression of a place where human dwellings (human-made features) are, perhaps, somewhat indiscernible from the surrounding land with its many hills and wind-blown sand dunes. Adding further to this sense, once inside, these dwellings revealed a maze of tunnels and doorways leading from one to the next.

Both from the air and from the ground, one can see the large round depressions of the sod houses where they once lived. I was even able to crawl through one of the openings that once served as an entrance tunnel. The wooden support beam was still in place and, although it was a tight squeeze, I managed to crawl through the passageway of this dwelling. Nelson described these passageways at Askinuk in great detail:

> The houses are clustered together in the most irregular manner, and the entrances to the passageways leading to the interiors open out in the most unexpected places. Sometimes one of these passages opens on the top of another house built lower down on the side of the mound, or, it may be, between two houses, or almost against the side of an adjoining one. (Nelson 1983 [1899], 249)

Passing through this entryway was a momentary event, but one I would always remember. As I went through I had a strong sense of touching history, but immediately noticed that my actions made my Yup'ik companions very uneasy. At the time I was truly puzzled by their look of concern as I examined the structure, wondering if it was unsafe.

After a few years and many more stories, I understood this sentiment better. I also came to see my own actions as foolish and careless. I had often wondered why the Hooper Bay ancestors had left this place. When I asked about it some would say that flooding might have been the primary reason, others simply said that they did not know the reason for this move, but the abandoned site of Askinuk seems to be associated with unsettling events.

I knew epidemics were another reason for the abandonment of villages throughout Alaska. "Too weak to bury all the dead, many survivors abandoned the old villages, some caving in their houses with the dead still in them. Their homeland—the tundra, the Bering Sea coast, the riverbanks—had become a dying field for the Yup'ik people: families, leaders, artists, medicine men and women—and *Yuuyaraq* [way of life]" (Napoleon 1991, 11). I wondered if this was the reason. As it turned out, my Yup'ik companions, familiar with their own history, culture, and oral narratives, had other reasons to be concerned about my careless actions at this place. The next several narratives, shared with me on several occasions, helped me to gain this understanding.

The narrative of "The Giant Footprints" goes on to tell how the sound of singing and drumming in Askinuk enticed the young Yup'ik girls to sneak out and head towards the celebration. They were excited as they followed the sound, but as they crossed the tundra the ground began to "roll" and move. At this point, one teller explained to me that the "earth used to be much thinner" than it is today. As the girls tried to make their way towards the sound of the music and celebration, they started to sink. The more they struggled, the more they sank down. They sank into the tundra and became lost to the world of the living. They became a part of another world. This world is not entirely separate from the world of the living, but they have never been seen again.

"Words Return"

In June of 2002, I returned to Hooper Bay to work with traditional council and community members on another grant-funded oral history project through the Alaska Humanities Forum. The aim of this project, entitled "*Paivciyaraq Piciryaramteneng:* Sharing Our Traditions—Searching for Meaning," was to continue the work we had started in the last oral history project. The council met to discuss and approve this project and I helped carry out the objectives outlined in the proposal. This time I returned to Hooper Bay with my son, then six years old.

One day my son and I were walking to the store when one of the council members, a respected community elder, stopped us. He asked me about the project and we talked about community plans for conducting further interviews with chosen elders. My son played nearby with a group of children while we visited. This was my son's first visit to Hooper Bay. He fit in and made new friends instantly. He was taken out to the beach to collect driftwood and made a trip to fish camp. It was on this trip that I cut my first fish. I was teased for months afterward that out of the hundreds of salmon strips hanging on the racks at fish camp, the family members could always look and say, "There's Holly's fish!" I still get teased about my clumsy fish cutting. We cherish the memories of that trip to fish camp and recall it often. I marveled at how readily my son had been accepted. It had, after all, taken me many years to know people and to become something other than a stranger. We adults, however, did not speak the universal language of "Pokemon" the way he and the other children did! His genuine love of dry fish and seal oil certainly impressed people and allowed him to fit in quickly.

As we watched the kids playing, we talked about other Hooper Bay elders the elder thought should be included in the project. I assured him that we would work with these individuals, who were respected for their wisdom and life experience. As I scribbled down their names on a scrap piece of paper, the group of kids began to get loud and one started throwing sticks. With what at the time seemed to be an abrupt shift in our conversation, he began to talk about the giant footsteps out on the land. I would later reflect on his telling and wonder if it wasn't intended not only to instruct me as I proceeded to work with elders but also to comment on the kids and their increasingly annoying behavior.

Like previous tellings I had heard, he explained that the footsteps were made by two young girls who had ignored the wisdom of their elders. He told me part of the story and explained to me that those giant footsteps were out there on the land today. He spoke as he pointed to the open tundra behind me where the deep depressions marked the tundra. He explained that they had not respected the Yup'ik behavioral rules and restrictions regarding menstruation. I was, admittedly, intrigued by one aspect of his story that I had never heard before, in which he said the girls "are now up in the sky." I immediately recalled

Edward Nelson's writings in which he had described a "sky land" in reference to Yup'ik narratives. This description was given as part of a creation tale in which Raven is mentioned. Nelson wrote of "the tale of the creation by the Raven, as the latter and the First Man were traveling in the Skyland" (Nelson 1983 [1899], 445).

I must have let my curiosity show because he seemed to know that this tale had piqued my interest. Smiling at me, he said, "You will hear about that one." Nodding his head with assurance he told me again, "You will hear more about them!" We then parted company. I found my son and we were once again off to the store. As we made our way up the hill towards the old part of the village, I wished that I had taken this opportunity to ask him more about this narrative. I had missed my chance again! Then, laughing to myself, I recalled the lesson I had learned so many times before. Words return. Stories and narratives, like the seals who have been hunted, return to those who demonstrate respect and patience (Morrow and Schneider 1995). Words return as stories find you.

This narrative was also shared with Helen Oswalt back in 1950 when she visited Hooper Bay. The following excerpt is taken directly from her field notes. She writes:

> Once there was very thin land here. Two girls were left in [a] hut their family built for their puberty (they wore hoods) while rest of village went to sealing camp. Girls heard dance [and] music, [they] knew they weren't allowed to go but wanted to. All who go to dances must take something so they took the leftak [*sic*] skin from the doorway and started out with it between them. After walking a while, they began sinking in the shallow ground and then began going up to the sky. They started back another way, and the same thing happened. They disappeared in [the] sky, but footsteps can still be seen here. (Oswalt 1951, 11)

This 1950 telling is similar in detail to the versions that have been shared with me over the years by various tellers at Hooper Bay. The elder who said "you will hear more about them" was right. Later that year, I found myself sitting with another elder as we recorded his life history, and he too wove this narrative of "The Giant Footprints" into his own story. As people connect their own life story to places on the land, they connect the stories of place to their own experience. Hastrup, in recording life histories in an Icelandic community, has similarly noted this aspect of discourse in relation to place. "We were not only met with a life history," she writes, "but also a life space" (Hastrup 1998, 112).

Clearly the story of "The Giant Footprints" continues to hold meaning for the people of Hooper Bay. That there are several similar versions is one indication. It is also very significant that this story is connected to a physical place out on the tundra. The giant footprints, the actual depressions, are manifestations of the power of this tale and serve as a tangible reminder of the importance of Yup'ik teachings and tradition. The footprints instruct listeners that the world can be a dangerous place for those who do not listen to and respect Yup'ik beliefs and the knowledge of elders. These footprints also make a strong statement about the relationship that Yupiit hold with the animate land, cognizant of human behavior and actions.

Another telling of "The Giant Footsteps" was shared with me in the fall of 2002 during a recorded interview. Interestingly, this telling would lead to another narrative that was very similar in content and form. The teller stated that his grandfather and father often told him the story and that he would see the footprints out on the land when he was hunting. The following is an excerpt from a recording in which he explains the giant footprints to me and another listener. He begins by telling this story of "The Giant Footprints" and how he has seen them many times throughout his life on the land. He then ties this place to another narrative and yet another location out on the tundra. A portion of the Yup'ik language transcription follows this translated English excerpt.

Elder: I used to go bow and arrow, bird hunting [at that place].
Holly: Yeah, you would see them?
Elder: Tamana [refers to that place spoken of. Out, over there, extended space]
Interpreter: *Ii-I* [yes] [nods his head in agreement]
Elder: Uh, growing up, the footsteps from these young girls, that just got into their [first menstruation]. Two young girls that just started having their periods.

Elder: Uh, [pause] they [the footprints] used to be deep when [I] was young, back then.
Elder: Those who had their first menstruation.
Interpreter: Yes.
Elder: Their footprints [or the path they took]. Can you translate this?
Interpreter: Yes.
Elder: At the time when I was a boy, it was deep [the water hole]. They [the girls] had a house up there, above the school. And where their house was we used to fetch water when we were little. It was very clear. Real clear water.
Interpreter: Under the ground?
Elder: Under the ground. Where their house once was. Have you seen the wood . . .
Elder: Yeah. Their path, they called Atrangkaat, which went down to the beach. At that time they used to have dances, down there, at Nuvugmiut. It is said that they went down to Nuvugmiut to the dance from their house. It is said that with young bearded seal [skins]. . . . If I forget some of it, too bad! They had young bearded seal [skins]. I think I forgot some of it.
Interpreter: Even though they were warned, even though they were told not to go down, I think, they went.
Elder: Yes. They had with them bearded seal [skins].
Interpreter: To give . . . you know when they dance they bring something to give away.
Elder: Yes.
Interpreter: When they went down to the dance, they say they went under the usual path; I think they went under the ground.

[Yup'ik language/Partial Transcription]
Elder: Imkut aglerraat.
Interpreter: Ii-i.
Elder: Tumellrit. Tamana *translate*-aryumaan?
Interpreter: Ii-i.
Elder: Tamaani tan'gurraullemni ilutullruyaaqut.

Enengqellruuk-gguq pikani *school*-arviim keluani. Enellragneng-llu mertatullruukut miktellemteni. Cuuqekaapiggluni. *Real clear water.*

Interpreter: Nunam aciani?

Elder: Nunam aciani. Enellragni. Imkut muragallret tangerrsar . . .

Elder: *Yeah.* Tamaa-i imkut tumellret, Atrangkaarnek pituit, kanavet imumun unavet cenamun. Tamaani-gguq yuratullruut kanani imumi Nuvugmiuni. Yuraliyarlutek atrallruuk-gguq kanavet Nuvugmiunun tavaken enemegneng. Amirkaneng-gguq . . . Ilii nalluyaguskumku, aull'! Amirkaneng pingqerrlutek. Ilii nalluyagucugnarqaqa.

Interpreter: Inerquumangermek, atrasqenrilengraacetek atrarlutek tuan' pillrungatuk.

Elder: Ii-i. Amirkaneng pingqer', cangqerrlutek.

Interpreter: Tun' . . . catul' . . . yuraraqameng naugg' ellitameggneng, ellitarkameggneng pitulriit.

Elder: Ii-i.

Interpreter: Yuraliyarlutek atrallermeggnek aciararutnillrulukek; aciararutnillruyagnarqait nunam acianun pulalutek.

It was interesting how this short narrative about the giant footprints led to a longer, embedded narrative in which a group of children also becomes lost when they failed to listen to the important teachings of their elders. Like the narrative of the giant footprints, the tale is about more than just getting lost. The children become, for a time, a part of the land. It illustrates the way that people can become a part of the spirit world, lost, sometimes forever, in another realm of existence. Human beings are not separate, but are instead very much a part of the world of spirits and other beings that inhabit the tundra, the waters, rocks, and other features of the world around them.

The Children Came Out at Volcano Mountains

Another elder began his telling by making a comparison between Halloween trick-or-treating and a ceremonial practice, deeply rooted in Yup'ik tradition, of going from house to house. He and his Yup'ik interpreter (a younger Yup'ik man also from Hooper Bay) co-constructed and crafted the story for me, a particular *kass'aq* who would be familiar with Halloween but whose understanding of Yup'ik ceremonialism was limited at best. He began his tale:

Elder: Trick-or-treat, different house, they give 'em, piece of, some kind of different treat. They kept going into houses till they fill their [he holds up his hands as he smiles at me, then pretends to reach into a bag or some sort of container. We all laugh as he reaches slowly in for a treat].

Elder: Any kind of, any kind of Eskimo food. Like, uh, Trick and Treat!

Interpreter: This was done before, uh, before Caucasian/white Halloween was even realized. They used to do that, nowadays they trick-or-treat at Halloween time, candies? But back then they did it <u>long</u> before Halloween was here. You know, Caucasian Halloween came around.

Holly: Yeah, yeah.

Elder: Native foods!

Holly: Right!

Interpreter: All kinds of Native foods! A very different kind of food [than Halloween candy].

He explains to me that there are some logs on the tundra "behind the school" where there are some "spring wells." "That used to be their house," and another listener remarks that he remembers them too. I quickly ask, "Oh, you can still see them?" Both nod their heads in agreement. The Yup'ik listener comments, "I remember those, when I was young too, we used to pack water from that spot. Water used to seep out from underground, and it used to be really clear. Clear and cold."

This elder goes on to explain to me that, back then, they used to have houses with tunnels that led from "house to house." The story continues as follows:

Elder: They used to, at that time, like Halloween, trick 'n' treat, even though they didn't know about it, they did it. Even though they were Yup'iks, although they didn't know anything about Halloween. Like Halloween, trick 'n' treat, they participated in a feast called Qaariitaaq [which was held in late October when they went from house to house wearing masks]. They carried with them wooden bowls, trick 'n' treat. When they enter a house, different house, they give a piece of, some kind of fish. They keep goin' into houses till they fill their pocket. Any kind of Eskimo food. Like a trick 'n' treat. Just like in Halloween.

Interpreter: Two of them? Or . . .

Elder: There were three of them.

Interpreter: Three youths.

Elder: It is said that when they went into one of the houses, they missed the path that went into the house, but instead went under the path, in those *qasgi* . . . , this was during the war. They say they went out through the ground. Like this.

Interpreter: They were trick or treating house to house, uh, some houses had tunnels that go into the house. And right in the middle of the sod houses they had these, uh, like a door where you could pop up and get into the house. Somehow, uh, they went under, under the ground.

Elder: They go <u>under</u> the ground.

Interpreter: Uh, here's the actual tundra [shows me with his hand].

Holly: Oh, <u>below</u>.

Interpreter: Yeah, they got below somehow. Under the ground and, uh, they couldn't come up. They couldn't get out.

Elder: Like an elevator.

Elder: They had another entrance under the door. There was a door and another one underneath the ground. And they come up through the middle of the floor.

Interpreter: When the three went from house to house . . . while they were trick-or-treating back then, when they went under they . . . what happened when they went under and went below the underground entrance?

Elder: Yeah, they went below the underground entrance, when they tried to go in through the underground entrance, they began to travel through the ground underneath the tunnel.

Their parents panicked and they could hear them down there. They were able to hear them.

Interpreter: And the parents, they could hear them, uh, being afraid. You know, start crying and bawling and being afraid, but they [the parents] couldn't do nothing, uh, even though they could hear them. They panicked, you know, like parents would. They recognized their son. [lowers his voice] No more sound after that. At first they made a sound, and later on, no more sound. Not far from my camp, trapping camp. Got, uh, mountains over there [place where the children were heard], they call Volcano Mountains. They're not real close to my fishing, trapping camp right there. Between, uh, home [Hooper Bay] and, uh, Bethel. One of those volcanoes they go throughout . . . young kids, they go throughout through Volcano Mountains.

Elder: And through that they disappeared. No more . . . more sound. You know those Volcano Mountains? Not far . . . camp? That [camping place near the] . . . Mountains.

Holly: I've seen [those mountains].

Elder: Oh . . . there.

Holly: That's a neat place.

Elder: Between home and Bethel.

Holly: Yeah.

Elder: They apparently went out through one of the mountains. One of those volcanoes . . . kids. When they went out, when . . . mountains. Those things, when . . . Amazing.

Holly: Did they come out at that place?

Elder: Right there [nodding his head yes] at Volcano Mountains, from Hooper Bay. Under the ground.

Elder: They come out.

Elder: Right . . . under the ground.

Interpreter: When they go throughout, *tamaan imkuut* [those over there/ones spoken about] one of those mountains [pause] when they were young, when they got lost underground. When they come out, they're really old [I gasp with surprise] really old!

Holly: Jeez!

Elder: Amazing! [nodding his head in agreement]

Holly: But they were aged?

Interpreter: They were . . . how long, how long [underground]?

Elder: I don't . . . [know how long under]ground.

Interpreter: They were just kids when they got lost underground and, uh, I don't know how long . . .

Elder: I don't know how long they been, been under the ground.

Interpreter: By the time they got out, you've seen those volcanoes?

Holly: Yeah.

Interpreter: Through one of them, they finally got out . . . by the time they got out they were old and aged.

Elder: One of those volcanoes, some of the mountain, cut it, blow up. Volcano. Lots of lava rocks around there.

Holly: Yeah, that's an amazing place. I remember the first time I saw it, I just couldn't believe . . .

Elder: Sometimes I go over there and, uh, collect for ivory, carving base.

Holly: Oh, the rocks!

Elder: *Ii-i,* lava rocks. They are made just like mud, looks like mud, but, uh, some flowers start growing on top of this, looks fancy too.

Holly: Yeah, the tourists like it?

Elder: *Ii-i!*

Elder: And after that, you know where Newtok is? They originally were from Kayalivik, the grandchildren, Naunraq and his family. They checked the place they came out from; they got curious and checked it. You know those coils of string, old type of string, they put a rock on the end and dropped it in. And before they reached the bottom it ran out. Pretty deep.

Elder: Whenever the rock touched the sides it would echo, it echoed.

Elder: At that time, you know Kass'aq? She told the story, they were from Qagatet, from Cuukvagtulit at Cuukvagtuli. They would do that because Cuukvagtulit wasn't far from there. If they want to live a long life they would stick their arm into the hole and stay there, if they wanted to live long.

Interpreter: There at the volcano?

Elder: Yes, at the place they came out, there at the volcanoes.

Interpreter: How much of their arm did they stick into the hole?

Elder: Maybe all the way in.

Holly: Yeah, one arm?

Elder: One arm. That is how Kass'aq's mother said it was done.

Elder: That is where I had a camp. Even I know that. When I used to ride around the volcanoes.

Interpreter: Yeah, uh the Volcano Mountains they're like maybe 75 miles from Hooper Bay, but they finally came out and then, uh I don't know how long it was, uh these people from Newtok, they're about, uh, so many miles from the volcanoes, it's Nelson Island, just above Nelson Island, just south of, from the volcanoes. They got curious to see, uh, when they found out, after they found out [about the children from Hooper Bay], uh, those ladies, you know, they were kids when they first got under, they came out old ladies. They [the people from Newtok] got curious and, uh, they took a good-sized ball of string to, uh, to that place that they [the children who became old] got out. And they tied a rock at the end of that string, ball of string. And they unraveled it and that ball of string, uh, [pause] unraveled all the way until, you know, there was no more. It didn't even reach the bottom. There was a good-sized ball of string. You've seen them threads, you know, them nets, how they make strings?

Holly: They never found the bottom?

Interpreter: They didn't reach the bottom.

Elder: No bottom. When they swing it like this, when they hit the wall, just like a wall, the echo from the great bottom of that hole echo through the echo of like maybe a wall. All the way around.

Interpreter: They, uh, stretched that ball of string. At the end when they couldn't reach the bottom. They started swinging the string and pretty soon they started hitting the walls and you could hear the echo from that, you know, when it hits, it echoes, the sound. Apparently, uh, one of those volcanoes, where those three young kids came out old ladies, uh, there's a saying that if you want to live long, go to it, stick your hand in there and, stick it in there for a while and, you'll have a long life. . . . It's what they, they used to do if they want to have a long life. Go to one of those volcanoes, one of those volcanoes that those kids got out of. By the time they got out they were old ladies. [His] old mother used to say that, that's, you know, one of the things they used to do.

[Yupik Language Transcription]

Elder: Tamaani pitullruut, like Halloween, trick 'n' treat, nallungermeng pitullrulliniut. Yupiungermeng, Halloween-aq nallungermegteggu. Halloween-alriit-gguq, trick 'n' treat, qaariitaalriit-gguq, qaaritaarluteng. Imkuneng, wooden bowl assigcirluteng, trick 'n' treat. Enmun itraqata, different house they give piece of, some kind of fish. They keep goin' into houses till they fill their pocket. Any kind of Eskimo food. Like a trick 'n' treat. Just like in Halloween.

Interpreter: Malrulutek? Wall'u-qa . . .

Elder: Three-auluteng.

Interpreter: Three youths.

Elder: Tua-i-llu enet-gguq iliitnun itlermeggni acitruulluteng-gguq, imkut im' qaygi . . . , anguyautellratni qanellruuq. Tamaani-gguq camaggun anengqellruut. Makucetun waten.

Elder: Elevator, elevator-aatun.

Interpreter: Just like his . . .

Elder: Iteryarait camkut atlingqerrluteng. Qaingakun-llu allameng, nunam qaingakun iteryarangqerrluni camaggun cali. Kanaggun-ll' natrem qukaakun enmun mayurluteng.

Interpreter: Pingayut augkut mikelnguut qaaritaallermeggni . . . while they were trick-or-treating back then, when they went under they . . . aciararulluteng qaill' pillruat?

Elder: Yeah, atliaggun camaggun-gguq acitruulluteng-gguq. Nunam-ll' akuliikuneglenglliniluteng acitruulluteng enemun iteryaaqellermeggni. Nunam-ll' akuliikun eglenglliniluteng. Taukut-llu angayuqaarit kapialliniut, qalrillagnaurtut-gguq nunam akuliineng tayima. Alaunateng, niitnaqluteng.

Elder: Tua-i-llu tavaggun tamalliniluteng. No more . . . more sound. Imkut nallunrilketen Volcano Mountains? Not far . . . camp? That . . . Mountains.

Holly: I've seen . . .

Elder: Oh . . . there.

Holly: That's a neat place.

Elder: Between home and Bethel.

Holly: Yeah.

Elder: Ingrit iliitgun anellrulliniut taukut. One of those volcanoes . . . kids. Maaten-gguq anut, when . . . mountains. Tamaani imkut, when . . . Amazing.

Holly: Did they come out?

Elder: They come out.

Holly: At that place.

Elder: Right . . . under the ground.

Holly: But they were aged.

Interpreter: They were . . . how long, qaill' taktatalriameng?

Elder: I don't . . . ground.

Elder: And after that, imkut nallunrilketen Niugtaq? Kayalivigmiungullrulriit, imkut tutgaraluyagaat, Naunraankut, taukut Naunraankut. Tauna anvillrat check-aryartull[rulliniat] paqtellrulliniat-am paqnayungluteng. Imkut pelacinat, coils ball-apaarrlugtun angtaluni, coil-aumaluni. Tauna-gguq, string-at imkut, old types string, iqua teggalqumeng kicirlukek kalevvluk'. Teqlipailegmi-gguq nangellruuq. Pretty deep.

Elder: Waten-gguq agtuutaqameng echo-rnaurtuq, akiuggluni.

Elder: Tamaani-llu ingkut Kass'aq nallrunrilken? Aani imna qanemcikellra. Qagatmiullruut, Cuukvagtulirmiullret, Cuukvagtulimi. Waten-gguq pituut, tavani yaaqsinrilameng kiani Cuukvagtulirmiut. Yuunertuyukata tavavet agluki hole-aq, talliat iterrluku uitasqelluku, yuunertuyukata.

Interpreter: Tauna-q' volcano-q?

Elder: Ii-i, tavani anvillratni taukut, volcano-ni yaani.
Interpreter: Qaillun taktatalriameng talliteng ekumaluki?
Elder: Maybe all the way in.
Holly: Yeah. One arm.
Elder: One arm. Tavaten-am-qa Kass'am aaniin qanrutektullrua.

Understanding the Story

The practice of going house to house, as the storyteller noted, may be like trick-or-treat but it has an older linguistic and cultural significance. According to linguist Steve Jacobson, although the *qaariitaaq* festival "predates contact with Europeans, the name has been adopted for Halloween" (Jacobson 1984a, 302). The Yup'ik word *qaariitaarvik* ("time for qaariitaaq") refers to the month of October and probably also indicates the time of year when such a ceremony of going door-to-door took place.

The Qaariitaaq Ceremony: The Asking Festival

According to Phyllis Morrow (1984) and Elsie Mather (1985), Qaariitaaq (origin unknown), also known as Itertaaq ("going in and out of houses"), was the first of several ceremonies that preceded the Bladder Festival.

> During *Qaariitaaq*, one or two men led the children of their village from house to house, carrying bowls. On the coast, children of both sexes participated; elsewhere, only the boys followed. At each house, the children were given food, such as dried fish, (but not *akutaq*) to put in the bowls. Coastal sources did not describe what the children wore; elsewhere, they were disguised and made strange noises, such as a ghostly humming. *Qaariitaaq* lasted for three days on the coast and was followed by *Qaarpak*. On Nelson Island it lasted four days. There participants were disguised only on the fifth day (which may correspond to *Qengarpak* described for the coastal villages). (Morrow 1984, 119)

Morrow identifies this tale as one that is commonly told in the Yup'ik region (1984). She notes that these children, as they went from house to house, "became lost on the way back to the *qasgi* [men's ceremonial house]." It seems that the time surrounding these ceremonies was especially dangerous. "It is probably safe to conclude that *Qaariitaaq* and *Qengarpak* [a related ceremony] were ritually dangerous times, during which precautions had to be taken against entry into the spirit world" (Morrow 1984, 123). This caution probably extended to the use of entryways and tunnels at this time.

I have already spoken about the discomfort of my Yup'ik companions when I crawled through one of the passageways at Askinuk. Underground passageways and entrances sometimes led people to unintended places.[5] Edward Nelson noted, in "the Big-lake district" (Hooper Bay region), "houses were of the ordinary kind, except that they . . . had extraordinarily long entrance passages" (Nelson 1983 [1899], 248). Lantis said that Yupiit, in fear of enemy attacks, "would dig extra underground entrances out from the *kazigis* and houses or would connect the buildings by secret tunnels. They would also dig secret hideaways for the children" (Lantis 1946, 168). Morrow goes on to say of the children in the story:

> Instead of going into the entryway, they went underground. The people inside the *qasgi* could hear them crying, underneath the building. In this way, they acted like the spirits of the dead, who gathered under the *qasgi* for ceremonies when the people invited them to come from the underworld. (Morrow 1984, 122)

The permeability of the land to the underground world and spirits must have been strongly felt as people lived in these underground houses and moved through these passageways. Living in underground sod houses, with passageways that led from one chamber to the next, one was never out of sight from those who were, themselves, unseen. A Yup'ik woman once shared a recollection with Robin Barker (1994) that expresses this sense of permeability and uncertainty. The speaker, Irene, tells Barker of the warnings her mother used to give her as she was growing up. Irene explains:

> She tell us about, not to make noises in the evening times, that they (dwarves) [*ircinrraat*] always watch us from the . . . we lived in a mud house, igloos, like underground, and then she'd say if we make too much noise, the dwarves are always watching us from the corners of the house. And every move we make or what we say are heard by them all the time. They listen. That when we're alone not to make too much noise that those little people will come out from each corner and (laughs) do something to us. (Barker 1994, 97)

These themes of "going underground," being watched, and becoming lost in another world are common motifs. Passageways and tunnels, then, always held the potential for misleading the living. This was especially true for those who were not paying attention and aware of their surroundings. In Irene's account we get a strong sense that these underground dwellings were filled with much more than human dwellers. Ircinrraat are beings that have been variously described to me in Hooper Bay as very small people (only a few inches high) or, sometimes, larger beings (maybe a foot in height).[6]

People at Hooper Bay, and in other Yup'ik villages, have told me that ircinrraat[7] sometimes like to tease and mock human beings. One woman told me that they were making their way up the slough towards the village one time when the ircinrraat started throwing mud and sticks at them. They hurried on their way until they were out of that place along the slough. Morrow tells us that they are often depicted as "half-human/half-animal beings" (2002, 335). Fienup-Riordan says that people describe them as "small people, two to three feet high, and some . . . describe them as dwarves." She goes on to say that "occasionally a person encounters *ircenrrat* as *yuut* (people), and later sees them as wolves or foxes or other small mammals" (Fienup-Riordan 1994, 63).

Of ircinrraat, Henry and Black said "they are dwellers of the underground" (Tennant and Bitar 1981, 251). Susan Hansen (1985) wrote that "people believed the *ircinrraat* lived underground at the base of an old house pole" (1985, 86). While ircinrraat are not mentioned in the story, a similar sense of the permeability of worlds is reflected in it, as in many stories told at Hooper Bay. Recall the young Yup'ik girls of Hooper Bay who ignored the rules surrounding menstruation and how they sank down into the tundra. There is another genre of Yup'ik stories that centers around a water creature known as *paalraayak*. Tales of encounters with paalraayak also speak to this sense of permeability between worlds. The stories demonstrate how quickly this world can change and the dangers it presents. "The land you're standing on" is a dangerous place for those who do not demonstrate appropriate action.

In the case of the young girls, it is a dangerous place for those who do not maintain proper respect of that knowledge. In the case of the Yup'ik hunter who was vulnerable to the frightening creature, we get the strong sense that he was spared because he recalled the important knowledge and associated narratives of his own elders. This knowledge allowed him to act appropriately in the face of danger.

These tales all indicate a permeable and ever-changing landscape and remind Yup'ik people of the illusory quality of the world in which we live. A Yup'ik sense of place is one in which the earth and world below defy simple definition. Different levels can only be reached with the help or intervention of the spirit world. Lantis wrote:

> Concerning the world levels other than our own, they were not so certain. Underneath this earthly level was a dark disagreeable world . . . very dark (place), to which went the souls of all who died a natural death. . . . There was no one entrance to the underworld. . . . Human souls just sank down through any crevice apparently. (Lantis 1946, 197)

During ceremonial times, humans and spirits often inhabited the same places, or the boundaries between worlds were diminished. In the *qasgiq* the dead (ancestors) were welcomed back through ritual offerings, but certainly not all of the beings from this "dark disagreeable world" would have been intentionally invited into the world of the living.

Yupiit held many ceremonies throughout the year and there was more than one Yup'ik ceremony that involved children going door to door (Morrow 1984; Mather 1985). Another Yup'ik ceremony that preceded the Bladder Festival was *Qaarpak*, also known as *Qengarpak*. Morrow and Mather describe this ceremony as one in which children, or those playing the role of children, go door to door and receive food. During this ceremony the actors are disguised in much the same way that contemporary trick-or-treaters are today. The following account describes this ceremony:

> During *Qaarpak/Qengarpak* ["Big Nose"], boys of marriageable age, each accompanied by a younger boy said to be "his child," made the rounds from house to house each day. They were disguised with old clothes and false noses (hence the name), whispered, and generally tried to make themselves unrecognizable. Two of the boys were given *akutaq*. The "children" who followed these older boys purposely acted "unruly," a behavior which was normally discouraged in children. (Morrow 1984, 119)

Note that this tradition of going from house to house, or door to door, is also practiced in the context of contemporary seal parties in the Yup'ik region. A seal party was "given when the men and boys of the village brought home the first seals of the season" (Fienup-Riordan 1990, 39). More recently, too, seal party items include much-needed goods such as disposable diapers and other household necessities. Of seal parties, Fienup-Riordan recalls "following the group to the next house for a repetition of the event" (Fienup-Riordan 1990, 39). Selaviq or "starring" (Russian Christmas), in villages with Russian Orthodox influence, also follows a similar ritual practice which involves visiting house to house and the distribution of foods, often including large quantities of candy and sweets. In this way, contemporary Yup'ik celebrations continue to follow this ritual of house-to-house processions.

A Gift to the Land

Each telling of "The Giant Footprints" explains how they came to be. The place of the giant footprints, like the place of the volcano mountains, exists as a tangible and concrete reminder of deeply rooted Yup'ik knowledge and contemporary shared values. Each telling and each allusion to this place reinforces the importance of respecting that, as elders remind their listeners, the land is marked in this place, not as an inanimate surface, but rather as an actor. The land, as actor, responded directly to the careless, disrespectful behavior of the young girls.

Significantly, these stories reinforce both the idea that people need to have an intimate knowledge of the land and the idea that the land and particular places on the land have knowledge of people. Canadian anthropologist Julie Cruikshank makes similar observations in her discussion of glaciers in the Saint Elias Mountain divide between Alaska and the Yukon Territory noting that glaciers "make moral judgments and they punish infractions" (Cruikshank 2005, 3).

If the land and particular places are actors, cognizant of human actions and words, they must also be places that "recognize" proper behavior when it is exhibited. If such places make moral judgments, as Cruikshank suggests, do they also reward proper behavior? The land's knowledge of the people is best understood through the narratives and personal accounts shared in day-to-day experience. This understanding, like most of the knowledge I have been given over time, would come in a most unexpected place far from the tundra of the Bering Sea coast.

It was at that aforementioned 2001 American Folklore Society session on the power of place, where we shared our oral history project and invited a Hooper Bay elder to retell the story of "The Giant Footsteps," which so well illustrated the important relationship that Yupiit have with the land. The particular elder we had asked to join us declined, as his health did not allow him to travel, so he suggested that we invite his sister instead. She also knew the story very well.

What proved to be most valuable was the time that the three of us spent together before our public presentation. We decided to find a room where we could prepare for our public talk. As we sat in an empty ballroom at the Hilton Hotel, we joked that we should, instead, have treated ourselves to lunch at the ritzy "Hooper Bay Cafe." After a few more jokes about the upscale decor, we concurred that they should add whale meat and seal oil to the menu if they wanted to use that name. We then settled into the business of preparing for our upcoming public talk. We listened to this respected community elder tell the story of "The Giant Footsteps" as she planned to tell it to our larger, intended audience.

What was most fascinating to me was the way that she embedded in this widely known narrative about the giant footprints a rather personal narrative. As she described the young girls sinking down into the earth, she suddenly turned to a similar experience that she had with this sentient land. Her story demonstrated the same lessons and highlighted the important relationship of respect that Yupiit maintain with the land.

She began by telling us of a young boy in Hooper Bay whom she had cured with water found at a certain location on the tundra. This small boy had suffered a terrible illness, which resulted in a serious affliction of his arms, neck, trunk, and face. She described how she went to this special place on the tundra to collect the water for healing this child. She explained to us that she wanted to thank the land (*nuna*) for the healing waters and that she felt she had so little to offer. She thought about it and finally decided that she would offer as a gift her sewing needle. This was, indeed, a significant gift, since she was well known for her skilled sewing. She often talked about making a *qaspeq* (a lightweight parka) or pair of *pilugut* (skin boots known in English as mukluks) and was always sewing for her many children, grandchildren, and great-grandchildren. She was also very skilled at making beautiful and elaborate Yup'ik Eskimo grass baskets.

Her description of offering this special gift to the land is a powerful one. She reenacted the careful placement of the bone needle as though she was doing it at the very moment of her telling. She explained to us that sometimes the land will reject a gift: not accept it from the person offering it. She laughed uncomfortably as she recalled how very nervous she felt as she gently placed the bone needle down into the tundra waters. Her hand still extended out, she stared ahead as though she was there, nervously watching it for a while as it floated on the surface. As she told this story her eyes remained fixed on a single object. She didn't see us, her listeners, or the room where we were sitting. She was watching that needle float on the tundra water. She was waiting to see if this gift would be accepted. Her face lit up suddenly as she described her great relief and joy at the sight of the needle slowly disappearing under the water. She knew that her gift of thanks had been accepted. "Oh, I was <u>so</u> happy!" she said as she fondly remembered this powerful life experience. This tale also gives us a sense of these complex and overlapping worlds. The needle, as a gift of thanks, had not been accepted until she saw it sink down into the other world. Left implicit was the parallel between the girls sinking into another world through the earth, and her needle sinking through the water to the spirits.

Turning to the Land: The Impact of Disease and Local Response

The above narrative eloquently demonstrates the complexity of the reciprocal relationship that Yupiit maintain with the land and spirit world around them, a relationship obviously deeply rooted in Yup'ik tradition. In this story we learn that the land and the water hold the power to heal people who have been afflicted with disease. On this subject, several important points need to be stressed. First, people can turn to the land for help when community members become ill. Second, the land and spirit world are active in healing. Third, even in the face of unbelievable epidemics, this relationship endures.

A sentient world makes the choice to accept or reject the reciprocal relationship with living human beings. The elder offered a gift of thanks but the land and spirit world made an active choice to either acknowledge or reject this gift of thanks. The teller's gift was heartfelt and respectfully offered in exchange for the healing waters. Also implicit is the knowledge that a less respectful person might have been rejected. The powerful connection between Yupiit and the land is demonstrated by this deep dependence. In the face of disease, uncertainty, and horrible suffering, people are given guidance and solutions from the land.

Euro-Americans, not having experienced pandemics in recent history, are removed from the fear associated with widespread disease. They have not been raised with a "collective memory" of what epidemics can do and how lasting the devastation can be on a community. Alaska Native communities have a much stronger sense of what it means to experience an epidemic. Like Alaska Natives throughout the state, Yupiit have historically contended with wave after wave of disease. In 1900, for example, a devastating epidemic swept over villages on the Bering Sea coast as it did elsewhere in Alaska. This "Great Sickness" killed thousands of Alaska Native people (Fortuine 1992; Wolfe 1982). "It was alleged that communities frequently lost 25 percent to 50 percent of their members, and that a quarter of western Alaska's Eskimo population perished" (Wolfe 1982, 91). Dr. Joseph Romig described how

Yup'ik people on the Kuskokwim River were incapacitated and suffering a "social breakdown" as a result of the "Great Sickness" (Wolfe 1982). According to Romig, who was floating downriver in 1901, during the height of the outbreak:

> The story is just about the same for every village. There were not enough well ones to care for the sick, and in many cases the sick were in serious need of care. . . . The misery of the people seemed to be complete. They were cold, they were hungry and thirsty and sick, with no one to wait on them. The dead often remained for days in the same tent as the living, and in many cases they were never removed. Those that recovered left the tent to fall on the dead as the only covering for the remains of relatives and friends. Children cried for food, and no one was able to give it to them. At one place some passing strangers heard the crying of children, and upon examination found only some children left with both parents dead in the tent. Thus the story continues from the source to the mouth of the river. (Wolfe 1982, 110)

Fortuine, who researched and wrote of this devastation, has stated that the epidemic of "smallpox in 1835–1840 and influenza and measles in 1900, caused such devastation that they must rank among the most significant single events in the recorded history of the peoples they affected" (Fortuine 1992, 197). Yup'ik writer Harold Napoleon, who was born and raised in Hooper Bay, poignantly describes "the survivors" and the subsequent aftermath of their world:

> Whether the survivors knew or understood, they had witnessed the fatal wounding of *Yuuyaraq* and the old Yup'ik culture. Compared to the span of life of a culture, the Great Death was instantaneous. The Yup'ik world was turned upside down, literally overnight. Out of the suffering, confusion, desperation, heartbreak, and trauma was born a new generation of Yup'ik people. They were born into shock. They woke to a world in shambles, many of their people and their beliefs strewn around them, dead. In their minds they had been overcome by evil.

> Their medicines and their medicine men and women had proven useless. (Napoleon 1991, 11)

These widespread epidemics, as subsequent chapters will reveal, were one "of a series of catastrophic and traumatic events" that deeply impacted Native peoples throughout Alaska (Pullar 1992, 182). The impact of epidemics has been devastating and lasting for the Native village of Hooper Bay (Napoleon 1991).

Although there were no known Western cures for these epidemics, Yupiit turned to the land and specific places on the land to heal the sick. Such knowledge included certain places to find plants or collect water for making medicine.

To varying degrees, people continue to rely on the land and water in order to cure illness and maintain health. Examining how specific places on the land are associated with healing qualities contributes to understanding the importance of place in the Yup'ik tradition. I recall a personal conversation with a colleague in Anchorage who informed me that people in the southwestern villages "don't use traditional medicines" anymore. His statement was incorrect. Four years later, when I had been ill for many days, someone offered me what they translated as "Eskimo medicine." It was a mixture of water and plants from the local tundra. I don't know what this particular plant remedy contained, but it might have been the commonly used medicinal *ayuq*, known to English speakers as Labrador tea or tundra tea (*Rhododendron tomentosum*, formerly *Ledum palustre*)(Jacobson 1984a, 98). In an ethnobotany guide compiled by Yup'ik elders in western Alaska, Hooper Bay community member Juliana Springer "said her grandfather was cured of appendicitis using a tea made from ayuq and the bark of a dwarf willow species. She described it as 'super-strong medicine,' and other elders agreed" Jernigan 2014, 106). The remedy shared with me did sooth my stomach, allowing me to get rehydrated before my illness got too serious.

My personal observation is that many Yupiit continue to look to the land and water for various kinds of healing. This place-based knowledge of where to obtain specific plants and water for healing is passed down from one generation to the next. It includes the use of certain waters for tea, a point to which I will return in chapter 4. I believe that most Yupiit today do subscribe to the germ theory of disease, but they don't think that negates the power of the land to heal. Perhaps this observation is somewhat misguided by the fact that not all aspects of daily living are presented to outsiders. Like aspects of worldview and spiritual beliefs, medicinal practices probably went underground as a result of missionization, a time when traditional Yup'ik healers were being challenged as helpers of the devil. But the use of modern medicine does not negate older forms and practices of healing.

In fact, contemporary medical anthropological literature has well documented that people often adopt new forms of healing without entirely abandoning their old forms of practice. John Janzen reminds us, for example, that a true understanding of any system of healing "should describe the full range of practices in a society, and it should explain how these practices coexist in a changing structure of customs and social relationships" (1978, xi). Certainly a case for "medical pluralism" can be made in the Yup'ik region, just as it could be for those in Western society who employ herbal teas or vitamins.

Traditional medical knowledge and practice is now somewhat guarded in Alaska Native villages like Hooper Bay. Early 1900s mission records describe the presence and use of Western medicines in Hooper Bay, and indicate that they were strictly controlled by the missionaries. Actually, this kind of control over access to Western medicine may also have been a reason why people in Hooper Bay protected their own forms of healing from non-Yupiit. What outsiders didn't know, they couldn't regulate or prohibit. This tendency to "protect" older forms of healing is parallel to the kinds of guarded behaviors that Yupiit employed after missionaries came into their communities and actively sought to erase and replace other aspects of their culture. A Yup'ik woman who was born and raised in another coastal village once told me that her elders were cautious when talking about traditional plants used for medicinal purposes, especially when non-Yupiit were present. This is an issue of control, one that will be addressed further in later chapters.

In the collective memory of the community, epidemics loom large. Consequently, in the minds and hearts of the elders, disease is an ever-present concern. In 1985, Simeon Harpuk, who was born in 1896, recalled for Susan Hansen this painful experience of surviving wave after wave of epidemic. He recalled "his mother taking him to the *qasgiq* when he was sick and the 'Yup'ik doctors' drumming and performing their rites to make him well again" (Hansen 1985, 202). Although it is unclear as to whether it was during the epidemic of 1900, Simeon recalls that all three of his sisters died during their youth.

As a young man he also witnessed "the big sickness" (influenza epidemic, also referred to as "the great sickness"). "They say [it] happened . . . right before Christmas." Hansen says that "so many people died [during this time] that the survivors took the bodies to a hill above the village and left them." He told Hansen that he left that place "not wanting to be constantly reminded of my kids being born and dying" (Hansen 1985, 203).

In the fall of 2003, a high number of influenza cases were reported throughout the United States and, once again, hit communities throughout Alaska. According to the CDC (Centers for Disease Control and Prevention), the influenza season had begun early and was more severe, reporting that by the end of May 2004, there were "152 influenza-associated deaths in U.S."

When a young girl in a Yup'ik village died of influenza that season, it brought back a flood of painful memories. One Hooper Bay community member remarked that village elders seemed to have a "look of fear on their faces." This individual explained that many elders felt the girl had gone outside too soon after being ill. Although she appeared to be well, she was not. It seems that the sick can be caught in a dangerous, liminal stage. This is a particularly vulnerable state of not being fully aware.

In any state other than full awareness, people, whether they are ill, asleep, or unconscious, become more vulnerable to the unseen world. In this way, awareness is inextricably tied to both health and sense of place. Being aware of your own state is particularly important when you are out on the land and more vulnerable. Part of knowing places is also knowing where you have to be particularly mindful or, more to the point, mindful of particular things. Stories of tundra encounters establish which places one should be especially wary of and also hint at the kinds of dangers these places present, in particular, what spirit beings are encountered at that place whether it be a ghost or some other spirit form.

Several of the subsequent narratives will demonstrate that sleep is a liminal and therefore potentially dangerous state. This seems especially true for those who fall asleep out on the land. A key to wellness, then, is to maintain a sense of appropriate awareness or *ella*. Those who are not properly cautious, who do not maintain proper awareness, become more vulnerable to the dangers of illness (Fienup-Riordan 1990).

Encounters and Awareness

Bad things can happen when you are asleep and unaware of your surroundings. The following tale, shared with me by a Hooper Bay elder who passed away many years ago, illustrates this vulnerability. A skilled hunter, he spent much of his life on the land. Through this lifetime of experience, he knew intimately the places where encounters were more likely and which places to avoid. He once traveled by qayaq and, after much paddling, pulls his craft ashore to rest. He flips his qayaq over and, leaning against the side for support, falls quickly to sleep. He is soundly sleeping when something forces him back to a state of awareness. As he opens his eyes, he sees before him a ghostly shape. The face of this being is very pale and decrepit, clearly no longer one of the living. What most surprises the awakening hunter is that this figure is not dressed in contemporary clothing, but rather an "old-style" gut-skin parka. That, too, tells this surprised man something about what he is dealing with in this encounter. He forces himself to become fully awake, fully aware and then standing to his feet he silently places his hand (palm-down) on the top of the ghost's head and slowly pushes the being back below the surface of the land. This he must do slowly and more than once before the ghost finally leaves him alone. He concluded this story by turning to his younger listeners and reiterating the importance of knowing about and maintaining awareness at these places.

Wisdom Lives in Places

Those who are familiar with Keith Basso's work on Apache notions of place know that he cogently demonstrates how "wisdom sits in places" in the Apache Southwest. He highlights the complexity with which Apache people experience and "sense place." Basso explains that "Apache constructions of place reach deeply into other cultural spheres, including conceptions of wisdom, notions of morality, politeness and tact in forms of spoken discourse, and certain conventional ways of imagining and interpreting the Apache tribal past" (Basso 1996, xv).

The Apache landscape is filled with places that serve to remind people of important Apache knowledge and cultural lessons.

> The knowledge on which wisdom depends is gained from observing different places (thus to recall them quickly and clearly), learning their Apache names (thus to identify them in spoken discourse and in song), and reflecting on traditional narratives that underscore the virtues of wisdom by showing what can happen when its facilitating conditions are absent. Drawn from different story genres, these narratives juxtapose a character whose mind is insightfully smooth with one or more characters whose minds are not. (Basso 1996, 134)

I once shared some of Keith Basso's writings with some of my friends in Hooper Bay. I did this because I wanted to share the kinds of anthropological insights that had influenced my thinking, but I also had been struck by some of the parallels to what I had been taught in the Yup'ik southwest. Those I shared it with were also intrigued by some of the parallels between Apache and Yup'ik notions of the land and sense of place.

When I asked one what he thought of Basso's article, he simply stated "scary!" I asked, "What do you mean scary?" He explained that some of the similarities were unexpected and that some of the knowledge recorded by Basso reminded him of his grandmother's teachings when he was growing up in Hooper Bay. He then began to talk about places on the tundra where they collected water and places they had passed when harvesting greens or collecting eggs. There were, she had taught him long ago, special places to go for the collection of water used in healing teas.

Viewing the Land as a Social Actor

He, of course, also noted many ways in which his Yup'ik cultural traditions differed from that of the Western Apache.[8] One marked difference has to do with the ways in which the land reacts directly to human action. Unlike the Apache examples, place does more than remind people of "the virtues of wisdom." The land is more than a stage[9] upon which actors live and respond to the world around them.

The Hooper Bay narratives illustrate how the land and specific places directly react and respond to the choices and actions of the living. This is an essential point in understanding place in the Yup'ik southwest and it is specifically what sets a Yup'ik sense of place apart from other ways of viewing the land. Consider the aforementioned narratives of "The Giant Footprints," "The Shaman's Grave," or "A Gift to the Land." All demonstrate that the landscape is much more than an inanimate place: it responds to the disobedience of children, to the social ills within the community, and to a gift given. Aware of human action the land and spirit world, reacting like a community member, are an active force.

Like people, the land responds both positively and negatively, depending on the context of the particular event or human action. There is a sense that when the community is not well, the land and spirit world are not well because everything is interconnected in a cycle of reciprocal influence. The land is like the seals that are reclothed and reborn. The birds and the flowers return in greater numbers when the land is properly treated, but also when the people living on this land are well. The land and spirit world are well when human action is guided by awareness (ella), respect, and proper behavior. Maintaining a balance between the human and spirit world (*Ellam Yua*) is essential for a healthy community and a healthy land. This is "sense of place" in the Yup'ik region.

The lore provides ample evidence to suggest that the relationship Yupiit hold with the land is longstanding. However, as Keith Basso states in the western Apache case, "In today's climate of accelerating change, its [the land's] importance . . . may well be deepening" (Basso 1986, 114). Certainly in the Yup'ik region one can argue that people see and understand the land as responding positively and negatively to contemporary issues and events and use the land's responses as a guide to behavior in relation to those issues and events. The land, in essence, is responding to a new and changing social setting.

Yupiit know and understand place on two levels. Place defines cultural notions of what constitutes appropriate and inappropriate behavior. On one level, Yup'ik places serve very much the same way that Apache places do. Places, by their very existence, remind people how to act. However, among the Yupiit, there is this other aspect of place that goes beyond a tangible marker for a particular narrative or set of cultural norms.

The land, the water, and the spirit world directly react to the actions of the living. On the one hand we see how water and land accept a gift of thanks from an individual who respectfully uses the healing waters. This narrative is also significant because it suggests that the land can be responsive to the actions of the living in a positive, reaffirming way. By demonstration of proper reciprocity and respect, this elder's actions have not only made the young boy well, they have brought a sense of well-being and harmony to the land. In contrast, things worsen in the community and people watch as the shaman's grave gets lower. Human action, then, can bring both sorrow and joy to a sentient land. Yup'ik wisdom "sits in places," but it also *lives* in places. For Apache, wisdom and guidance come from the land. Chase Hensel adeptly expressed this notion, stating that "for Yupiit, pain and sorrow come to the land as well" (pers. comm. February 2004). This is a marked and unique aspect of place in the Yup'ik region. In chapter 8, specifically, I will demonstrate how this Yup'ik sense of place has translated to new marks on the land.

4

"Too Many Otters in That One Place!"

STORIES OF *PAALRAAYAK* AND OTHER WATER CREATURES

The narrative about offering the sewing needle, presented in chapter 3, expresses not only the ongoing, reciprocal relationship that many Yupiit maintain with the land but also the significance of water. Water is often used as a means of healing. Another Hooper Bay community member told me that, when she was a child, her grandmother always sent her to one particular pond for tea water. It was a long way from the village and extremely difficult to get to during bad weather, but the water from this specific location was necessary for its healing qualities.

While some possess the ability to heal, other kinds of water pose a serious threat to human well-being. An integral knowledge of place shapes the relationships people have with those different places. People learn that some ponds hold the potential to heal, while other bodies of water are places where heightened awareness is essential. As noted in the last chapter, for example, George Moses cautioned his listeners about a particular lake that "acts in unusual ways." This chapter looks more closely at Yup'ik relationships with water and bodies of water.

Water and Rebirth at Askinuk: Yup'ik Eskimo Worldview and Practice

During that first trip to Hooper Bay back in 1996, I learned just how significant water is in Yup'ik cosmology. I was invited to go with a small group of young people out onto the tundra to collect greens. Eager to take part in day-to-day activities and gain acceptance in the community, I readily accepted. Eventually we found ourselves making our way along the sand dunes and grassy mounds of the old village described by Edward Nelson during his visit to Askinuk (Hooper Bay) in the 1880s. As previously described, this place consists of a series of large, earthen mounds where the Hooper Bay ancestors once lived. We climbed up these large mounds to gain a better vantage point. From Askinuk one can see for miles. According to one community member this place is often referred to simply as Nuvugmiut, or "the old village."

Coming down off the mounds in the direction of the coastline, I spotted a pond on the tundra. I headed straight for the small, round kettle pond located just below the old sod houses. The water, I remember, was extremely clear and still. As I approached, I was astonished at the sight of literally hundreds and thousands of bones scattered on the pond floor. The bones were so dense that one could not see the bottom of the pond. I guessed that they were the bones of seals and perhaps other water creatures. Those who had hunted them had, at some time in the past, respectfully returned these bones to the water.

A hunter from Hooper Bay once told me about a song his grandma would sing to her grandchildren, reminding them not to leave any meat on seal bones as they ate (wasting meat was disrespectful). The song lyrics are the words of the seals and their bones and are sung in a taunting or haunting way. It goes something like "you didn't eat it, you didn't eat all of the meat from the bones." Robert Brightman talks about Cree values and beliefs in a similar way. "You got to eat the whole works" is a notion that extends beyond a concern for waste. The spiritual connection to game is complex for Yupiit as for Cree and in both cases involves concepts of respect for and reciprocity with the animals that are hunted and consumed (Brightman 1993, 213).

> The careful disposal of uneaten food, bones, crumbs, and other residue at the Watt Lake "eat-all" parallels Eastern Cree practice. Tanner's (1979, 166) statement about the Mistassini, that "it is as if every morsel must be accounted for," is apt. Like other large bones from game animals, the bones of animals eaten in wihkohtowin are either burned, placed into the water, or,

> especially in the case of skulls and antlers, suspended in trees. (Brightman 1993, 224)

The sight of all those seal bones reminded me of one of my favorite black-and-white photographs that I discovered in the hundreds taken by the Disney team back in 1946. It is an image of a Hooper Bay woman offering a drink of fresh water to a seal that had just been taken (figure 4.1). I always wondered what the photographers had understood about this particular image. Only a few months before his death, we had taken it to share with the husband of the deceased woman who had been photographed with the seal.[1] It was a powerful and deeply meaningful experience to see his face light up when he saw her again. We never recorded a single word that day, but we felt something much greater had been accomplished.

I have since wondered if his reaction was not only to the long-forgotten image of his deceased wife but also to the recollection of an important and essential act, the offering of fresh water to the seal, which meant so much to this Yup'ik hunter who had spent most of his life out on the land. How much knowledge this single individual must have come to gain over the years as he traveled and hunted to provide for his family. I often think back on our visit and wish we had had more time to learn from him, but I am always comforted in knowing that we gave him something that can't quite be put into words.

Hunting luck is deeply connected to respectful actions of all types. I recall an incident at Hooper Bay in the summer of 1997. I had been invited to share tea and *akutaq* with a community elder. I was particularly honored to share this akutaq because it was made in the old style with "mouse food" (*anlleq*), the seeds and roots collected from vole caches in the tundra. After we finished eating I offered to help with the dishes. Just as we were finishing up, her grandchildren came bounding through the door, proudly displaying a dead loon they had just shot on the tundra. Loons are not sought for food and also have spiritual significance (Morrow and Volkman 1975). The elder was upset with their actions and warned them that killing this bird without reason could cause them all trouble, though she never explicitly stated *how*. Diminished hunting luck is only one of the possible troubles that could result from their careless action. Specific Yup'ik beliefs about loons suggest

FIGURE 4.1. Offering fresh water to a seal. Alaska & Polar Regions Collections & Archives, University of Alaska Fairbanks

that they are particularly powerful and sentient creatures. Offending such a creature, then, certainly held the potential for affecting the family's luck by disrupting the balance and harmony between the human and the spirit world.

Several other researchers have noted that hunting success was directly linked to the proper treatment of animals, including not wasting them (Fienup-Riordan 1990; Fitzhugh and Kaplan 1982; Mather 1985; Morrow 1984; Morrow and Hensel 1992). Beliefs about the proper treatment of animals are common among cultures of the Arctic and sub-Arctic. Alan Boraas said that among the Dena'ina Athabascan, "a bad attitude [not observing prescribed rituals] resulted in the animals, which were believed to be both sensate and willful, withdrawing and not allowing themselves to be hunted" (Boraas 2002, 9; see also Boraas and Peter 1996). Among the Koyukon (Nelson 1983) and the Cree (Brightman 1993), a similar relationship exists between hunters and those they pursue. In the Yup'ik case, Hensel notes that "success in hunting or fishing meant that the individual was in harmony with the world and had behaved correctly" and, conversely, lack of success followed on improper behavior (1996, 41). In addition to affecting hunting luck, improper and disrespectful behavior towards animals could precipitate other misfortunes.

The bone-filled tundra pond at Askinuk is a place of importance because it reminds people of many deeply rooted Yup'ik beliefs that continue to be a guiding force in contemporary Yup'ik lives. Water not only has protective and healing qualities. Water also has the potential for renewal and rebirth. This is part of a continual cycle that does not end with death. The seal hunters of Hooper Bay came to this place to ensure the proper treatment of game, thus ensuring the well-being of both human and spirit world. As Ben and Eliza Orr note:

> Seals and seal hunting figure heavily in cultural and ceremonial iconography and storytelling. Among the coastal Yupiit, a young man's first seal kill is the occasion for an important ceremonial distribution; his first bearded seal marks his passage into manhood and eligibility for marriage. In numerous other ways, seals and men are portrayed as existing in close reciprocal relationships. Like human beings, seals continually pass through the cycle of death and rebirth. (Orr and Orr 1995, xiii)

Clearly this was an important place to the ancestors of the Hooper Bay community members. I believe that it remains an important place to this day because it marks the land and serves as a tangible connection to the past, as well as the spirit world in which Yupiit play an integral, ongoing part. This tundra pond serves to remind and instruct people about the important and delicate relationship that they must maintain with the animal/spirit world.

In general, ponds are important places in day-to-day experience and, as such, figure prominently in Yup'ik folklore. Susan Hansen, in a 1985 study, recorded the following:

> Two miles north of Petmigtalek, a dry lake exists. In the center of the lake is a pile of bones from sea mammals and other animals. Four posts indicate where former sod houses were built. Spear points were sometimes found in the area and small implements such as a tiny board on which boot soles and parkie trim were cut and formed. Other small implements were found. The users of these tools were small people or *ircinrraat.* (Hansen 1985, 85)

Cyril and Anna Okitkun told Hansen about another tundra pond that was also specifically associated with ircinrraat. They said that "in the middle of the lake there was a pile of sea-mammal bones, all kinds of bones" (Hansen 1985, 240). This pond was located at a place (old village) where ircinrraat lived. In this case, the ircinrraat are also respectfully returning their game to the water. Thus, these beings must also demonstrate appropriate awareness in a place filled with sentient others.

It should now be clear that Western concepts of water and land do not easily fit with those of the Yupiit. When we speak of "the land" and "the water" we are easily able to compartmentalize these places on the landscape as distinctly separate realms. This distinction is much less clear when Yupiit speak of such places.

A Big Fish, "Like You Wouldn't Normally See"

Hills, ponds and other land features often mark other specific places with known associations to ircinrraat. As Hansen observes, "Hills and grassy knolls . . . [are] associated with spirits and the remains of the dead" (1985, 89). A Yup'ik teller shared the following story with me a few years ago. This woman was born and raised in a small village upriver from Bethel. As we talked about various creatures that exist on the land and in the water, she explained how the tundra is inhabited by many unseen beings. In response to my questioning, she explained that people don't always know what it is that they have encountered when something happens out on the land. She told me that many people in her village, during Russian Orthodox Christmas (*Selaviq*), had been afraid to travel alone because of recent sightings. In this instance people had been seeing the ircinrraat, often called "little people," but there was also some implied connection to a water/land creature that had been encountered. She explained:

> There's this place called the little hill, and, and, the weird thing is they say, they [ircinrraat] exist in places that are kinda hilly, you know, they live under the ground. That's what they usually say, um, and, this place is, hunters have to pass by it all the time and it's very shallow, it's like, in the summer when it's deep, it's only four feet deep and they have to push their [boats], it's small section and the only hill is right by it and the hunters or people passing by it have to push their boats through. And, um, this family was pushing their boats through, you know, slowly and all of a sudden, you know, um, a big fish comes out, you know like you wouldn't normally see. Like, I don't know how long that they said it was, maybe six feet or so. I mean it just came out of the water and splashed its way through, I mean those kinds of things happen in that area!

In this contemporary story the Yup'ik travelers are forced to get out of their boat and portage at this particular place "called the little hill." There is a sense that as they step onto the land they are in a place that is marked in some way. The condition of this place (very shallow waters) facilitates human entry into the spirit world. Places of portage seem to bear some similarity to the passageways between worlds. Moses, for example, told his listeners about the place called *Qemirrluar* (see chapter 3) and very clearly points to the fact that it was "a portaging place from the beginning." Like Qemirrluar, the place where the "big fish" appeared is marked by unusual occurrences. We are never told what causes the "high winds" of Qemirrluar, but in the above narrative "a big fish . . . like you wouldn't normally see" warns travelers to pass with care (respectfully).

Emeq: Water as Place, Water as Protector

Fresh water is a basic element and essential to all life. This essential quality is reflected in the cultural beliefs and practices of people throughout the world. The significance of water and its symbolic connections, however, can only be understood within a particular cultural framework. For example, what water meant to early missionaries is not what it meant to Yupiit in southwestern Alaska. Recall the image in figure 4.1 of a Hooper Bay woman offering fresh water to a seal that her husband had just killed. Understanding this single act is central to understanding Yup'ik worldview. Fresh water is offered to the seal as a sign of respect. Like the ancestors who returned during certain ceremonies, game animals who "return" also thirst for fresh water. This sense of renewal and return is symbolically marked by the offering of fresh water, which serves to welcome those who reenter the world of the living. In the case of the seal, this act ensures that the game animal will continue to return to the respectful hunter.

Consider the various ways that water is potentially viewed. Water has clarity and, as such, is parallel to a window. Water has strong associations to "seeing" or "insight." Windows and doorways, as I later discuss in more depth, are direct openings or entryways to the spirit world. A pond's reflective, mirror-like quality might also suggest that humans can *see* into the spirit world at such places. On the other hand, water can also lack clarity and thus conceal what exists below, thus impairing one's vision or insight. Water not only sustains life, but also contains and conceals life. This becomes especially important in terms of travel.

Water transportation is a routine part of life in southwestern Alaska. The late Hooper Bay elder Angelo Hoelscher said that he once traveled "over to Bethel. It took them about thirteen days to row to Bethel, and about nine days to return home; they were almost wintered in that year because of the ice" (Miller 1982, 20). The many waterways of southwestern Alaska continue to dictate the necessity of water transportation, making water central to Yup'ik daily experience. Wendell Oswalt wrote,

"The entire region south of and inland from Hooper Bay is commonly known as the Big Lake district; this name well may be applied to the entire area, for it is honeycombed with both large and small lakes and ponds" (1952, 47). Community members often express unease about traveling over bodies of water, frozen or otherwise, and understandably so when one considers the number of drowning incidents that occur in the region each year. According to the state's Department of Epidemiology, the number of drownings in Alaska is ranked among the highest in the nation. KTUU reporter Samantha Angaiak stated, "In communities nestled along the banks of rivers like the Kuskokwim, the water provides a way of life but has also claimed many lives" (KTUU, November 5, 2014).

The caution around *emeq* (water), however, is deeply embedded in a sense of place more generally and extends far beyond physical threats. The subsequent stories of *paalraayak* will demonstrate how water can be healing and protective on the one hand and threatening on the other. For example, it is not uncommon for people to place a small bowl or saucer of water at the entrance to their home. It is even more commonplace to see this done at fish camp or berry camp. A small container of water at the entrance to a tent protects those inside from many, many different kinds of danger.

Agnes Henry and Mary Black of Kongiganak said that Yup'ik "people would take a small amount of water from a container and let it drip to the ground" (Tennant and Bitar 1981, 245). Sometimes the water is thrown or flicked from the fingers around the room, providing protection from potentially harmful spirits. Water as a protectant somewhat coincides with, but also far predates, the use of holy water in the church context (it is also more widespread than the Yup'ik Eskimo tradition).

I have thought about the knowledge surrounding the protective quality of emeq and wondered when I first learned it. I probably heard about it in settings where ghost stories were shared with me, but only later realized that I had truly internalized this knowledge when I needed it most. It was in 2002, as part of a tribal repatriation consultation visit with elders and community members from Hooper Bay. We had made this long journey from the village of Hooper Bay to Washington, D.C., to reclaim the ancestors who had long been housed at the National Museum of Natural History. On this same trip we had also been invited to visit the National Museum of the

American Indian's Suitland, Maryland, facility where many Yup'ik Eskimo objects were housed. Our small group boarded an NMAI shuttle bus on the National Mall and headed out to Suitland where we were greeted by NMAI collections staff. There were several collections to visit and a full day planned.

We followed our hosts down windowless corridors, dark hallways, and numerous staircases as we made our way from one storage location to the next. One room we entered had large, double steel doors located in three places on the same wall. We entered from the center doors and found ourselves in a large, sterile room with rows of metal carts. On each cart and each shelf objects sat with labels that read "Yup'ik Eskimo" or "Yukon-Kuskokwim," etc. We were asked to gather around large, padded tables where we were provided with white gloves as they systematically brought the trays of objects to us for viewing. So many objects surrounded us and there was a general excitement in the room as we "discovered" one treasure after another. Two of the men in our party, both known for their skills as hunters in the community, picked up a spear point and speculated as to how each was made, wondering if that particular one had been used or simply collected at the time of manufacture. After more than an hour, we encountered an object sitting on a tray that none of us were prepared for.

It was a dark, feathered object and it almost instantly commanded everyone's attention. Dangling at the bottom of this bag made of deep black, shiny raven feathers (or, perhaps, the breast of a raven) were raven's feet. The members of our group immediately became concerned over the object and quickly assessed that this object had probably belonged to "a shaman from another village." The younger of the two elders shook his head and motioned to me in a way that suggested this was not a good thing. I asked the museum staff if we could have the object removed from the room before we continued our work. Recognizing the level of our immediate concern, the staff quickly suggested that we take a break. They assured us that they would return the object to its permanent storage location before we continued our work of viewing the remaining objects. We were all relieved at this prompt suggestion and took our leave.

After some time in the break room, we were rejoined by our hosts, who assured us that the object was no longer among the items in the room. We thanked them for their respect and understanding as our group made its way back down the corridor. When we got to the middle door, one of the staff members pulled out her key fob and swiped the magnetic door pad. Nothing happened. As we stood waiting to re-enter, she swiped it again. Still the door did not click and open as it had that morning. Looking strangely at her colleague, she said, "Huh, that has never happened before." It was at this point that the senior elder in our group turned to the younger community member and spoke to him in his Yup'ik language. The younger man then turned to me and said, "Can you get some water?" I knew exactly why we needed water and asked the staff member if she could take me back to the break lounge. I rambled through the mostly empty cabinets until I found some shallow bowls and a saucer. "Perfect," I thought to myself, recalling similar shaped vessels and saucers of water placed at the entrances and windows of Yup'ik homes. I placed water in a cup and carried the vessels back to the doorway where our party waited. I was instructed to place a little bit of water at each doorway. I carefully did so and then returned to the middle doorway. The staff member swiped her key fob again, the door clicked, and we were able to enter. Very little was said, but I still remember the elder's face when the door easily opened for us. It was an expression of relief and certainty. I knew then that we were safe.

In the summer of 2013 I took a group of my undergraduate and graduate students to the Sugpiaq Alutiiq village of Nanwalek to work in their tribal, community museum. The village of Nanwalek is situated on the southwestern tip of the Kenai Peninsula in lower Cook Inlet. The community is located some two hundred miles south of Anchorage and is accessible only by boat or plane.

We lived and worked in Nanwalek for three weeks during which time community members freely shared aspects of their culture.[2] My students learned Sugcestun[3] words, they learned to cut fish, they learned to make grass baskets, and they learned the stories of that special place. Not surprisingly, among the stories shared were those of encounters with ghosts. One such tale described an encounter while sleeping out on the land in a tent. The haunted occupants had to "tear a hole" in the tent to escape and then threw water on the ghost to keep it from pursuing them further. The water caused the ghost to "melt" (pers. comm. 2013).

I have seen instances when water is not readily available and spitting has been used as a form of protection. This seems to have the same effect as fresh water. One Hooper Bay missionary, clearly not understanding the purpose, recorded in the 1920s that "people spit everywhere" (AM Collection 30, 20). Given the popularity among Yupiit at that time of chewing tobacco mixed with fungus ashes (*iqmiq*), the missionary would likely have seen this "constant spitting" as a purely secular activity, parallel to one with which he was familiar in his own society, and some of it may have been. While it is impossible to know how much, given the lack of specific context, it is likely that this behavior served more than one purpose as it does in contemporary contexts today.

Water is not the only element that offers protection from the spirit world. Mather and Morrow note that "anointing oneself or one's house with oily soot or making motions of encasing oneself was a way to form a protective barrier against the supernatural" (Swann 1994, 47). Fienup-Riordan also notes the importance of using food scraps and soot from a seal-oil lamp as a means of bridging the human and spirit world (Fienup-Riordan 1994). The aforementioned missionary, in response to the constant spitting of churchgoers, placed "a can full of ashes in every room and in church" insisting that he would "make them spit in it" (AM Collection 30, 20). It is likely that this priest had no idea how spit, ashes, and soot, in Yup'ik worldview, served as a protection against dangerous beings in the spirit world.

Hawkes also notes the use of soot by a shaman before appealing to the spirit world. "Before commencing his part [in the ceremony], the shaman daubed soot from the *kazgi* wall on his breast." In a footnote to his description of the shaman's commencement of this ceremony, Hawkes states that "this was supposed to put him en rapport with the spirit-guests" (1913, 17). A Yup'ik author writes that a shaman gained his or her visions through "a pot of water" (Kawagley 1995, 32). Elements like water and soot, I believe, not only allowed for contact and "rapport" with the spirit world, but protected the shaman as she or he bridged the spirit world and that of the living.[4]

Water, however, is cast as both a protector and a vehicle for spirits that may be dangerous. There is also a sense that the very water one drinks can be of potential harm to those who are not aware. Water seems to not only have protective qualities in that it serves as a barrier, but also holds the potential for containing harmful forces, particularly for the careless or unaware. If drinking water is not guarded then it can become a dangerous element. Sometimes water draws bad, unwelcome spirits and brings danger. A Yup'ik story Hansen calls "The Bad-Hearted Shaman" speaks of "a spirit [who] is reborn through an old woman when she drinks his 'essence,' from a water dipper" (Hansen 1985, 78).

In 1899, Edward W. Nelson, during his travels up the Bering Sea coast, noted that his Eskimo companion would not drink from an uncovered water container. Nelson explains that this man's son had only recently died. There was a need to guard the water, thus protecting the one who would drink it.

> I learned that for three to four months after the death of a son the father must not drink from an uncovered vessel, for if he does he may swallow some impurity from the shade that might be present, and die. . . . During the journey I noticed for some days that whenever he drank he inserted a small dipper beneath his fur coat, and then lowering his face under the collar drank from beneath. On inquiry I was told that this was because his son had died a short time before and he dared not drink from an uncovered vessel, fearing that some emanation from his son's shade [his ghost] might get into the water and, being swallowed, do him harm. (Nelson 1983 [1899], 422)

The importance of water was again reinforced for me shortly after the birth of my daughter in June of 1999. She was very lucky to have a Yup'ik name, Cugmi, bestowed upon her as a newborn baby. The one who named her was very specific in the way that I, her mother, was to present her new Yup'ik name to her. I was carefully instructed to "give her her first taste of fresh water." It was explained to me that this was very important because my daughter would be "thirsty" for fresh water. The deceased person for whom she was being named is drawn to the water as a gesture of being welcomed back. I carefully followed that instruction with sincere respect for the treasured gift we were given.

In Tennant and Bitar (1981), George Beaver, of Bethel, describes a similar way of welcoming the baby:

> When a child was born and received the name of a person who had died, the dead person's relatives, for example his mother, treated the child as if it were the dead person. If a girl died and a baby was named after her, and the mother of the dead girl heard about it, she would prepare food and make Eskimo ice-cream. She would fill a dish with food and some ice-cream and take it to the newborn baby.
>
> In one hand she would hold a dipper filled with water. Upon entering the house she would place the dipper of water in front of the baby, then sprinkle drops of water on the baby's head and body. She would then present the dish, addressing the new baby by her daughter's name. (Tennant and Bitar 1981, 61–62)

Upon my very next visit to Hooper Bay, during which my daughter was still an infant, I was presented with a bowl of *akutaq*, a small package of dried *maklaaq* (bearded seal meat), some dry fish, and seal oil. Again, I was carefully instructed to feed her this food. When I returned home I gave my daughter her first taste of Yup'ik food.

We are honored that she has a Yup'ik name and family tie. By the time she was four years old, she asked everyone she met what *their* Yup'ik Eskimo name was. She was saddened to learn that not everyone has a Yup'ik name, but was very proud to speak her own. I continue to be amazed at some of the similarities and occurrences that tie my daughter to her *ateq* (namesake). Yupiit expect that namesakes will show such resemblances, but for me they have often seemed uncanny. Cugmi, now a teenager, stays connected to her family by sending along baked goods for them whenever I visit Hooper Bay. In turn, I always return home with a gift of seal oil and dried fish for her.

This "first taste of fresh water" is a symbolic gesture which, in essence, welcomes back her ateq or namesake (the one she was named for). Like the seals and other game who return to the respectful hunter, those who are loved and respected return again to those they loved through the ones who receive their names along with offerings of water. This is a vital and ongoing part of Yup'ik daily life. The recycling of names, along with the return of animals, is part of a general sense of connectedness to the spirit world. This cycle of renewal is a theme that permeates every aspect of Yup'ik worldview.

Wooden Spoons and Ladles

There are no strict boundaries between land and water. Water can have protective, healing, and renewing qualities, but it can also hold many dangers for the unaware. Narratives of place and stories of the water creature known as paalraayak, in particular, demonstrate this aspect of Yup'ik worldview quite well. Paalraayak, one of many creatures who inhabit the water world, was described by Edward Nelson during his 1899 expedition as crocodile-like in appearance. Some of the descriptions offered to me also describe "jagged teeth" but sometimes vary in terms of the creature's shape.

When I was at the Smithsonian Institution's National Museum of Natural History as part of the repatriation consultation, I first saw the dozens and dozens of wooden spoons and drinking ladles that had been collected by Nelson in the Yup'ik southwest. We stood with our inventory list in hand, knowing that we were about to view spoons and ladles. What I did not expect was to see paalraayak and other water creatures painted on water utensils, carved wooden dishes, and serving trays (figure 4.2). I was puzzled, at first, that such a creature would have a prominent place on something associated with drinking water. My understanding of such creatures was that they were to be feared. Why, then, was the figure painted on tools for dipping and consumption of water?

This fearsome creature appeared over and over again. Shelf after shelf contained wooden spoons and wooden ladles used for dipping and drinking fresh water. Large wooden bowls, like the ones used for serving akutaq, also displayed the water creatures. It was painted on a traditional-style *qayaq* (kayak) from the region, too. Now resting on a storage shelf and covered with plastic, the paalraayak on that kayak silently peers out of the darkness, still demanding the attention of all those who pass down this aisle.

One elder smiled broadly as he examined the red-painted paalraayak figure swimming across a wooden ladle that had been handed to him by the museum staff. I don't think I shall ever forget the wise, knowing look on his face. He was silent for a moment. He seemed to be a long way away, but he commanded our attention. We could see him thinking about something, remembering. Then he shared with us the following narrative.

"Too Many Otters in That One Place"

One time I, uh, followed three otter tracks, by snow machine. I followed, on my way, getting more and more [tracks]. I get into this slough, go out, to the main river. Getting more and more [tracks]. Comes on, the side of that river [the river bank]. And I kept following it. And there's a little, small slough, so I had to run alongside . . . , stopped my snow machine, take my .22 [rifle] and follow it. They go into same one hole, that small [shows us about a twelve- to fourteen-inch hole with his hands] about that wide from here. About that wide. They all get into that hole. I take my ice pick, .22 I got, make that hole a little bigger. It's, uh, about that high [holds his hand up]. Make it bigger. I go in there and, [pause] the heat really warmed that water up from that slough. Just like heater!

It was cold weather that day too. And what I saw when I make it open, when I look in, they finally. . . . That water underneath the ice start coming up and down. The ice is about that high [showing us with his hands above his head]. The water from all of them otters, come up and down. Lots of otters come out! Sounds like, uh, sounds like bunches of little puppies, small puppies. Gee [drawn out with great emphasis], I don't know how many? Lots. I load up my gun. I, I tried to . . . I remember that, what my dad and my grandpa told me cause there's too many in that one place. One place, [lowers his voice] right there. I saw biggest one. I saw the biggest one. I pull it out through the ice. It didn't want to come out. There were too many. I think about, think about that, uh [pause] what my dad told me. Not to get that much otter. So I quit, I stop. Catch [lowers his voice] only one [pause]. Ah, jeez! [shaking his head in disbelief]. That little creek, nothing. No water, full of otters. That much, that much otter [shows us the expanse with his hands]. They said no more than twenty, I could keep shooting. Get as much I want. I shot one [he laughs nervously as he holds up one finger]. If I get more than twenty, they turn out *paalraayak*.

Holly: They turn into . . .

Elder: *Ii-i* [yes] and what I'm standing on [the tundra] turn[s] out all water.

Holly: The land?
Elder: The land. No more land. Only water.
Holly: *nunapik* [tundra]?
Elder: *nuna* [land, earth].
Elder: *emeq* [water]!

This paalraayak narrative demonstrates how delicate the balance is with the spirit world. This hunter describes his encounter with "too many otters," indicating that there was an unseen force that required him to act appropriately. He sensed that there was something different or special about this particular place on the edge of the shore ice. As a hunter, he found himself faced with a situation in which he needed to demonstrate respect and constraint.[5] To act irresponsibly, in this case taking all of the otters, would have upset the balance of the human-spirit world. It would, in this instance, have placed this hunter in great danger from paalraayak. His chances of survival would become even less certain as the ground below him transformed into water: "What I'm standing on turn out all water." This transformation would ultimately place him in the world of paalraayak, leaving him defenseless. Again, we are reminded through narrative that the world can be a dangerous place for those who ignore Yup'ik teachings and knowledge. The unseen world is all around us. It is cognizant of human action, aware and watching all the time.

Contemporary Narratives of Paalraayak and Other Water Creatures

In the autumn of 2002, I sat alone with two friends as we discussed stories we had heard in the past about the land and the water. I asked the younger man (then in his mid- to late fifties) about paalraayak and what stories he had heard about the creature as he grew up in Hooper Bay. Instead, he told me a story about another water creature that was created by a Hooper Bay shaman to keep the bay open and clear.

Teller: Uh, shamans produced that by their shamanism, to keep our bay, channel open. And there's a few, recently, they sighted it a few times.

Holly: Is it one, or more than one?
Teller: I don't know, probably just one.
Elder: One. [audience/listener]
Teller: *Ii-i.* [pause] to keep the main channel open and clear.
Elder: Keep it open.
Teller: Just like snow removal ya know? [said teasingly and we laugh].
Teller: There's quite a few men that have sighted it. He [pointing to the other teller] and my Uncle saw it surface when they were out seal hunting . . . surfaced, a big old head surfaced [he laughs], they didn't know what it was. They turn around and took off! [they both laugh nervously]

To this day, this creature is said to prevent the bay from filling in. This is important for many reasons. If the bay were too shallow and allowed to fill in then the large barges could not arrive in the spring. The barges deliver the vital supplies that are needed for building construction and the fuel that is needed to operate snow machines, four-wheelers, and skiffs. Later that same month the teller described this creature as "kinda like a big insect." He went on to say that it is the size of the table in his kitchen, stretching out his arms to demonstrate.

Only the month before, I was sitting in a large city airport with an elder from Hooper Bay as he spoke of paalraayak. Ironically, we were sitting at a table next to a Rosetta Stone language cart. As the cart's demo tape switched from Italian to French, and then to German, this Hooper Bay elder raised his voice to speak over the background noise as he spoke in his own native Yup'ik language. He told his stories of paalraayak in Yup'ik to his Yup'ik listeners, stopping only briefly to make sure that I got the gist of his tellings.

This elder told us to be aware when out on the tundra. He warned us that if we should encounter the creature that we should step over it. He described in both Yup'ik and then in English how it appears. Its back is "spiky like, sticking up like needle fish or porcupine quills." He went on, telling a story of an old woman who was out on the tundra when she encountered paalraayak. She followed this wisdom and stepped over the creature the way her elders had instructed her to do. When she did this, she "became young again." Her teeth, it is said, came back in sharp like those of an otter.

One Yup'ik listener, nodding his head in agreement, added that his own father had warned him to be aware and watch for such creatures. There is a water creature that appears with many heads coming to the surface. His father told him that if he encounters such a creature he should "get out!" I was, again, riveted by these many tales of water creatures and let my enthusiasm show. I soon recognized my error as my Yup'ik companions teased me and rebuffed my overzealous behavior. They laughed and told me that perhaps they would give me a Yup'ik name, calling me Paalraayak! I retorted that this would certainly not help me fit into the community. I stated that I would cease my eager questioning at once. "*Ii-i* Paalraayak" (okay Paalraayak), they continued.

Those who have spent any time in a Yup'ik community know that teasing is commonplace, and it serves an important purpose. I have been indirectly instructed not to ask so many questions. My role is to listen and learn. Again I remembered my very first night in Hooper Bay and the important lesson I was supposed to have learned then. This is the way that certain narratives come back to you again and again throughout your life. I sat quietly listening for the remainder of our visit.

Edward Nelson's travels along the Bering Sea coast in the 1880s taught him a lot about paalraayak (*păl-raí-yûk* in Nelson). In his field journal Nelson wrote:

> A strange, crocodile-like animal, known as *păl-raí-yûk*, is painted on the sides of umiaks and on the inside of wooden dishes by natives along lower Yukon and Kuskokwim rivers. A mask from the tundra south of the Yukon mouth has this animal drawn down each side of the face. According to the traditions of the people in this district the climate in ancient times was very much warmer than at present and the winters were shorter. In those days the mythic animals referred to were abundant in the swampy country between the two rivers, being more common near the Kuskokwim, where the climate was more temperate than on the Yukon. . . .
>
> In those days the waterfowl and other birds came back from the south in February and the snow melted during that month and the water ran into the passages of houses as it does now in

> April. At that time the păl-raí-y ûk lived in lakes, creeks, and marshes, where it killed men and animals for food. Several of the lower Yukon Eskimo recounted the killing of the last one by a hunter whose wife the beast had caught and devoured while she was getting water from the lake. In the tale of the creation by the Raven, as the latter and the First Man were traveling in the Skyland, the Raven cautioned his companion not to drink from the lakes which were passed, because in them were animals he had made that would seize and destroy any one who ventured near. These were *păl-raí-yûk*. . . .
>
> In one of the Raven tales a large beast is described as having been seen haunting a dry lake bed overgrown with tall grass while Raven and First Man were journeying in the sky land. It is said to have rested by lying down on the tips of the growing grass, without bending the stems. When this animal was killed by the Sky people it was necessary for them first to place logs under it, for when dead it became so heavy that it would sink into the ground as will a lean seal in water. (Nelson 1983 [1899], 444–45)

Nelson's descriptions of this creature also say that it has "a long head and six legs, the hind legs unusually large and the fore ones short, with the small middle pair hanging from the belly. A fine, thick fur, like that on the shrew-mouse, is said to grow all over its body and is thickest about the feet. On the back of the head are a pair of thick, short horns, which extend forward and outward and then curve back at the points. The animal has small eyes and is very dark colored" (Nelson 1983 [1899], 445).

Nelson further states that "in the drawings of this animal on umiaks, at intervals along the body are open spaces, inside which are represented parts of a human body, showing the belief in its having eaten such food. It was said to live in the water, where it lay hidden among the grass, whence it suddenly rushed to seize a person on the bank or to attack kaiaks [*sic*] when crossing its haunts" (Nelson 1983 [1899], 445).

Nelson's description bears some resemblance to descriptions of water creatures found in other Native North American cultures. My

FIGURE 4.2. *Qantaq* (wooden dish) collected by E. W. Nelson. Catalog number E45494, Department of Anthropology, Smithsonian Institution. Photo by Donald E. Hurlbert

previous experiences of living and working among Algonquian groups had taught me to take the matter of "crossing its haunts" seriously. Among the Ojibway, Odawa, and Pottawatomi peoples of Canada, "Mishipizheu" is both feared and respected. Canadian archaeologist William Fox notes that this creature's "power to create storms was greatly feared by mariners . . . and Aboriginal travelers are regularly documented as propitiating the great underwater panther with sacrifices" (Fox 1992, 27). I had often wondered why my Anishinaabe teacher routinely placed pinches of tobacco in the water as we traveled from shore to shore on the waters of Georgian Bay. There was an uneasy quality about those trips that would someday seem familiar as I found myself out in boats with friends at Hooper Bay.

Closer to my Kenai Peninsula home, but much earlier in time, is a similar account from the Dena'ina Kenaitze Athabascan people. The first Russian Orthodox priest at Kenai recorded this account in 1860.

Father Nikolai Militov (Hegumen Nikolai), who had been appointed by Ivan Veniaminov (later canonized as St. Innocent), reported:

> In September I visited the Chkituk village, where I sang a funeral service for a Kenaitze who had become ill and soon died from a fright. He had seen some scary animal-like monster that was coming from the water. Soon this native lost his speech, his mind became cloudy and within three days he died. (Znamenski 2003, 84)

Richard Nelson, writing about Koyukon Athabascan places, said that "a nebulous but still threatening spirit power is associated with many places on the land, bodies of water, or stretches of waterways" (Nelson 1983, 35). These diverse traditions share a common discomfort about traveling on water where dangerous, unseen creatures may dwell.

"Land Was Pretty Far Away"

Edward Tennant and Joseph Bitar recorded a tale with Edward Hooper of Tununak who recalled an experience he had while spring seal hunting with his cousin and older brother (Tennant and Bitar 1981). This encounter with a water creature occurred somewhere between Nunivak and Nelson Islands. Hooper's narrative begins by describing a place where they had been weathered in for days. He recalls:

> The water was close to where we were and it was very windy, so we went up on the bank and pulled up our kayaks, using them as windbreakers. The wind became stronger. The water below formed small whirlpools and sent up a spray. As we waited there under the *Kalukat*, snow covered our kayaks.
>
> The next day dawned the same—bad weather with blowing snow. We were stuck there for three days. The water was still close to us and would send up a spray now and then. While we were there, our cousin began clowning around for us, saying

he would pretend to freeze when the time was right. . . . As we prepared to leave, our cousin was singing away and telling us that he was going to perform magic. . . .

When we were ready we went down to the ocean, to the point where the mountain ends. Our cousin went up to the ridge to see how far out the ice was in the ocean. He beached his kayak, climbed up, then came back down, while we floated in our kayak and waited for him.

Before we left the area, a seal surfaced. Just as it surfaced our cousin shot it and hit it. We helped him beach it. He told us the ice was not too far away and wanted to go out there. . . . Before we reached the ice, we spotted something huge ahead of us. We had no idea what it was. We thought nothing of it because we had never seen anything like it.

I for one was not scared. We figured there would be some seals on the ice, so we kept on going. We were getting close when I thought I heard something breathe. My brother was some distance ahead of me. I looked and saw something huge following us, with its mouth wide open.

Its eyes looked as if they were rolling. Its teeth seemed to be like those of a mastodon, only different. We did not know what it was. It was covered with seaweed, the kind that grows in areas where certain edible mussels are found.

When that enormous thing was following us with its mouth wide open, I think I was afraid for the first time. I thought it was the size of an island, maybe twenty-five yards long. Its back was very rough. We fled toward the ice. When I looked again, I saw how, when it lifted its tail, it splashed huge volumes of water. It was very close behind me. If it had caught me in its mouth, both I and my kayak would have disappeared from view. . . . Our cousin was still coming, but not straight for us. Then the huge thing dove. We waited for it to gobble us up, but it did not surface. When I stood up, it surfaced close to the ice just where we were headed. "Well," I said, "it can eat us up if it wants to. I'm leaving."

We continued on our way, but that creature did not bother us again. At that time I thought that this must have been the scariest thing I had ever seen because it was so gigantic. . . . And to make matters even worse, land was pretty far away. (Tennant and Bitar 1981, 49–53)

Again, there is a sense here that "crossing its haunts" is not a matter to take lightly. Encounters with water creatures are not uncommon, but we get the sense that this particular incident may have been out of the ordinary. Elder Edward Hooper concluded his narrative of this frightening encounter by stating: "This story is based on my personal experience. I did not hear it from anybody else" (Tennant and Bitar 1981, 53). Each encounter and each retelling of the experience reminds Yupiit that the unseen world exists. Two hunters from Hooper Bay told me that some creatures, although seemingly familiar, may not be what they appear. Certain seals are to be avoided.[6] They told me that seal hunters need to be particularly cognizant of those they hunt. They said:

Hunter 1: And those *pugcuaraat* [small surfaced seals] when they go seal hunting, *pugcuaraat* that are black, the small ones, they're not to touch. When you follow them it'll take you in the wrong direction.
Hunter 2: When . . . myself. One time before anything happened to Naka and my father we went out to get wood. I took an aim and it was very, very black.
Hunter 2: Real pitch black. Yeah, . . . face. But it didn't come up. It didn't come up again after that. It's . . . black light.
Holly: The seal?
Hunter 2: No . . . [it will] vanish.
Hunter 1: Direct you . . .
Holly: Yeah?
Hunter 1: Direct . . . [you off a] distance.
Hunter 2: The *maklak* [bearded seal].
Holly: *Maklak*?
Hunter 2: Yeah.
Hunter 1: It is said that they try to let you make a mistake. That's what they [our ancestors] said. Those are also prohibitions, their warnings not to do them.
Hunter 1: Not [to] go for it.

In this narrative, the Hooper Bay hunters are talking about seals who appear at the surface. Surfaced seals[7] watch human beings and observe their actions; this relates to the strong sense that the spirit world is all around us and always watching. The tale recounts the experience of these men, who as they collect driftwood are being observed by this particular seal. This observant creature, however, is marked as somehow special because it appears with a face that is "real pitch black." This indicates to the hunters that, although it may seem to be presenting itself to be hunted, there may be dangers associated with its pursuit.

This exchange with the two hunters has always reminded me of one of my favorite Yup'ik tales about a boy who goes to live in the world of the seals. "In the spring the boy swam through the ocean with his host [a seal], viewing human hunters from the seals' perspective . . . he and his host approached a good [respectful] hunter, whom they allowed to overpower them" (Fienup-Riordan 1994, 3). In the narrative given by the two hunters it is clear that there is potential danger and that one who lacks appropriate awareness can be led to "make a mistake." Both stories reinforce the notion that this world is watchful. The world is a place where one must remain aware and maintain respect in order to be both successful in hunting and remain safe out on the land or sea (see figures 5.1 and 5.2). The following story is told by a Yup'ik man from Hooper Bay in response to my questions about the creature known as paalraayak.

A Place Where This River Goes Up to Kashunuk

Going home from hunting, uh, my cousin and I, we were in an 18 footer and I was driving, he was sitting in the front. Going home, going home from up, way up Kashunuk. It's a river, you know, where the Chevak River goes. That river and then this river goes up to Kashunuk and then up where we go berry camping.

We got to the, we got out of the river and we turned and [pause] . . . and then that land, you know sometimes the bank, when it erodes there's big chunks of land, you know, drifting. I thought that's what it was, on the beach. And the tide was low. Enough, you know that you could see sand bars, in the bay.

We were going along and all of a sudden, that land that I saw, I thought it was land that I saw, I thought it was land. It starts sinking. And I yelled at my cousin to, look at it, but by the time he looked up, it had submerged . . . yeah, gone under. And I told him what I just saw. He didn't believe me, of course, because he didn't see it! [laughs] So, when I got to that area, I beached up, right on the mud, you know, kind of freaked out, to pass it. Finally I told him, "Well, let's go!" So we started going out, and about half a mile out [speaks in Yup'ik] that Island between Hooper and Chevak, in our bay. I was going at a good clip, maybe half the speed of a twin forty horse? We came upon these, uh . . . [speaks in Yup'ik] uh, it start, you know when you're under water? When you're kicking your feet? When you're almost at the surface, the water will, you know, just like boiling water.

Holly: Bubble?

Teller: Yeah, not quite bubble, but just like when it's boiling.

H: Rolling?

T: *Ii-i-* [yes] came upon those and I said '*Tangtaamaa*! [look at those] look!' Shit, I sat down and just went around, went around right close to the, shallow part, just gunned the motor and took off!

When asked how he knew that this was paalraayak, he recalled a hunting trip many years ago when he and his cousin first learned this important lesson. He remarked that it was "taboo" to hunt or pursue such creatures. The teller explained that he and his family members saw something surface in a tundra lake near the Askinuk Mountains. The young men were eager to pursue this creature. His father knew immediately what it was out there in the waters of that lake. When his father saw their enthusiasm he quickly warned them of this hunting taboo and the potential danger of disturbing the creature. The teller told me of this earlier experience in which he learned about such creatures:

And those are one of the taboos not to, see them or, hunt them [paalraayak]. I think we saw one when we were going back from hunting . . . my dad, my cousin, myself and other cousins when we were going home from, geese hunting, from the end of the mountains. Going home we stopped by and, we rest up there. And there's a little kind of lake, small lake right by the mountain. [Joseph] saw it and, and he got, what do you call it? *Piigalik*? Really wanted to get it!

And my dad, I guess heard stories of certain *paalraayaat* like that in that area before, you know? He warned us, "don't, don't go for it." But, we were young and we knew it all [he laughs] you know. We didn't know nothing about that [paalraayak]. But, uh, it didn't pop up again. So in that sense I guess we were lucky!

The Land You're Standing On: Paalraayak and Yup'ik Connection to Place in Southwestern Alaska

The many stories of encounters with paalraayak and other water creatures are central in understanding the significance of place among the Yupiit of southwestern Alaska. Paalraayak is not, for many Yupiit, a "mythical" creature of the past. Paalraayak is a dynamic and powerful force in the natural, spirit world. The tales of "Too Many Otters," the aforementioned narrative of the seal hunters at Nunivak, and this last narrative of two young, overzealous hunters all emphasize the importance of respecting the game that one harvests. This is not, however, all that they do.

These narratives also show us how a sentient world responds to spoken words and human action. The stories stress the central and ongoing theme among the Yup'ik Eskimo people that human action and human speech must demonstrate respect and moderation. The Hooper Bay elder had prefaced his telling at the museum by stating to his listeners, "*Makut* [these things] . . . my grandpa and my daddy told me not to, even if I see that much otters [and] I shoot more than twenty. If I pass over twenty, if I shoot over twenty otters it would turn out [to be] *paalraayak*!"

This tale illustrates the ways in which Yup'ik sense of place and perspectives of the land differ greatly from Western views. Overuse and wastefulness constitute not only improper but also dangerous behavior: "No more than twenty." One is reminded time and time again to observe the practices that are considered appropriate. The encounter that occurred between Nunivak and Nelson Islands reminds listeners how essential proper behavior is in terms of actions. While the teller did not specifically call this water creature by the name paalraayak, it is clear that "clowning" around and joking about the use of "magic" can be seen by the sentient world as a sign of disrespect. This seems to be a common thread in many narratives of place. Lack of appropriate awareness and speaking carelessly can result in a deadly encounter.

Taking too many otters, against the wisdom of one's elders, can result in a direct encounter with the much respected and feared paalraayak. On yet another level, the tale of "Too Many Otters" also generally instructs listeners to be properly aware of those circumstances that appear "unnatural." Improbable events (so many otters in one place) signal uncharacteristic behaviors in the natural world. Hence, such events signal danger for those who are not properly aware of their surroundings. Edward Hooper concluded his personal narrative by explaining that his father told him, "Those things [water creatures] do not bother people except when they are protecting their young" (Tennant and Bitar 1981, 53).

The Hooper Bay elder gave us a sense that, perhaps, these were something more than otters as he described the puppy-like sounds and nature of the otters. "Lots of otters come out! Sounds like bunches of little puppies, small puppies. Gee [drawn out with great emphasis], I don't know how many? Lots." Were these young otters, or could they have been the young of some other creature? Something wasn't right, and this Yup'ik elder knew that. Perhaps this hunter's sense of danger was informed by many years spent on the land and water, as well as other experiences. By drawing from his experience and the narratives of his own elders, he was able to demonstrate safe and appropriate action during this encounter.

Boundaries became fluid and we, as his listeners, get a strong sense that this watery place he describes is inhabited by those of the spirit world. "To make matters even worse," he says, "land was pretty far away" (Tennant and Bitar 1981, 53). One young Hooper Bay hunter told me, "Uh, those creatures, even if you're on land, it'll turn to water. The land you're standing on! The land. The ground, just like water." This transitional world is one that Yupiit know to be dangerous. The very land that you stand upon turns to water below your feet.

Careless action and careless words, on the part of human beings, can dissolve the boundaries between worlds. The fur-bearing otters that you track hold the potential of transforming from small creatures to a powerful paalraayak. This tale serves as a specific warning to hunters, while at the same time reinforcing the general understanding that the land is a place of uncertainty. The tundra, the ocean, and the lakes are places that may not be what they seem, since one can become the other. Place is permeable and uncertain. Human awareness and proper action are essential to keep one safe in such a world.

A Place Called Cape Romanzof: What Couldn't Be Seen

Imagine the ways that this spirit world is disrupted, then, when outsiders damage the land and water with contaminants. Contamination is a kind of disrespect. It disrupts the reciprocal relationship that Yupiit have always maintained with the land, the water, and the beings of the spirit world.

It was not until my second summer in Hooper Bay that I began to see the notices tacked on the Traditional Council office bulletin board or taped on the board at the small store where I bought my food and other supplies. The public notice warned all Hooper Bay residents not to harvest or consume any fish or game taken off Cape Romanzof or the surrounding area. Cape Romanzof is located north of Hooper Bay on the Bering Sea coast, south of the Yukon Delta (Michael 1967, 349). Through inquiry I soon learned that this place had always been an important source of food and resources for the Hooper Bay and neighboring Yup'ik villages. Edward Nelson reports "a summer fishing village" at Cape Romanzof (Nelson 1983 [1899], 249). Hooper Bay elder Mike Simon recalled that "in the spring time he used to go to Cape Romanzof for spring camp where he used to hunt seals" (Miller 1982, 18). Erma Tomaganuk said, "In the summer time we used to go to cape Romanzof there we caught herring fish and tomcods" (Miller 1982, 14). Like their ancestors before them, the people of Hooper Bay have long hunted, fished, and collected plants and driftwood from Romanzof.

In the 1840s, thirty-five years before Nelson explored the Bering Sea coast, Russian naval lieutenant Lavrentiy Zagoskin documented and described geographic place-names. He referred to this place as Cape Rumyantsev. The Russians also called it Cape Graf (Count) Rumyantsev (Michael 1967, 349). Over one hundred years after Zagoskin's travels along the Bering Sea coast, the United States military visited "Cape Rumyanstev." These visitors would leave a lasting mark on the land. It was 1952 when the U.S. Air Force chose this place to build a long-range radar site. According to the *Tundra Drums* newspaper, a major spill occurred at the site thirty years ago. A documented fifty thousand gallons of diesel fuel seeped into the earth and water, along with "other spills" that have not been publicly identified or measured by the Air Force.

On September 26, 2001, Yup'ik community members from Hooper Bay, Chevak, and Scammon Bay went to the site to see the military's cleanup efforts for themselves. While the project manager for the U.S. Air Force environment restoration program described monitoring procedures, the Yupiit looked on. The *Tundra Drums* reporter wrote: "Men from Hooper Bay could be seen in the distance hauling some of the 177 old barrels that had been scattered by wind into and around the upper Fowler Creek area" (Denning-Barnes 2001, 24).

One Hooper Bay elder recalled the times spent at this place, gathering clams on the sand bar that divides Kokechik Bay from the open sea. Certainly, all of the Yupiit present would have similar memories and stories of this beautiful place, but "what seemed beautiful to the eye, raised questions of what couldn't be seen." The Air Force project manager was quoted as saying that "this is one of our worst sites. We have no way to tell how much spilled" (Denning-Barnes 2001, 24).

A November 28, 2003, *All Things Considered* report for National Public Radio posted a web page on the Cape Romanzof case, stating that Hooper Bay residents link present community health concerns to this contamination. The 2003 report states that "although there is no scientific evidence, the Yup'ik Eskimos are increasingly worried that abnormalities in the fish and wildlife and their own health problems are somehow related to the contaminants left behind by the military . . . the people of Hooper Bay are determined to find out themselves" (Arnold 2003).

It is a stark irony that the *Tundra Drums* newspaper article was simply titled "Unseen Concern." When outsiders look at the Cape

Romanzof case, they identify with it in terms of contamination or resources lost, but that is only part of the story. To understand the relationship that Yupiit maintain with the land is to understand that when pollutants damage the tundra and the waters they have done even more than take away their places to fish and hunt. The loss of these subsistence resources can have a devastating impact on a community that relies so heavily on subsistence. Less tangible is the loss that results from no longer having safe access to an important *place*.

This is a place where Hooper Bay, Chevak, and Scammon Bay ancestors also hunted, fished, and gathered plants and driftwood. This is a place, like elsewhere, that is inhabited by those of the spirit world. What happens to the important balance between the human and spirit world when an important place is contaminated and abandoned? How will the pollutants and acts of ignorance affect those who seek to maintain this balance? This Yup'ik connection to place is completely missed by most outsiders.

The concern that Yup'ik knowledge is so often dismissed was shared at the regional meetings of the Alaska Native Science Commission. When Oscar Kawagley said that "landscape forms the mindscape," his comment was in relation to a call for an equal treatment and respect of Native scientific knowledge by the outside community.[8] It was also aimed at non-Natives' lack of understanding of Natives' spiritual connection to the land. Another participant then added that when outsiders lack this understanding, "it hurts the people!" Certainly Yupiit know and expect the U.S. military to be completely ignorant of this fact. "What couldn't be seen" is far more complex than what most outsiders will ever know and understand.

In chapter 5, I will explore more about the importance of human awareness and proper action in relation to the land and demonstrate the ways in which Yup'ik places are permeable and often indefinable. I will also show how human action is directly linked to this notion of place and the understanding that while people learn about the land, the land learns about people.

5

"Assiituq!" The Land Can Be a Dangerous Place

UNDERSTANDING THE IMPORTANCE OF CAUTIONARY TALES

As I think about the various encounters Yupiit have described to me, I realize that they take many forms. While often associated with specific places, other narratives reveal something about general dangers "out on the land."

One genre of stories that is tied to particular places consists of encounters at abandoned villages. While no longer inhabited by the living, such places are seldom described as "unoccupied." Like these, tales about dangers more generally on the land embody shared knowledge about places and keep people from harm. But stories less tied to specific places emphasize what to do when such encounters occur, as opposed to which places to avoid. What is often implied, but not explicitly stated, is that we can't always tell by looking where these abandoned places are located. Such encounters, often described as occurring out on the land, also occur closer to home, in or around the village.

It was Friday night of Thanksgiving weekend. We were all looking forward to the long weekend break. Among the most anticipated events of winter are the basketball games between villages, especially the championships. Players travel by snow machine from village to village in order to compete against one another. I have never been a big sports fan, but I have really become a fan of the local basketball teams. I look forward to the visiting that always accompanies a game. I was really looking forward to traveling to the neighboring Cup'ik village of Cevv'aq (Chevak) that night because it would give us a chance to go visiting, but it would also mean a long snow machine ride. Everyone enjoys such trips when the weather allows. As elsewhere in Alaska, people welcome a chance to get out of the house and get some much-needed fresh air.

That evening one of my friends had decided that the weather was just too bad to make the trip. Desperate for an outing, I almost begged her to go. She never responded directly to my pleading, but instead sat down and began to tell me a story.

A Dark Figure

That night, the wind was blowing off the ocean and driving snow straight across the tundra. The winds were whipping against the walls so strongly that it shook the house. She explained to me that it was a night just like this when she was returning from Chevak and almost got lost in a whiteout. She described her fear as she desperately tried to see the trail before her. She explained to me that it is very easy to get disoriented and end up heading out to open water. This, she told me, had happened to people many times before.

She went on to say that she suddenly "saw a light" out in front of her. She felt relief at having seen what she believed were the tail lights of another snow machine. Following another snow machine is much easier than trying to find and keep the trail by yourself. She increased her speed, but could never catch up to the lights. She said, "People see it, but never catch up to it." When she finally got closer she could only vaguely see the rider, which she described to me as "a dark figure." She suddenly had the sense that something was wrong. She stopped her snow machine. She explained to me that she was very close to "open water." Had she gone any further she would have been lost.

She told me that, the next day, community members saw her single track "way out on the ice" and that there were "patches of open water all around." She went on to say that some people in Hooper Bay had been watching her approaching lights and described the way that she dangerously turned out towards the open sea. This "lone" snow machine, she said, "draws people off the trail." She told me how very frightening this experience was for her. She then reiterated that it is *dangerous* to travel in such conditions. I nodded my head to indicate that I understood. We spent the rest of the evening indoors visiting, very happy to be safe and warm.

Consider the following narrative, which also describes an encounter with a "dark figure." This story, shared with me in 2003, took place in Napakiak in the mid-1990s.

> Every once in a while people will, you know, say they saw [this] figure, or something. Not even related to, you know, certain dead people and, [pause] like for instance about three years ago I think it was, I guess a couple of people from Napakiak, you know, um, one of 'em was outside working on his snow machine in the dark, but he had a small light you know and he thought he heard somebody back there and he thought it was his wife and he [saying] "oh, hi honey," you know still working on his snow machine and, and somebody tapped him on the shoulder. And, uh, he looked back and, [pause] and it was just a dark figure. It was nobody else, it was a dark figure that was just watching him—doing nothing. And he looked back, and I mean he just kept [laughs very nervously], he just kept working on his tools and the figure walked away.
>
> And that same week, I guess this guy was drunk, drunk on his four-wheeler, a lot of four-wheelers there, and he was driving and winding really fast through town, and all of a sudden he looked back and saw that same figure was running behind him, you know, even though he was going like sixty miles an hour it was still right next to him and still going.

A Very Bright Light on the Tundra at Kashunuk

The church frequently offered its own interpretation of mysterious encounters. Analogous to the aforementioned incidents where "a light" draws people away from the established trail or a dark figure (sometimes associated with a light) pursues travelers, a tale described by an Alaska missionary in the 1930s also recounted an encounter, by a villager named Ulroan, with a bright light as he made his way to the outhouse one night. This encounter, we are told, took place in the fall of

1927 shortly before the Kashunuk Mission was opened. The frightened man reported that the light came from the direction of the mission building and that as he ran back to the shelter of his tent the light crossed over him.

Completely ignorant of Yup'ik beliefs, the missionary attempted to explain this event as some kind of blessing or sign from God. Ulroan may or may not have accepted the missionary's explanation, but since the time of missionization Yupiit have sometimes associated mysterious encounters with concepts drawn from Christianity, such as devils (and may also make other connections, such as with concepts of the supernatural drawn from Hollywood movies). Similarly, anthropologist Carol Zane Jolles, in a discussion of contemporary Sivuqghhmiit (St. Lawrence Island Eskimos) beliefs, states that "Christians in the community interpret events within a Christian framework, but the events themselves reflect an older world view" (Jolles 1989, 14). Agnes Henry and Mary Black of Kongiganak, speaking of encounters with spirits, recalled an incident from their early childhood. They said:

> When we first moved here [village of Kongiganak] we were young. When we played outdoors and were having fun, a bright light would flash at us from upriver. It was very bright. We would feel strange and sometimes we would stagger. When that happened we ran into the house very frightened. (Tennant and Bitar 1981, 247)

Several Yupiit, over the years, have warned me about a certain kinds of light "like a flashlight" or even a "ball of light during the night." One time I went to the beach to collect driftwood with two women from Hooper Bay. As we made our way back along the beach, one asked if I knew the stories about the "giant hand" or "the fireball" that comes from the ocean. She pointed out in the direction of the ocean behind us, and alluded to the story of two boys who were "making too much noise" and were attacked by a fireball coming from the ocean. It actually didn't occur to me until later that this may have been a cautionary tale alluded to for my benefit, and I wondered if I had been talking too much or too loudly (made too much noise) again?

In the summer of 1950, Helen Oswalt, a University of Alaska Fairbanks student at the time, wrote about a "fire person" at Hooper Bay.[1] According to Oswalt, this light was a bad sign and often meant that someone would soon drown. "On the ocean, it does not look like a person but has three bright beams. This [light] has been seen many times and is still seen today" (Oswalt 1951, 12).

In 2013, anthropologist Katrin Simon-Sakurai documented the following tale, which also refers to a spirit (a large hand) that sometimes appears in the form of a fireball. She wrote:

> The itqiirpak (which is also referred to as the fireball, the fire hand, the large hand, or the sea monster) is said to be a sea creature that can be encountered in various shapes. According to elders, several hundred years ago a male itqiirpak attacked the neighbouring community of Hooper Bay. James Akerelrea said to me when I asked him about the appearance of this spirit that "the itqiirpak has a large hand and every finger has a mouth that swallows everything and leaves out the bones" (October 25, 2008). Akerelrea further explained that the male itqiirpak burned through the entrance to a qasgiq (men's house) and killed ill-mannered children. Hooper Bay elders defeated the male itqiirpak; however, the wife of itqiirpak survived. (Simon-Sakurai 2013, 61–62)

Clearly, seeing a light out on the tundra is a dangerous sign. I've been told that following it will get you lost. "Don't go after it. You will never catch up to it." They call it *malirqeraa*.[2] According to Jacobson, *malirqe-* means "to chase game". I once asked, "It's trying to lead you off your path?" The person responded "Yeah, you get into a spirit world where nobody would find you. You'd be in that spirit world forever."

"A Black Shadow . . . Assiituq!"

> One time I see it, with snow machine . . . good trail, hard and slow. . . . I see that, uh, *tarenraq* [tarneq], shadow, going back and forth, inside of that light. Going back, <u>black</u> shadow. . . .

When I get a little closer, that far [he motions with his hands] it tried to start going back and forth inside that light. I finally turn around, before I get run out of gas. Make it to my camp. . . . I think I, did three times, I did follow it, after last time I didn't follow it again. . . . If you follow that all the way [pause] you'll get lost.

I looked at this man and naively asked, "Were you scared?" He immediately responded to my question by saying "*Ii-I*! *Assiituq*!" (Yes! It is not good!)

Elder: Do not do that. It is not good to follow a light in the dark. If you follow it, even snow machine, you absolutely won't catch that light.
Interpreter: That light used to come around to Qungagtetuli, that light.
Elder: Yes.
Interpreter: Was it to make you make a mistake, something to follow?
Elder: It is to make you into an *ircinrraq* [little people], to let you make a mistake.
Elder: I saw something's shadow, I see that a, now what do you call a *tarenraq* in English?
Interpreter: Shadow?
Elder: Shadow. Goin' . . . my tent.
Holly: Were you scared?
Elder: Yes. It is not good!

[Original Yup'ik Telling]
Elder: Elpengungerpet-llu aturyaquniu. Unugmi kenurraq maligcunaituq. Maligeskuvgu, even snowmachine, angungaitqapigtan kenurratuuq.
Interpreter: Nunam tekicaurtellruuq tamana Qungagtetulim avatiini, kenurraq tauna.
Elder: Ii-i.
Interpreter: Cameng alarcitaa, maligcitaaq?
Elder: Ircinrurcitaalria. Alarcitaarluni.

Elder: Cam tarenraa. I see that a, tarenrat im' canek piaqekait?
Interpreter: Shadow?
Elder: Shadow. Goin' . . . my tent.
Holly: Were you scared?
Elder: Yes. Assiituq.

He then turned to a younger Yup'ik listener (the interpreter) and elaborated in Yup'ik what he had seen. The young man, in turn, then spoke to me in English as he described this figure further.

> He just warned me, there's a certain light. If you see that light, like a flashlight, or even a ball of light during the night. <u>Don't</u> go after it. [pause] You will never catch up to it. That's what they call *illacitaa. Malacitaa* [a "dark figure"]. [They then both repeat the two names for this dark figure several times before continuing.] He [the above elder] got tired of seeing that at night so he chased with his snow machine as fast as he could. He finally got close enough, and he got close. Kind of close enough to see that, you know, it was kind of like a window. And there was a shadow of a human walking back and forth, pacing back and forth. So, he realized what it was and just quickly went back to his camp.

This description of the shadow appearing "like [at] a window," pacing back and forth, is suggestive of unrest. This kind of encounter suggests that this particular place is a danger to the living because it is an entryway to the spirit world (as was hinted at in earlier discussions about windows and doors to other worlds). One man from Hooper Bay described the danger of this "dark figure":

Teller: They even have what they call a "Black Rider."
Holly: Black Rider?
Teller: Yep.
Listener: *Ii-i* [<u>yes</u>] [pause] sounds like that.
Teller: All black!
Teller: When you're riding all alone like that. That's why they [the elders] <u>always</u> tell us not to go alone.

Holly: Really?
Teller: . . . that you'll have somebody, and . . . pull you off in the wrong direction.

I have encountered numerous narratives about danger taking the form of dark figures or dark beings throughout the Yup'ik southwest. One Yup'ik teller, with whom I had been talking about ghosts, wanted me to understand that there are many different dangers and harmful forces that people encounter. She wanted me to understand something important about her cultural tradition, something she assumed I would have no understanding of, and perhaps no respect for. Sometimes people disappear and we never learn what happened to them or why.

They Found His Tracks, But Never Found His Body

Missionary accounts frequently detailed the disappearance of community members. In one such account a local man was out hunting geese and never returned to the village. He was assumed to have drowned when they found his tracks leading into the slough, but never found the man's body (Alaska Mission Collection 30). In yet another account, from November of 1942, Fox wrote, "Three men were carried out to sea by the storm and drowned. The anchor rope tore, thus leaving them adrift in a small boat and at the mercy of the waves" (Hooper Bay Collection Part 2, 439). These brief accounts recorded by missionaries in the 1940s and 1950s reflect a very real aspect of life in this region. Many people are lost on the tundra. Some are never found.

Southwestern Alaska, with its many lakes, ponds, ocean shores, and vast expanses of land, is a beautiful place but it can also be dangerous. This understanding is a part of the knowledge that Yupiit pass on from generation to generation. People go out on the land and water: sometimes they do not return. Cautionary tales, personal narratives, and ordinary discourse all serve to inform and prepare community members for dangerous situations. Sometimes it is not clear why a person is lost, but for Yupiit there are many plausible explanations beyond what the local newspapers report.

Old Sites and Potential Dangers on the Tundra

In a previous chapter I described a community project in which we dragged out a huge area map for recording place names. I described how men gathered around this map, transforming it with their narratives. One genre of stories that emerged from this gathering had to do with dangerous encounters with ghosts and other spirits on the land. One man, pointing to a place on the Kashunuk River, simply said to the others, "This is an old site." The other men were silent. He turned to them and said in Yup'ik, "lots of ghosts, spirits." I immediately recognized the word *aliurtuut*. This word loosely translates to "a thing which appears unexpectedly" or a "surprise visitor," an "apparition" or "ghost" (Jacobson 1984a, 55).

He explained to his listeners that he and some other men had recently camped "down river and opposite" that site (on the other side of the river, but within sight of this place). Apparently two of their group saw what they thought were flashlights at the spot. Thinking they would meet other people there, they prepared to go over in one of the boats. The teller and another member of their party stopped them before they pushed off from the shore and told them they should not go. When daylight returned the next morning, they saw nothing but an old abandoned site. Clearly, this was a dangerous place for the living. Only prior knowledge of it kept them from being lured away from the rest of their party.

If One Has No Water in His House or Tent

One summer night, after a wonderful meal of duck and rice, I found myself sitting around the kitchen table as my host recalled stories from his past. Four generations of listeners and myself constituted his audience. This Hooper Bay elder recalled a ghost-like encounter from many years before. He talked about being out on the land alone in the early spring. He had stopped to sleep next to his dog sled when he was awakened by a "figure" rising out of the tundra floor in front of him. The figure was dressed in an old-style fish-skin parka. (Before the influence of missionaries, I should note, hunters were dressed like this, in their hunting attire, for burial.) He described how the figure's

FIGURE 5.1. Hunting on the Tundra. Courtesy of James H. Barker 1981

skin was wrinkled and old looking. The teller explained that he was in danger because he had lost awareness during his sleep.

Before he became fully aware, the parka-clad figure began to suck his toe. He said it had attempted to suck from him his life, his *ella*. There is a description of and reference to such a figure in the *Yup'ik Eskimo Dictionary*. Linguist Steven Jacobson notes that Yupiit are vulnerable to a certain being known as *Meriiq*, which is described as a "being which will suck the blood from one's big toe if one has no water in his house or tent" (Jacobson 1984a, 234).

The young Yup'ik listeners and I were warned by the teller to keep fresh water with us if we go out onto the land. Again, as described in chapter 3, there is an emphasis on the essential, protective qualities of water. Furthermore, he told us that he was only able to overcome the "figure" after he fully awoke and regained his ella (awareness). Once he regained his awareness the figure instantly and dramatically dropped back into the tundra. What saved the man was his knowledge about ghosts and what to do in the event of an encounter—in this case, to attempt to fully wake up. He concluded his telling that night by re-emphasizing that water can prevent such an encounter from taking place. He restated this fact many times during his narrative, using this tale to teach vitally important lessons.

Places Where Nobody Camps

The following narrative also illustrates things one must know to go out on the land and return safely. This story was recorded with John Moses in the Yup'ik village of Akiachak (located some 150 miles southeast of Hooper Bay). The following excerpt is taken from that 1977 Bureau of Indian Affairs Alaska Native Claims Settlement Act interview. The interviewer (identified in the transcripts only as "Fox" and no connection to the Fox discussed in subsequent chapters) was recording place names and information on previously marked maps that contained (numbered) places/sites. Through an interpreter, Moses spoke about various places on the land in his Yup'ik language. The interpreter then repeats/retells what Moses has said in English for Fox (the ANCSA interviewer). The interpreter also seems to be part of the dialogue, asking questions and clarifying what Moses has said.

As happened in Hooper Bay, working with maps quickly became much more than an exercise in recording place names. As they moved across the map, Moses's stories colored the places and brought them to life. And just like the Hooper Bay elders and other community members, Moses recalled places that are dangerous and warned his listeners accordingly. In the following excerpt he points to a tributary of the Johnson River where, as a boy, he spent time with his grandparents.

> Interpreter: When I was a kid, probably I was three or four years old, I was staying with my grandparents—that's one, either one, of these two pictures.
>
> Fox: Uh huh. This place here, are there a lot of graves there? Like was there a trading post there or something, like marked on the map?
>
> Interpreter: The Johnson River, going up river that's very old, very many old graves in every, probably in every camp you

stop by there's going to be some graves. Even on people . . . place where the Yukon used to be here. Where great (?) related to the Yukoners . . . used to be some, right here . . .

Interpreter: There's another one right here, it's called Ayaiggluk.

Fox: Yeah, that's Number 4 there.

Interpreter: There's another old camp . . . he can't remember the name . . . Amiyugaq.

Interpreter: This'd be another name. It's named after a really small . . . [inaudible] . . . play around with. It could be because somebody found one there or they made a lot of 'em or something.

Interpreter: George's father used to be here in springtime. [Interpreter repeats the Yup'ik word *puskiaq* several times, then:] Ghost town. [laughs]

Fox: Does that mean there's just nobody there now or does it mean that ghosts live there?

Interpreter: It's just old spirits, bad spirits that kinda live there. Weird stories, . . . they can blow up the window, let it land down in the river.

Fox: What kind of . . . well, does he know some of those stories? Why do they think, why are there bad spirits there or what is a bad spirit?

Interpreter: Why these spirits happen we don't know. There's probably bad things going on . . . (?) . . . Probably a murder, maybe.

Fox: What sorts of things have the bad spirits? . . . What sorts of things have happened there?

Interpreter: I don't know. I'd like to find out so . . . [inaudible] might come up and we'll find out [laughs].

Fox: Has he heard of some of those? What are some of the things that have happened?

Interpreter: Only one man's story he can tell.

Interpreter: So called village man, his name is [John] . . . He and one of his friends from down river, they were going to spend the night up there. Then all this time they had this weird feeling that it was snowing. That's how they knew that it was going to be something. And then during that period they could feel that spirit, you know, someplace around them. Their dogs also were scared, you know. They were down on the ground, scared and barking a little. And after they went someplace else to spend the night, then they went back, they saw this window that used to be on top of this old sod house. It was blown off! It was blown off, so the next day they went back, they checked to see what happened. Bad spirits must have blown it away. Must have gotten mad. . . . They didn't find no tracks of anybody that would do something like that. That window that blew out was just staying there so nothing would take it out, you know? Then the next day, everything that was on the window, the mud that was weighing it down, it was all scattered around the house, outside the house not inside. . . .

Those are places where nobody camps. Used to be some places, many years ago people living there, but nowadays nobody like to camp, people . . .

Interpreter: There's many people got some stories from those days when they'd go dog teaming all the time up back and forth, Akiachak and those camps up there. (Moses 1977)

Windows as a Portal to the Spirit World

Yupiit often tell stories and personal narratives in which windows are a point of entry, or some kind of a portal to the spirit world. The following excerpt is taken from a tale told by Peter Nick at Russian Mission in the mid-1970s:

> The young boy "sees" animal-spirits and follows them across the Yukon River to Arumalria. They disappear underground and the boy follows until he reaches the "window" that leads to their underground *qasgiq*. He peers through this window and becomes so absorbed in their activities that he watches them (as in a trance) all winter long. The "underground" house and seal-gut window probably indicate that the boy is looking into "another world" or a spirit dwelling. (Hansen 1985, 78)

The appearance and repetition of windows in Yup'ik narrative reinforce understandings about the permeable nature of the human and spirit worlds. Morrow reminds us of "the need to form a protective barrier between the living and the dead" (Morrow 1984, 131). Likewise, Fienup-Riordan says that "Yup'ik discourse" maintains "boundaries and passages between worlds" (Fienup-Riordan 1994, 7). This motif of a window suggests something significant about the ways in which beings (human and spirit), literally, "see into" the other world.

The Hooper Bay elder told me that "it was kind of like a window . . . and there was shadow of a human walking back and forth." In the narrative that John Moses shared, the Yup'ik hunters have clearly chosen a dangerous place to camp. They wisely move their camp because they feel something dangerous exists in this place. Their dogs, too, have sensed this. They return the next day to find the window of the old sod house blown off. "They went back, they saw this window that used to be on top of this old sod house. It was blown off!" This suggests a power beyond that of human nature or human ability. To further establish the eerie nature of this incident, the teller states that the Yup'ik men "didn't find . . . tracks . . . those are places where nobody camps" (Moses 1977).

"Old spirits, bad spirits that kinda live there . . . they can blow up the window, let it land down the river." I think that the "bad" spirits are centered at the window because the windows of sod houses were places where not only the smoke of the living once passed, but also the opening through which the dead exited. Edward Nelson wrote that "by means of cords the body is usually raised through the smoke hole in the roof, but is never taken out by the doorway" (Nelson 1983 [1899], 311).

George Moses Sr., in his narrative (see chapter 3) about the lake where "unusual" things happen at Qemirrluar (the name that translates to "bit of a broad hill" and is known as a place where high winds are encountered), explains the importance of knowing these places and their names. "All those lakes were named, 'cause in those days many things could happen, you know, like somebody might get lost. The only way to come back if your dog team runs away, the only way you can come back is by these, the names of these places, the lakes" (Moses 1988). Knowing place names is important.

What is implicit in his statement is the fact that "knowing" these place names goes well beyond the ability to simply list or map them. Place names do not simply allow you to find your way home by connecting point "A" to point "B." The very names themselves tell people important information about a particular site. Names are often imbued with cultural descriptions that instruct and remind people where to camp, what to avoid, and why. This too, then, becomes an important part of the necessary knowledge, and these understandings may be the "only way to come back" (Moses 1988).

In March of 2004, while examining an ANCSA map with Robert Drozda and Louann Rank, we noted a place next to Qemirrluar, called Ircenrraat Egalrat. The handwritten note on this map, from the Russian Mission area, indicated that this Yup'ik name meant "the window of the ircenrraqs" (pers. comm. Robert Drozda and Louann Rank 2004). While Yup'ik place names are often descriptive, this one caught my attention because of the specific connection to a window. The "window of the ircinrraat" suggests that perhaps this place, too, may be a place of entry into and from the spirit world. It certainly tells Yupiit something significant since there are prescribed ways to act around ircinrraat. It also suggests that lakes, like windows, may also be viewed as a passageway between worlds.

An interesting incident took place in Hooper Bay during the 1930s when the local community members informed the priest that "there are footprints on the windows in the church and in your room, too" (AM Collection 30, 472). The missionary would later write in the *Indian Sentinel*, "Sure enough, there they were. I saw them myself as soon as I entered the chapel. It was very cold inside and out, and the windows were heavily frosted except for a succession of clear spots. They gave the impression of a trail that a child with red-hot feet might have made by running up and down the windows" (AM Collection 30, 472). The priest could not have understood the significance of this event as Yupiit understood it. Instead, he tried to offer a scientific explanation of how the footprints got on the church window. This story, though, indicates that Yup'ik understandings of the land and particular places easily carried over to understandings about human-made places as well.

Among Yupiit, windows and doorways or other passageways continue to be places where the spirit and human world converge and intersect. In contemporary tellings about "modern" structures, the significance is similar.[3] I will address this point, especially in relation to human-made buildings, again in later chapters. Turning back to the various narratives by Moses and Hooper Bay elders, places on the land that are associated with "windows to another world" are certainly not good places to camp or rest. Camping and resting involve sleep, and sleep involves a diminished sense of ella, so choosing the right place to camp is as important today as it was in the past. Embedded in these Yup'ik place names is the cultural information necessary to make appropriate choices and actions.

It is understood that places considered not safe for camping are places that are already inhabited. In 1996, a Yup'ik woman told me the following story:

> This hunting crew, these men were going out to hunt and they stopped by a riverbank to camp out until the next day. And there were other people there, but they didn't hear any other boats pass by, or anything, but they kept hearing voices at night, one of them did. And, um, they didn't know what it was and he [the one who heard voices] was just so tired that he collapsed and forgot about it.
>
> The next morning they went down and checked their motor and all the little, you know, the wires and stuff were pulled out. And they had to find a ride home and somebody had to haul their boat back. And they didn't hear any, you know, there was not much people and it was during the night too. So, they kind of had the idea that it was, you know, the *ircinrraq*, [teller lowers voice to whisper] or somebody else who was out there.

Hooper Bay tales reflect that ircinrraat are sometimes "more helpful," sometimes "playing tricks," but can be dangerous "depending on where you camp." One of my favorite stories of ircinrraat from Hooper Bay, because it vividly illustrates Yup'ik knowledge of place, is the following narrative I recorded in 2001 about two hunters and their personal experience.

"We Are Trying to Live in This World of Ours"

From my own experience I know of three or four occasions [encounters] and a few others with my in-laws and cousins. One experience I had with my cousin on a hunting trip during the fall season for white-fronted geese. I believe this was our second or third trip in so many years. Each time we would walk to our blind which is about three quarters of a mile roundabout, by an old big, big lake.

Each year we are sitting in our blind we would start hearing humming, like a hum of a distant generator, although this last season when we went we decided to stay in and wait till the chill of the morning was more warmer, we headed up to our blind by mid-morning. After what seemed like an hour of sitting we, or I, realized that I was in a trance like state and there was this loud humming, seeming all around us. I glanced at my cousin who was sitting about four feet to my right, staring at one spot.

Right off I knew something was wrong and I slowly stood up and gave a warning to him [his cousin], although it took him a couple minutes of comprehending my warning. I moved a few feet away from my shotgun and looked at the hill we had been sitting on and just started talking. I talked about how we both have families and how we are trying to catch some game and, like them, we are trying to live in this world of ours and that we did not mean any harm and that we were sorry for intruding. By this time my cousin stands beside and starts doing the same [speaking to them]. We've returned every year since that incident and haven't had problems after that.

After we had talked, seemingly for a few minutes. After we sat we finally realized the weather was super calm and felt like in the seventies ["hot" weather] temperature wise. We finally looked at our time and realized we had lost all afternoon, since our watches were at six o'clock. We had lost all afternoon and did not even realize what was going on till the time we suddenly became aware.

We were told we had a close encounter, but we did the right thing according to the elders. We did not actually see the *ircinrraat* as you and I see each other, but thinking back the experience gives me the chills still.

These Hooper Bay hunters were in real danger, but having regained their sense of ella, were able to recall their elder's teachings. Once they had regained their awareness they were able to act on the words and stories of their elders. This saved them from an otherwise dangerous situation. These hunters demonstrated a sincere respect for the spirit world and made an appeal that was heard. The ircinrraat were listening. As long as they continue to maintain awareness and respect (demonstrate appropriate action), they will be allowed to return every year to this hill.

People at Hooper Bay have warned me about using or speaking the word *ircinrraq* (singular form). One person told me explicitly that it is "not good to say the word." Perhaps this is equivalent to "making too much noise" and an invitation to dangerous beings of the spirit world. Speaking the word can make these beings come to you. Similarly, I have been told that "too much noise" will "wake up the dead."

There is a strong connection between "making too much noise" and demonstrating improper behavior. I was once told of a young Hooper Bay girl who had stayed out all night with her friends. As she made her way home early the next morning she was pelted with mud and tiny sticks by unseen beings. She was being admonished for her actions of the night before (partying too much) and I am told never did that again! She learned how one's own actions can bring about dangerous and unwanted consequences.

Sometimes encounters, as in the above narratives, are not of a serious nature. This was recently the case at Hooper Bay. According to a community member, "the village dogs were making a ruckus" in the middle of the night. This, says the teller, "happened sometime before snow started falling." As the family slowly opened their door to investigate the cause, they carefully peered around the corner and spied a small ircinrraq. "It was sitting right on our steps, sitting and panting. It was tired from being chased by loose dogs." When they momentarily looked away, it vanished.

Other times encounters can be quite serious and life threatening. You may recall the Yup'ik woman who as a little girl feared these beings who lurked in the corners of underground houses. Even when there is a humorous element, such as when ircinrraat mess with the "wires and stuff" of a boat motor, there can be a serious undertone. Tampering with a boat motor can prove to be very dangerous if one ends up stranded on the tundra or out on the open ice.

Stories and Accounts of the "Hairy Man": Careless Words and Cautionary Tales

Ircinrraat are not the only ones who are known to inhabit certain places on the land. Myriad seen and unseen beings surround the living and the potential for encounters is always present. It is easy when out on the tundra, with its vast expanses of treeless, open land and the ability to see for miles in any direction, to think that you are alone. Through stories, those who are under this false impression are instructed about and cautioned against such careless notions.

During one of my stays in Hooper Bay back in 1998, I received an invitation to go out on the tundra to collect bird eggs and greens with a woman from the community. I was so eager to get out on the land and away from the hours of work that we had been doing in the office that I accepted without hesitation. Once we were out very little was said as we walked along, our eyes peeled on the tundra floor. After a long silence she told me how glad she was to be out of town, out on the land. I enthusiastically said to her that I felt very comfortable collecting greens and eggs in a place where one does not have to watch out for brown bears. I told her that, at home on the Kenai Peninsula, I always felt some concern over berry picking with my kids. Here, in this place, I could just pick without having to look over my shoulder and always be listening.

She quickly nodded and then, without hesitation, alluded to a story often told about a being or creature known as "Hairy Man." Pointing in the direction of the nearby Askinuk Mountains, she explained to me that she had just recently heard of other community members seeing him "up at the mountains." She told me that she is afraid when she has trouble sleeping at fish camp or up at her berry camp at night. She said that she especially thinks about him when she is alone at her camp. We both agreed that we were glad to have each other's company.

FIGURE 5.2. Seal hunters out on the ice. Courtesy of James H. Barker 2004

I had carelessly expressed overconfidence and ease with the land. My discourse was potentially dangerous for both of us. She immediately referenced this tale in order to caution me about my overt statements in relation to this place. I had expressed a reckless disregard for the power of words and the very real dangers that exist on the land. My careless use of words typified *kass'aq* behavior. Her allusion to this particular being and the associated stories about recent sightings served to remind me that I lacked appropriate awareness.

On that level, the teller was using her narrative to instruct and caution me. But perhaps more importantly, her words served to undo my words. My careless act of speaking was diminished as she reestablished her own position. She used this narrative to make her own awareness (ella) known to the sentient world around us. In this way, her cautionary tale made the place somewhat safer again.

The Hairy Man stories certainly extend beyond the reaches of the Askinuk Mountains and the community of Hooper Bay. In fact, these tales are found beyond the Yup'ik cultural tradition. A close friend who was raised in her small Athabascan village on the Yup'ik-Athabascan border told me that she too had heard "a lot about Hairy Man" especially when she was a young girl. She recalls the fear that these stories instilled in her and told me that she "sure as hell took it seriously" (pers. comm. October 2003). Some of these Yup'ik tales, as we have seen, are serious lessons. For those who do not know or respect this knowledge, there are potentially devastating outcomes. Some are less serious in nature but remind listeners that it is an uncertain world and that to return safely one must remain vigilant.

In fall of 2014, I was sitting in my office at the university thousands of miles from the tundra when the phone rang. On the other end, a familiar voice greeted me with "Waqaa, Holly!" I immediately recognized the voice as that of a friend from Hooper Bay whom I had worked with on many collaborative projects over the years. He shifted to English, "Didn't you get my e-mail message?" I admitted that I had not quite waded through the week's backlog and apologized, but quickly scrolled to the bold highlighted message. He said, "I saw another Hairy Man and it was in the news!" I scrolled down and clicked on the embedded link. As I glanced at the story text, my friend went on to say, "I even got video footage with my camera!" The news article appeared in the *Delta Discovery*, a Native-owned and operated publication "dedicated to the free exchange of ideas and issues of the Yukon-Kuskokwim Delta" (*Delta Discovery* 2014). The story page featured a slightly blurry image (taken from the moving footage) of the large, hunched creature approaching the rotting walrus carcass that had washed ashore along that stretch of the Bering Sea coast. The article, titled "A Bigfoot Seen along the Hooper Bay Beach," chronicled this account. As I began reading, he said, "That is the video picture I took back around the 4th of July of my sighting of Hairy Man!" He knew I would have the context for understanding this well-publicized sighting and that I would link it to other tellings shared with me over the years. I expressed my excitement over this coverage. He then laughed nervously and said, "My cousins are really teasing me about seeing a Big Foot and even *kass'aq*s are teasing me here!"

The paper chronicled his encounter and quoted him, "Later that day at the post office, I learned from a cousin and her husband that while clamming in a nearby area they came upon large footprints. Another person told me he had found unusual footprints that had toenail or claw marks and when he compared them with his own size 10 shoes, they were bigger by 5 inches, more or less. He had been fishing for humpies, but when he found the tracks he upped and took off for home" (*Delta Discovery* 2014).

The sidebar of this online news story contained an "ad-like" box featuring a rough sketch of a hunched-over, hairy, ape-like creature. The caption read "Hairy Man Stories, AKA Bigfoot." Below was a link that lead to a series of similar reports that have been chronicled over the past year in the region. In all, I counted thirty-seven different documented accounts dating back to February 6, 2013. The stories ranged from encounters in Nome to small Yup'ik villages south of the Kuskokwim River region. In June of 2014, for example, the *Delta Discovery* reported, "Two geese hunters who are from Bethel are the most recent eyewitnesses of a large, hairy, Bigfoot-like creature on the tundra near the community of Bethel."

I think one of the most important aspects of my friend's story is what he said at the end of the interview. The intended audience is his own community and, likely, those of younger generations. He concludes by stating,

> After the sighting, I told fellow Hooper Bayers about the creature. In hindsight, maybe I should have kept this to myself, but I wanted the community to become aware of other beings and creatures that live with us. There are creatures out there. My grandmother instilled in my mind daily when I started hunting around eight-years-old, saying to me, "Do not ever panic when you encounter something that is strange." She told me, "One of these days, now that you are traveling to the wilderness, you will meet creatures that live with us, but they don't trust people." (*Delta Discovery* July 23, 2014)

The Church Bell at Hooper Bay

When people go missing, the community goes to great lengths to find them, and they take into consideration not only the physical conditions of their disappearance but also the possibility that the one who was lost encountered some perilous nonhuman beings. There is also an understanding that such individuals, even when found, may have entered a liminal state. Church documents from Hooper Bay describe how the bell of the old church originally was used at the Kashunuk Mission. After severe floods forced the people of Kashunuk to relocate, the bell was brought to Hooper Bay for the Little Flower Mission. The bell served one purpose for the missionaries, the announcement of mass, but a much more practical application was soon employed by the community members. The following account was written in the church diary for the year 1943 at Hooper Bay.

> Every once in a while our bell does emergency duty. And as the bell is just now ringing, and has been ringing almost constantly for the past three hours, the idea for these lines came to me. We are living on a wicked coast. Storms are very frequent all the year round. . . . A storm last fall carried three of our Eskimos out to sea with their small boat, and none of them has been heard of since. And that has this to do with bells. When one of these blizzards that hit us frequently in winter catch any of our hunters out on the tundra for foxes, or at the seashore for seals, about the only chance they have of finding their way home is to be led there by our bell. And so early this afternoon when some of the hunters failed to return one of the men came to ask for permission to toll our bell so as to guide in the straying hunters. . . .
>
> To my people here no explanations are necessary when the bell begins to ring on a stormy winter day, and not at regular time. But Father Covert who is still rather new here, came running in excitement: "Why that bell?" "Oh, nothing special," I replied, "a few of the hunters got caught in the storm and we are trying to help them home with our bell." Father breathed a sigh of relief: "I thought we had a fire somewhere and so dashed over here to see you! Thanks be to God, we still have not had to ring the bell for a fire." (AM Collection 14, 425)

Three years later, in 1946, another entry in the church diary for the Little Flower Mission, *Historia Domus*, simply read: "Three men from Kashunuk lost on the ice. After much delay Gov. [government] planes sent to search. They searched 5,000 sq. miles to no avail" (AM Collection 13, 37). In the summer of 1950 when Helen Oswalt visited Hooper Bay, she also wrote that "three Kashunuk men . . . drowned when out on ice; ice broke, [they] put [the] dogs in [the] kayak but too heavy, tipped over" (Oswalt 1951, 6).

"The Elders Say the Man is Still Somehow Alive"

In a state as vast as Alaska, search-and-rescue teams are crucial. The above accounts establish the ongoing regularity with which people are lost on the tundra and upon the sea. Sometimes the cause of a disappearance is known; other times it is not. The seeming apathy of the two missionaries aside, this historic description does shed light on the fact that going out on the land can be dangerous. It illustrates one of the strategies that Hooper Bay community members employed to locate missing people many years ago.

The missionary who wrote about the church bell's "emergency duty" in Hooper Bay probably had no idea that the dangers of going out onto the land extend far beyond contending with below-zero temperatures and whiteout conditions. The natural and spirit world can present many unseen dangers for those who are not aware of their surroundings. Winter weather in a Bering Sea coast village can be very harsh. I can remember many nights when the winds whipped so violently that the entire house shook as I lay awake in my bed, listening to it smash against the house and howl outside the rattling windows. The weather itself is understood to have ella, as do other elements of the natural world (animals, plants, land features). Writers Eliza Cingarkaq Orr and Ben Orr perfectly describe the animate nature of the weather when writing of the ferocious winds on Nelson Island:

> Six hundred miles south of the arctic circle, Nelson Island has a harsh maritime Climate, with the third highest prevailing winds in Alaska. Particularly in winter, these winds beset the Island for days on end, stirring up fierce gales that make travel

> and subsistence activity perilous. It is then that the Yupiit say that *Ella*, the weather, whom they view as possessing will and animacy, is hunting for victims and will not abate until someone dies. (Orr and Orr 1995, xii)

In the Yup'ik region, search-and-rescue knowledge extends well beyond the use of a flare gun and first aid kit. Especially in the Yup'ik villages, a team needs to be equipped with the knowledge of their elders as well. A few years ago two Yup'ik men, traveling by snow machine, were lost in the region on Christmas Eve. In early January the body of one man was found next to his snow machine. The second man, however, was not located (Irwin 2000a). By the end of the month the Alaska State Troopers had called off their search, but Bethel's Search and Rescue team continued to look for the lost man (Irwin 2000b). Throughout the Yup'ik region, concern grew as the weeks passed. People spoke of this man who was lost on the land, and rescue team members reported finding signs of him.

Searchers came across snow shelters on the tundra and nearby footprints that had been left behind by the missing man. The local newspaper, the *Tundra Drums*, reported, "Searchers have found at least two manmade shelters during their search. . . . However, the waning conditions of the shelters indicate his strength was fading" (Irwin 2000b). The *Tundra Drums* continued to report that "searchers and other travelers . . . [have] reported finding traces of [his] footprints. The tracks were followed until they seemed to disappear into thin air. Broken spruce tree branches, snow caves, windbreaks and even an igloo were discovered southwest from the area [where his companion was found]" (Active 2000).

Throughout the region there was much talk and speculation regarding his whereabouts. The longer he was missing, the more concern community members expressed over the disappearance. Weeks went by, and some speculated that he had died on the tundra, saying that he had probably lost his way and frozen to death. Many others did not find this to be a satisfactory explanation. What became a central concern for many Yupiit was that he was believed to exist in a liminal stage as he remained out on the tundra. Many indicated that this was a dangerous situation.

In the 1890s, Edward Nelson wrote of a similar danger in his discussion of "shades of the dead." Nelson describes this "shade" in terms of "evil," which oversimplifies the Yup'ik understanding of such a state. He does, however, provide a useful description of the way in which a person lingers "in the vicinity of their life." Nelson notes that this kind of being, figure, or ghost is particularly threatening to the living because the "shade" remains with the body. He writes:

> From the people with whom I talked I obtained a suggestion of a third kind of shade, which is supposed to remain with the body and to possess evil powers, which, however, seem to be limited, but I could not obtain more definite information about it. The shades of the dead are believed to linger for some time in the vicinity of their life scenes. (Nelson 1983 [1899], 422)

"Somewhere There, Perhaps in the Place of the Dead"

I can't overemphasize the permeable and illusive nature of the human and spirit world as experienced by Yupiit. Phyllis Morrow and Elsie Mather, in their analysis of a Yup'ik tale, also describe this liminal stage of existence. The telling of "Uterneq: The Woman Who Returned From the Dead" (in Swann 1994) gives listeners and readers a strong sense that there are no well-marked boundaries between the world of the living and the world of the dead. The story of Uterneq, with its variation from teller to teller, is essentially about a woman who returns to the living world in order to instruct Yupiit about the Elriq Ceremony and the proper treatment of the dead. Elriq (which translates to "throwing away") was a ceremony that allowed the living to care for the dead. The dead were given food, fresh water, and new clothes.

If proper procedures were not followed, then the ancestors would not return from the place of the dead during this ceremony, leading to a break between the worlds of the living and the dead. This ceremony and the story of Uterneq illustrate the permeable nature of the living and spirit world, an essential theme that weaves in and out of Yup'ik narrative and discourse with many variations. The authors remind us that "like many other Yup'ik concepts, ideas about the dead are nondefinitive and open-ended, consisting of multiple terms and descriptions that follow from each person's traditional knowledge and personal experience of things spiritual" (Swann 1994, 39). Consider the following excerpt from one telling of the Uterneq story:

> When the living relative left on earth, one who lost a loved one, did not take part [in the Elriq ceremony], the dead person, the one for whom he had cared, would stay behind, feeling unloved, somewhere there, perhaps in the place of the dead. (Swann 1994, 41)

One winter day, during the time when this man was still missing, I sat with a woman in Hooper Bay drinking tea in her home. I asked her if she had heard about the missing man. She began to describe a trip to Bethel, over 150 miles away by air, in which she had taken her elderly mother to the hospital. They were required to stay in Bethel for several days while her mother underwent treatment. Her young daughters were able to stay with nearby family members, but she needed to be close to the hospital. She told me that she had been very afraid of sleeping at the hospice home because residents had reported "seeing him around the hospital." He (the missing man) had been seen by locals near the high school as well.

She told me that he was probably hanging around the hospital because this was the place where they had brought the body of his travel companion after he had been found frozen on the tundra. She told me that she was especially frightened because her bed was located right next to the outside wall and window of the tiny room where they were staying. Her discomfort with the window again indicates that these are places where the spirit world enters the world of the living. She explained that this caused several sleepless nights and that she was very glad to finally be back in Hooper Bay.

She went on to say that he was able to do things that most human beings can't do. She described how he could travel across the tundra at very high speeds and traverse large bodies of water with ease. This, she indicated, made her very uneasy. As she related this information, we heard footsteps coming up the stairs of her house. They came into the *elaturraq* (enclosed exterior storm porch) and stopped. We listened and waited to see who it was, both expecting to see one of her young children come bounding through the door. No one came in and no one knocked.

We paused and looked at each other. I could see that she was concerned. As she turned back towards the door, I suddenly stopped to think about what we had been talking about before the interruption. We exchanged a nervous glance. After a few moments she rose to her feet and slowly went over to the interior door. She opened it and saw no one. Again, we looked at each other, each waiting for the other to speak. Then in a low voice she informed me that we should not have been talking about him. I nodded my head to indicate that I understood. We ended our words and never again spoke of this incident or the missing man.

However, he continued to be a concern for community members. Village search-and-rescue teams in the region are equipped with the Yup'ik knowledge that tells them how to behave when such a being is encountered. Rescue team members in the Yup'ik southwest also turn to the wisdom and experience of their elders during these times.

People in Hooper Bay talked about the need to keep some food and fresh water with them when out traveling on the land or the sea. They explained that this is done because spirits are often drawn to certain foods and, like other beings in the spirit world, thirst for fresh water. The aforementioned tale of "Uterneq, the Woman Who Returned from the Dead," describes the way in which a young man is "able to reach into her [Uterneq's] plane without fully leaving his own." This he achieved by rubbing food scraps on his body. "He picked up some of those food scraps and rubbed his arms with them." The authors note that such food scraps "belong to both worlds" (Mather and Morrow in Swann 1994, 47). Food scraps were often dropped on the floor as offerings to the dead: Food, as a substance, sustains the living, but it also sustains the dead. Recall the seal oil left at the place on the tundra where the Hooper Bay shaman is buried. Food and water maintain a relationship between the living and the dead, and can help in retrieving a lost soul. Food and water connect the living and the dead, but water is also used to maintain boundaries and can protect search team members, hunters, and travelers from the potential dangers that come from unwelcome encounters.

After the Alaska State Troopers canceled their search, the Bethel Search and Rescue team turned to the Yup'ik elders for guidance on the matter. One young team member said that "the sightings and footprints left by someone missing for so long in the cold was something we couldn't understand and so we needed to hear from the elders what we should do next." Another young man at the meeting stated, "Okay, the elders say the man is still somehow alive. . . . I've never experienced anything like this before in my life, but have heard stories about it. What am I supposed to do if I see him?" (Active 2000). In response to these questions one Bethel elder explained:

> You must be very careful with him. Don't startle him. Coax him back to reality, speak to him with your mind. And most importantly, try to touch him. His spirit is keeping his body moving. He will be very thirsty. Give him some water and try to touch him. And if you can't, spit on him. Your spittle is from you, a living human being, your spit will cause him to become very weak and collapse. (Active 2000)

Respected elders from villages throughout the Yup'ik region spoke to the crowd. An elder from Tuntutuliak explained that "those who get lost in the wilderness become like animals being hunted. They are hard to apprehend and unpredictable in their behavior" (Active 2000). An elder from Napakiak was quoted: "You can't catch a wild bird with your hands, it'll fly away if you try to touch it. It's the same with these people who are lost." According to the reporter, a younger man from Nunapitchuk told the elders that "he's heard about several ways to touch a lost one. On the clothing and on the flesh. Which was best he wanted to know?" (Active 2000). The Napakiak elder responded, "I think touching him on the flesh is the most powerful and that will help get him back into our world" (Active 2000).

Still another elder from Kasigluk spoke to the young people, telling them, "If you lose your bearing, stop. Don't continue. Stay put. Later you will realize where you are and then can continue." He recalled his own experiences of being lost on the land and how he would "hear shouts and commands, such as a dog musher would make to his team, around him. But there'd be no one around. Or he'd see people milling about and when he'd go to them, it would only be grass waving in the wind. Or he'd see a rabbit bolt and stop and when he'd go to it, it would be a small snowdrift" (Active 2000). Another man from Quinhagak continued by telling the audience, "We grew up hearing these things and we didn't make them up. These are our beliefs, traditions, and customs" (Active 2000). This statement was probably directed not only at the Yup'ik youths, but also at the non-Yupiit who would have attended this public forum.

An elder from the village of Akiachak recalled for the audience an incident in which he himself had rescued a hunter. This hunter, the elder explained, had disappeared when he was out hunting for muskrat in the springtime. Yup'ik reporter John Active wrote:

> One day while searchers [in this elder's rescue team] were resting, the man appeared before them as he fell to the ground. Later, when the missing man recovered, he related that he had been standing before the searchers for a while, but then became very dizzy and fell down. That's when the missing man appeared to them. [The rescuer] sent the searchers back home to report that the missing man had been found, and that [he] was going to prepare the lost man for his return home. The man whistled like a bird when he tried to speak. As the man recovered he began to speak. [The rescuer] asked him how he got around.
>
> The missing man told him when he came to a river, he simply stepped across it and lakes were like puddles on the ground. Wherever he wanted to go, all he had to do was think about it and he'd be there. (Active 2000)

This report ended with one elder's closing remarks to the rescue team and other audience members. This Akiachak elder encouraged the rescue team to continue their efforts to find this missing man. He instructed them by saying that "if he is making tracks or there are still sightings of him continue to search. . . . We are Yupiit and these are our beliefs" (Active 2000).

James Barker underscores that "implicit is the understanding that one must be wise in knowing what to prepare for and equally prepared for the unknowable" (Barker 1993, 13). This protection is especially important when facing dangers that come from unexpected encounters with bad, angry, or unknown beings or spirits. The first part of this elder's statement was aimed at his younger, audience members, whom he was telling to "continue to search," but his final remark was also aimed at a non- Yup'ik audience: "We are Yupiit and these are our beliefs."

From such statements we sense the sort of underlying tensions that not only characterized this public meeting, but the interrelationships that exist in villages throughout southwest Alaska. It was, after all, a well-established fact that the Alaska State Troopers had already declared the search fruitless. In this sense there is a tension between the approaches and thinking of these two groups who were involved in the search.

It is generally understood and expected that most non-Yupiit do not know the stories and the embedded cultural knowledge that informs listeners of which places to avoid and why. It goes well beyond the notion that kass'aqs lack knowledge, however. Implicit is the notion that even when given the opportunity to learn such things, they often do not respect the wisdom Yup'ik elders are trying to impart. As we shall see in subsequent chapters, this ignorance can have a significant and lasting outcome for those who debunk knowledge about places and the beings who inhabit them. This expectation of ignorance is embedded in Yup'ik narrative discourse and reflects ongoing tensions between Yupiit and non-Yupiit.

6

Angalkuut

SHAMANS, ENEMIES, AND OTHER VILLAGES

In chapter 2, I described a single grave on the tundra, known to be that of a shaman. Like other narratives previously discussed, the story of this grave and how people behave around it gives a sense that humans are a part of a sentient natural-spirit world. As we have seen, living in such a world presents many unseen and often unidentifiable dangers; these can often be reduced or obviated if people know what places to avoid and what to do if they have an unexpected encounter.

Sometimes, however, potential threats come in a recognizable form, that of the human kind. Shaman stories illustrate how people relate to each other through places and their associated narratives, but they also reveal important understandings about a specific type of human-made place—contemporary villages. In the Yup'ik region warfare was once common and enemy villages posed clear dangers. In contemporary times one may not always know where dangers lurk, whether in a familiar neighboring village or one less familiar, but it seems that in contemporary times, as in the past, traveling to another community can make one more vulnerable. In fact, traveling to another village, in some ways, parallels the kinds of dangers one might encounter when out on the land.

A Yup'ik woman at Hooper Bay told me the following story in 1996:

> This is a story that was told to me . . . [about] one of the health aides. . . . This is a story about shamans though, mostly. And

> . . . [she] was visiting a certain, you know, she visits villages all over the place, to see how their health aide programs are doing. And I guess in one of the villages . . . one of her friends who's a health aide . . . was having like, really weird dreams, like about dogs, you know chasing her. And it's just this <u>one</u> particular, it was a dark black dog who was just <u>chasing</u> her, you know. He kept chasing her.
>
> And in her dream, every time, I mean she had the same re-occurring dream for [pause] about three days and, um, the dog just kept getting <u>closer</u> to her before she woke up, you know. And so she went to an older person [community elder] in the village, you know, an elder. And she asked for advice and, and the elder said, "The next time you go to, go to sleep leave a 2x4 or a big stick by your bed" and, and she did that for one night and the dog got closer. And then the next night after that, when the dog got closer to her, in her dream, she grabbed that big 2x4 stick and started pounding on the dog.
>
> And that morning, at about [pause] like six o'clock in the morning, you know, she woke up after that dream and she got a call, um, saying, you know, there's this person that, in the village [a community member] that is hurt. And she went over to that house and [pause] it was an old woman who was weeping, you know, like a dog on the floor. And she had, like six ribs broken on her back. And so, you know, she figured out who it was that was bothering her, so [laughs nervously].
>
> Interesting huh? Yeah, like every once in a while when my mom has a <u>bad</u> dream, you know, she'll regard it as something really big, you know. And she worries. . . . So, dreams are a big thing I guess.

This story, identified by the teller as "a shaman story," and recorded during the summer of 1996, was said to have taken place sometime in the late 1980s or early 1990s. It was shared with me because the teller wanted to stress the fact that such dangers still exist. She stated that I (as a kass'aq listener) probably wouldn't expect these dangers to be active, but she wanted me to understand something important about her culture and her Yup'ik upbringing. She became very serious and lowered her voice as she began to share the story. We were not in a public setting where others might overhear, but she remained cautious with her words. It was clear from my attentiveness that I understood little about the various kinds of dangers people potentially face. She chose this account of a shaman attack to demonstrate her point about such dangers.

Hooper Bay has a strong history of well-known and powerful shamans. In Hooper Bay, and in other villages, I have heard strikingly similar accounts of shamans who take the form of a black dog, bird, or other dark creature. These are terrifying tales and leave no question that such dangers exist.

Guarded Words and Narratives

Shamanism is a sensitive subject, one that I don't raise lightly. The narratives that I have heard, only some later recorded, suggest that the powers associated with shamanism are not simply a subject of the past but rather a contemporary issue as well. Because I have been taught that words have power and because words do hold the potential to make things happen, I will never write down certain stories and narratives. Real people, in contemporary settings, deem this a dangerous undertaking. This chapter is included to share those aspects of knowledge that I think can be presented in a published form.

Shamans and Times of War: A Precontact History

There is ample evidence to suggest that Eskimo peoples, like groups everywhere, experienced periods of peace and periods of conflict. "Bad shamans," those who present dangers and hold the potential to harm others, used a special form of discourse or spell to achieve their goal (Burch 1988). Paralleling the Yup'ik Eskimo notion that words hold the potential of power and action, here is Burch's brief description of shamans and this form of discourse. He states that a shaman's spell was a source of "supernatural power" and that "a spell is a word, or a series of words—spoken in some cases, sung in others—which produces a specific magical effect, such as killing a wounded whale, moderating a severe windstorm, or defending a person from the attacks of ghosts"

(Burch 1988, 101). "Dangerous people," or bad shamans, were probably most often from opposing villages. Thus, not only did enemy warfare present a real and ongoing danger but there was also an ongoing threat from the words and actions of enemy shamans. These threats came during times of war and periods of relative peace.

I began this work with a discussion of the various stereotypes that, from the time of contact, have plagued Eskimo peoples throughout the north. Another stereotype that has long been held is that Eskimo groups were not war-like. "The smiling, innocent Eskimo" was "the one at war with nature," but never with other groups (Brody 1987, 21). Eskimo peoples are still portrayed by the outside world as a people who battle their "harsh" environment, not each other. But this "nonviolent character of Eskimo social interaction has been emphasized at the expense of the violence and warfare that are a real part of their history and tradition" (Fienup-Riordan 1994, 146).

Recent oral historical, archaeological, and ethnohistorical research yields a different picture of Eskimo peoples and the past. Researcher Ernest "Tiger" Burch, for example, argued that Eskimo groups of northwest Alaska actually comprised distinct nations and that most Eskimo groups in Alaska regularly warred with neighboring Eskimo and Athabascan groups (Burch 1998). The elders he interviewed "expressed the view that constant warfare in northwestern Alaska" contributed to lowering the populations of this region. He goes on to say that "a raid or battle that led to the deaths of only 100 people would eliminate 20 percent to 30 percent of the population" (Burch 1998, 322). Yup'ik oral traditions also describe raids and violence between groups. In Hooper Bay, stories not only recount these wars but also specifically mention which neighboring villages were their enemies.

Ethnohistorical records from southwestern Alaska also substantiate the fact that warfare was not uncommon. In the early 1840s Lieutenant Zagoskin reported that, among the *Magmyut* (Hooper Bay ancestors), "disputes have long since broken off all their contacts with the coastal dwellers of Norton Sound but it seems they still have some relations with the *Kvikhpaymyut* [Yukon proper] people with whom they have also been feuding for a long time" (Michael 1967, 210). Similarly, Edward Nelson wrote that "the *Magemut* are said to have been stronger in battle than the Yukon men, and a larger number of the latter were always killed in conflict between these two people" (Nelson 1983 [1899], 329).

Almost thirty years later, in the Hooper Bay–Kashunuk District, in August 1928, a missionary reported that "one blind old man about 95 years of age explained the number of graves by telling me of a war the people of this district had with their neighbors to the north. He says his own relatives were captured and carried into exile . . . it would explain why there are so many graves here" (AM Collection 30, 72). During a 1950 summer visit to Hooper Bay, Helen Oswalt wrote about a community member who proudly shared a "trophy" from past encounters with the enemy. "The man used a three-pointed spear with human bone in the middle, and he hunted with it only once a year for eiders. All passing in front of the spear died" (Oswalt 1951, 11).

Even more compelling than the ethnohistorical and archaeological records are the accounts of Yup'ik Eskimo wars and shaman feuds that exist as a part of the living oral tradition in this region. Shaman tales often depict the Nunivak Islanders and their shamans as dangerous enemies of the Hooper Bay people and their neighbors. At the village of Chevak, linguist Anthony Woodbury recorded a shaman story with Chevak elder Thomas Moses. In this narrative the Nunivak shamans present real danger for the people of Chevak. Recorded on November 9, 1978, this firsthand account recalls the actions taken by shamans at Chevak to protect themselves against this unseen but clearly known threat. The original text is provided by Woodbury in both the Cup'ik and English languages (Woodbury 1992). This excerpt, translated by Leo Moses and Woodbury from a longer recorded narrative, describes the powerful ability of shamans to travel about and potentially harm others.

The Old Shamans

Long ago the shamans
Used to contact their familiar spirits
In my very presence;
I watched this myself.
Now at one time

they were troubled by some Nunivak shamans,
from Nunivak Island down that way.

As they were passing time quietly
in the qaygiq,
they suddenly began conjuring,
having just seen those
shamans from Nunivak . . .

The shamans were on the floor,
all of them
around the opening to the entrance passage,
squatting down . . .

They were saying that right then, at the
mouth of the Qissunaq River [Kashunuk River],
those Nunivak shamans were approaching . . .

Now when the Nunivakers went into
the front chamber of the qaygiq,
They tried and tried to go down the
entrance passage,
but it was not very wide . . .

They kept trying,
and one made it;
then two others went down at once,
but they got wedged in together,
and could not go down farther . . .

Oh, they found that they had gotten
nowhere, so they just came back up
from the entrance passage.

Those two shamans had gone down and
then come right back up.

> They did not capture them, and
> so they fled . . .
>
> And once again, this is the end of my story.
> (Woodbury 1992, 53–55)

This shaman story from Chevak gives us a strong sense of just how permeable the world is in terms of proximity to the spirit world. The shamans, in this case, do battle through the entry passageways of the *qasgiq*: "They tried and tried to go down the entrance passage" (Woodbury 1992, 54). The imagery of openings that lead to the other world is reinforced throughout this telling. The Chevak shamans were gathered "around the opening to the entrance passage" (Woodbury 1992, 54). Through this portal they have the ability of a deeper vision than that of ordinary people. You will recall the Paalraayak narrative of a place where the Kashunuk River flows. When the enemy shamans from Nunivak reach this place at the mouth of the Kashunuk River (Qissunaq), the Chevak shamans have the power to see them coming.

The following story about a Hooper Bay shaman was published in 1955 and is similar in content, at least in terms of which shamans presented a threat to the people of Hooper Bay and the surrounding villages. A word of caution to my readers: unlike the narrative provided by Woodbury, this older publication appeared under the title *Medicine Men of Hooper Bay*, and is undoubtedly far from the version told by its original Hooper Bay teller. The author, Charles Gillham, was a U.S. Fish and Wildlife Service biologist who had spent time working in Hooper Bay during the 1950s.

Morrow accurately describes these Hooper Bay tales as presented by Gillham in "a very un-Yup'ik fashion" (Morrow 1995, 37). Missing much of the cultural significance behind the tales, he instead offers his readers a "moral of the story" ending, or inserts his own moral judgments. He writes, for example, that "someone was always telling a story, and the Eskimo men did spend too much time in there [in the *qaygiq* or men's house] sleeping" (Gillham 1955, 7). For this reason I offer only segments of these tales about the shamans of Hooper Bay, choosing to eliminate Gillham's stereotypic and naïve commentary. One tale begins:

> For a long time . . . they had no Medicine Man at Hooper Bay. At last the "Never Sleepy Man" came. . . .
>
> He was a good man and cured the sick. He spent much time looking around in the ocean to see just where the seals and the fish were. Often he brought them close to Hooper Bay and made it easy for the people to get them. He could walk under water like Neshmuk [a past Hooper Bay shaman], but he usually swam like a seal. . . .
>
> In the Kashim at Nunivak were two very powerful and wicked Medicine Men. Although they sat with their eyes closed and appeared to be sleeping, they saw the "Never Sleepy Man" in their medicine as he popped up out in the channel of the ocean. "We must kill this powerful Medicine man who swims so far from his home," they told each other. "He will take all our seals and our fish. There will be none here for us. . . ."
>
> "He is sure to come back this way," said the Medicine Men, "so we will change the channel from out in the beautiful harbor to make it flow right through the porch [probably refers to the entryway or passageway] of our Kashim. . . ."
>
> They . . . changed the channel that went from Nunivak to Tununa [Tununak]. The water now flowed through the porch of the Kashim. (Gillham 1955, 7–8)

In spite of Gillham's ignorance, a lot of cultural understanding can be gleaned from these tales. Clearly, this narrative casts the Nunivak Islanders and their shamans as dangerous enemies. This is in contrast to a subsequent tale collected by Lantis in 1946, but it too will demonstrate that shamans were known and greatly feared for their powerful abilities.

Battle at Hooper Bay

The same year that Disney came to Hooper Bay, anthropologist Margaret Lantis was publishing her research from Nunivak Island. She collected numerous tales on Nunivak, which is located many miles to the south of Hooper Bay in the Bering Sea. She recorded Yup'ik Eskimo lifeways and ceremonial customs and documented local narratives.

One narrative, in particular, recalls an alliance between Hooper Bay and Nunivak. This narrative, entitled "Battle at Hooper Bay," describes the way that leaders from Hooper Bay, Nelson Island, and Nunivak joined forces to battle enemy groups from the north (Lantis 1946). These enemies are referred to by Hooper Bay community members simply as "Yukoners" (Yukon Eskimo groups).

When Helen Oswalt briefly documented this account in 1950, she more explicitly identified the enemy as "Mt. Village people." Much like Woodbury's recorded tale of the shamans who came from Nunivak to Chevak, the tale begins with "a shaman from Mt. Village." The tale begins, "Long time ago there was only a village close to the beach [Askinuk], and lots of graves at [the] school house area." In this tale some hunters from Hooper Bay try to kill a seal, but "it went to Chevak, and then [the] men followed it back to that side [the mukluk was a shaman from Mt. Village]." The people of Hooper Bay "hid in a hollow beneath a hill" as the Mt. Villagers attacked and the battle proceeded from there (Oswalt 1951, 22).[1]

Woodbury has also referred to this narrative. He wrote that "well known among those from the coastal region around Chevak is the story of a great battle at Hooper Bay between the inhabitants of Hooper Bay, Qissunaq [Kashunuk], Nelson Island and Nunivak Island on one side, a war party from the Yukon River region on the other" (Woodbury 1992, 14). This is the version recorded by Lantis in the early 1940s:

> (Nunivakers and the people from Nelson Island and Hooper Bay fought together as partners.) When they were ready to fight one time, two kayaks from Nelson Island came to Nunivak to get helpers. Nunivakers went back with them to Nelson Island. They met two kayaks from Hooper Bay. Then they all went up and joined together there (at Hooper Bay).
>
> Two Yukon men [their enemies] came at night and looked over their kayaks. They saw that there were Nunivakers at Hooper Bay [from the larger kayaks—Nunivak kayaks are larger than any mainland ones]. The scouts then went back and told the others that there were Nunivakers there, that they were dangerous. The Yukon people decided to kill them all.

There were three famous fighters at Hooper Bay. *Tau'ka'xco'ax* was the first one. The second fighter was *mănli'tax*. The third fighter was *ki'yugan*. The Hooper Bay men had large buckets of water ready. The Yukon people shot arrows through the skylights, all but the two scouts. They did not come with the others. The Hooper Bay people put the children in the underground hiding place[2] and gave them salmon eggs to chew on. They stuck to their teeth. The children were busy getting the salmon eggs off their teeth and did not cry. The men gathered in the kazigi; they stood in the center singing songs so they would not be killed. They used their bowstrings in place of drums [hit bowstring with arrow].

Four Yukon men come in and sat in the entrance [passageway] of the kazigi, two men at the outer end, two at the inner end. Before they had started to sing, when their enemies shot through the skylight, tau'ka'xco'ax's son had been killed in the family house. An arrow went through the boy's eye and stuck in his mother's arm. She pulled it out and threw it on the floor.

When the men got ready to go out from the kazigi, tau'ka'xco'ax went out first, with his brother right behind him. He told his brother to go straight out with him. The men all moistened their mouths in the big bucket of water before they went out, so it was empty when they left. (There were two kazigis there at that village [Hooper Bay]. The women came to the kazigi where the men were [through the underground passage] and told them to go to the other kazigi. If they came out from the other kazigi, the enemy would be facing the sun and could not see them. But the men stayed where they were.) Tau'ka'xco'ax started out of the kazigi. This was the third fight in which he was the first one to go out to fight. The two men in the entrance tried to catch him but he dodged all the arrows. When the women called out [a kind of call to battle], the men all went out, Hooper Bay men first, then Nelson Island, then Nunivak. They had arranged it that way. Tau'ka'xco'ax continued to dodge even though he was fighting alone.

While everyone was fighting, the women called out that the Yukon men were running away and the Nunivakers were chasing them. When the Yukon men tried to get into their kayaks and get away, they were all killed except one fighter. They let him live, so he could go home and tell his people that they had lost.

While they were fighting, an old man went into the storehouse and was eating as much as he could when the women found him. They poured urine on him and killed him this way. The Hooper Bay people cut off the heads of the enemies they had killed and put them in a row. Also they cut off the privates of the men they had killed and put them in a seal poke. They threw the bodies in a pond. They completely filled the pond. One man threw a stick as far as he could along the row of heads. It landed at the middle of the row. He threw it again, from the middle, and it landed almost at the end of the row.

Tau'ka'xco'ax made a grave for his son and his nephews who were killed. He did not weep for them while he was burying them. Then he put a skin on a drum. He began to dance in the kazigi. Tau'ka'xco'ax sat on the bench and wept for his son when the people began to sing. He composed the song and taught it to them. He made up the song while he was making the drum. (Lantis 1946, 306–7)

The Rest of the Story

This tale of the "Battle at Hooper Bay" continues to be told in the community today. In 2003 I sent copies of the 1946 Nunivak version to Hooper Bay for comment. One friend, eager to set the record straight, phoned me and said, "This is Paul Harvey, are you ready for the rest of the story?" He then proceeded to literally correct all of the details of the Lantis version that did not match his own grandmother's telling from Hooper Bay. Several interesting contemporary aspects of this narrative have been shared with me from the perspective of Hooper Bay tellers.

The narrative, documented at Nunivak Island, depicts the peoples of Hooper Bay, Nelson Island, and Nunivak Island as allies against raiding groups from the Yukon. This element of the story is very similar to the contemporary Hooper Bay tellings. "Paul Harvey" told me that indeed there were "two Nunivak shamans" who had helped the people of Hooper Bay win this battle. In 1950, a Hooper Bay elder told Helen Oswalt they "used to live at [the] old village across [the] way where tunnels connect houses [Askinuk]." He said that they "used to fight Yukoners there, but never went to the Yukon. Yukoners would burn houses if [they] could; people [at Hooper Bay] hid under houses." According to this elder, there were "only two exits from [these] tunnels" (Oswalt 1951).

The pond that is mentioned in the above narrative is a known, identifiable place that community members associate with a specific location on the tundra. This place, I am told, is very near the present-day village. This is the pond where they "threw the bodies [of their Yukon enemies]" and "completely filled the pond" (Lantis 1946, 307). This is a compelling element of the story since, as we already know, placing animal bones in a freshwater pond signified rebirth, renewal, and respect. I wondered why Hooper Bayers would treat the bodies of their enemies similarly to the way they treated game or if it held an entirely different symbolic meaning. Unlike the seals, who it was hoped would return to the respectful hunter, one wouldn't want their enemies returning, would they? Perhaps this is the essential difference, seals are reborn when returned to the water whereas placing humans in the water does not return them to their origins.

A tale of a Point Hope (Inupiaq Eskimo region) battle may shed some light on why the enemy dead at Hooper Bay were placed in a pond. A Tikigaq (Point Hope) man who has been shot "full of arrows" by his enemies struggles to find an appropriate place to fall down. We are told that he has rejected a specific place on the sea ice. The tale continues:

> They shot Nigliq full of arrows. But he didn't want to fall there on the sea ice. Nigliq said to himself, "it isn't a good sight, the bones of animals and humans, drifted in together. They don't look good together, mixed on the beaches." That was his thought. Nigliq tried to get to shore. To the beach at Tapqagruk. He had to reach shore. He was full of arrows. His mind told him to reach land before falling forward. (Lowenstein 1992, 113–14)

A footnote to this narrative states, "'It isn't a good sight, the bones of animals and humans. . . . ' Nigliq fears being butchered like an animal" (Lowenstein 1992, 113). This may lead us to some understanding about the treatment of the bodies at Hooper Bay. Perhaps this treatment signified a final insult on the enemy dead and their living relatives. Edward Nelson also noted treatment of the enemy dead, saying that among the Magemut, "the dead were thrown in heaps and left" (Nelson 1983 [1899], 328). Oswalt, too, said that the people of Hooper Bay would "leave [the] body alone where killed"[3] (Oswalt 1951, 10).

Other details also vary in contemporary Hooper Bay tellings. At Nunivak, it was said that the Yup'ik warriors "all moistened their mouths in the big bucket of water before they went out, so it was empty when they left" (Lantis 1946, 306). Hooper Bay tellings describe a *qaltaq* or *qamyaq* (a large wooden bucket or pail) filled with "seal oil, not water!" One man told me that they used a feather for dipping into the seal oil. It is not entirely clear from Lantis's account if this was just an act of "moistening their mouths" in preparation for the intense, physical demands of fighting, or if this water was somehow used to protect them as well. The contemporary Hooper Bay tale variant with seal oil furthers this second possibility but, of course, we can never say with absolute certainty.

One important element of the contemporary variant involves the capture and killing of the old man who stole food from the Hooper Bay community. The Hooper Bay version also contains an old woman who sits on top of the qasgiq to keep watch for the enemy. This is clearly an important role, one that is filled not only by an older person, but by a female. It was, I am told, the women of Hooper Bay who caught and killed the thief. Unlike the version from Nunivak, however, these Hooper Bay women did not kill him by pouring "urine on him" (Lantis 1946). Again, there is the notion that urine is a particularly powerful substance. Urine buckets would have been commonly present in the qasgiq on a day-to-day practical level,[4] but "urine also had magical properties, and was used in ritual contexts" (Morrow 2002, 341). In the Hooper Bay version it is not the use of urine, but it is the women themselves who kill this man by "sitting on his face."

By sitting on his face they suffocate (according to the teller) this man, but what is not explicit is the possibility that it is the power of these females that kills him. "In Yup'ik society, urine, feces, and menses were treated in a somewhat parallel way. All were subject to social regulation, all had potential magicoreligious power, and all were used in mundane and ritual contexts" (Morrow 2002, 342). We are not explicitly told that these women are menstruating, but either way, these women literally killed this man with their own power. According to Phyllis Morrow, women, generally speaking, can affect a man's hunting luck by simply stepping over him whether menstruating or not (pers. comm. May 20, 2016). In any case, we know that the women killed him and that this fact is both met with humor and, at the same time, guarded. Hooper Bay men during steam bath, for example, will joke that "at least he died happy!" This inside joke, however, is never told in the presence of other Yupiit who are from the Yukon area, especially those from Mountain Village. Nor is this joking discourse employed when a man is present who has kinship or ancestral ties to this Yukon village. "Yukoners," I am told, can become very, very angry by the insult of this telling or allusion to this Hooper Bay tale. "That's something that's not talked about!" This joke is reserved, then, for a particular audience, one that is specific to the community of Hooper Bay.

Transcending Time: A Shaman's Message

In May of 1996, a wonderful exhibit opened at the Anchorage Museum of History and Art. This exhibit brought together Yup'ik masks from collections around the world. They came from as far away as Berlin, bringing together a phenomenal representation of Yup'ik mask-making and ceremonialism. "Agayuliyararput: Our Way of Making Prayer" had received wide attention everywhere that it traveled. I was fortunate to have participated in the opening ceremonies both in Bethel and in Anchorage. The smaller version of this exhibit had opened in Bethel earlier that winter during the month of January.

It was *the* weekend to be in Bethel, Alaska. Besides the long-awaited opening of the mask exhibit, we attended the Alaska Humanities Forum's Communities of Memory Symposium and the Kuskokwim 300 Sled Dog Race. There was Yup'ik Eskimo dancing at the exhibit opening, tales of Yup'ik elders and bush pilots at the symposium, and free burgers out on the frozen Kuskokwim River at the start of the sled dog race. It was very cold and windy that weekend. I can vividly recall the weather, probably because several Yup'ik people had been commenting on it during this exhibit opening. The exhibit organizers had chosen a Yup'ik mask known as *Negakfok* (following Edward Nelson's original spelling; contemporary spelling "Negeqvaq") for the exhibition catalog cover. Identified on The Metropolitan Museum of Art's website as "the cold-weather spirit," it was said to represent "the north wind or, more eloquently, the spirit that likes cold and stormy weather" (Metropolitan Museum of Art 2000–2013). Its white spots are said to represent snowflakes, and the many wood danglers clattered when moved giving a voice to the spirit of the north wind. This particular mask had been collected by A. H. Twitchell in the early 1900s (Fienup-Riordan 1996). From the time of the first opening at Toksook Bay on Nelson Island, Yupiit commented that *Negeqvaq* (north wind) had been making its presence known. This, again, is directly linked to the notion of *ellam yua* and the animate qualities that the weather is known to possess.

Negeqvaq was not the only one to make its presence felt during this traveling exhibition. Another mask, obtained on the Yukon by well-known collector Johan Adrian Jacobsen, seemed to have an impact on many of those who walked into the Anchorage Museum of History and Art's gallery on opening night. The oblong, red-ochre-colored mask boasts an actual raven's head protruding from the open mouth of the figure identified as "*Tullukarokaak Kinakut*" or (*tulukaruguaq kegginaquq*, "imitation raven mask") (see Fienup-Riordan 1996, 216–17). Equally disquieting were the two raven's feet, nailed upside-down on either side of the mask's forehead.

I was struck by it right away and pondered over its possible meanings. Was this a representation of Raven the Creator? Was raven controlling or controlled by the figure represented in the mask? Out of curiosity, I stood and watched as others came upon it. The reaction was the same nearly every time. Both Yupiit and non-Yup'ik audiences seemed uncomfortable by what they saw, some explicitly associating the mask with that of a shaman.

Those who have worked with Yup'ik material culture know that there are no specific criteria for identifying objects that have been made by, or for, Yup'ik shamans. This powerful mask, fashioned from the feet and head of a raven, seemed to transcend time. Its intention may have been to alarm and frighten its viewers, and although it was probably never intended to survive into the present day (masks were often burned after the ceremony for which they were created came to an end), this mask's powerful presence still commanded the attention of its audiences and instilled a level of reverence. Was this mask made and worn by a shaman? Fienup-Riordan (1996, 217) notes that Yup'ik carvers "did not frequently present raven masks." The encounter with this mask may have served as a reminder to those who entered the museum gallery that we too were travelers, and as such, vulnerable in unfamiliar places.

Dreams and Visions

A brief survey of the anthropological literature will, for the most part, suggest that shamanism is a thing of the past. It is treated as a past-tense subject. Introductory texts, for example, talk about shamanism and present it as a past practice, one that is part of an older and no longer extant belief system. Wendell Oswalt (1990) wrote that the practice of Yup'ik Eskimo shamanism was "to gain power over spirits. Once this was accomplished, he could seek advice from them in dreams or visions. Spirit helpers could be found in animate forms, such as birds, or in inanimate ones, such as mountains or ponds" (36). This description, which casts "mountains and ponds" as inanimate objects, is an accurate portrayal for Western thinkers, but it is not necessarily so in the Yup'ik sense.

The above description assumes a great deal. It is true that, in the past, dreams and visions played an important part in the practice of shamanism. However, what is suggested by this and other descriptions is that powerful dreams and visions are no longer important aspects of Yup'ik experience. Firsthand experience has taught me otherwise. Many Yupiit are observant of dreams and their potential power. Dreams can guide people, but they can also bring unwanted dangers. At the beginning of this chapter I presented a contemporary story about a village health aide worker who was attacked by a shaman in her dreams when she visited another village. These dangerous powers are eventually countered by taking the appropriate action (in this case the use of a big stick) while in a dream (liminal) state. This indicates that, perhaps, a person maintains some level of *ella* when they are asleep. This awareness during sleep and dream states seems to vary from person to person. Like those on the land, sleeping persons can be prepared, aware, and protected to greater or lesser degrees.

Narratives commonly reflect a bad shaman's ability to harm people through their dreams.[5] Certainly, a person's awareness is diminished during sleep. A person is also more vulnerable during sleep. Consider the following account recorded by a Hooper Bay missionary sometime between 1927 and 1928. In this incident, like the previous narrative of a woman who is chased by a black "dog," harm comes to a woman as she sleeps. Of course, the missionary who reported this incident, transposing all references of evil spirits into Christian terms (as "devils"), probably lacked an appropriate understanding of the cultural significance of this account. It was reported that:

> Nuyailak [was] attacked as if in dream (though she says she heard the clock all the while) by two dogs with human heads. She says they were devils and tried to pull her around grabbing her by the neck and mouth. She came to have her neck [apparently injured during the attack] painted with iodine. (Alaska Mission Collection 30)

This account is a terrifying one. This woman, who "heard the clock all the while," had at least partially lost her sense of awareness (ella) and so became vulnerable to the unseen world. This account is similar to others that Yupiit have shared with me. In it, the victim is being attacked by two dogs "with human heads." We can never say with absolute certainty what cultural significance lies behind the imagery of dogs with human heads. The "human heads" may suggest that, indeed, the source of this danger is human, although dogs are sometimes said to have "persons" (*yuit*).[6] Dogs, as we will see in subsequent chapters, have perceptive abilities and heightened awareness of their surroundings.

Although these shaman stories are distanced by some sixty years or more, in both cases the attacker comes in the form of a dog. In both instances the dreamers seem to maintain some level of awareness but not enough awareness to prevent the attack. In the case of the second account, although she was aware enough to hear the clock "all the while," the dreamer seemingly lacked enough awareness to thwart her attacker. Thus, she arrived at the mission with wounds that needed treatment.

Some contemporary stories are just too dangerous and personal to tell, especially in light of the understanding that discourse can actualize events and words can make dangerous situations worse. Words are never to be spoken (or, as I have recently been reminded, written) without carefully weighing the outcome first. The aforementioned tales were ones that their tellers felt could be shared with my readers, but others are considered too dangerous for a broader audience. Thus, as I stated in my introduction, I have decided not to include certain events and stories, among them stories of shaman attacks.

At the conclusion of her narrative about the health aide worker, the teller reinforced the point that "dreams are a big thing." Hugh Brody's *Maps and Dreams* illustrates the ways that dreams guide action among the Beaver (Athabascan-speaking) people of northwest British Columbia, too. Brody describes how dreams ensured a successful hunt, stating that "there was no mistaking, no doubts about the efficacy of such dreams" (Brody 1982, 45).

Dreams and visions remain a vital and ongoing part of other Native American cultures as well. Among the First Nations Anishinaabek (Ojibway and Odawa), dreams are viewed as significant contemporary experiences (Hallowell 1992). Anishinaabe people often pay close attention to dreams. Dreams are considered in terms of their power and potential meanings. Sometimes they come in the form of welcomed guidance, other times they bring real danger.

Spirit Protectors, Shamans, and Dreams

As previously mentioned, danger often takes on a "dark" shape or appearance of some kind (Jolles 2002). Sometimes it is believed to be a person with shamanic powers. Sometimes the danger is undetermined. People seem more concerned with how to behave in such instances then they are with specifically identifying it. One young hunter in Hooper Bay told me how he had felt a dangerous presence one time when he was out on the land at a place he later decided "must have been an old village." He indicated that perhaps this was another person who was trying to harm him, though he did not explicitly explain what the danger was. He explained to me how, suddenly, a bird appeared in the sky and drove it off. He told me that it was probably his protective spirit that had driven this bad thing away. Similarly, in Gambell on St. Lawrence Island, Carol Zane Jolles reports:

> Power bestowed through individual acquisition of a spirit assistant was open in theory to all members of the society. This acquisition of a spirit assistant has been interpreted by some within the community as the establishment of a relationship with those intangible powers ultimately subject to Apa [word used to describe a spirit being and, now, God]. . . . In practice, the act of taking a spirit into oneself (*tughneghnakutqa*) was generally reserved for those strong ones in need of spirit assistance in hunting or in curing. Most often shamans acquired such power. (Jolles 1989, 18)

Jolles also noted that among the St. Lawrence Island Yupik, among whom she worked, "many are reluctant to speak about shamans, who regularly dealt with a multitude of spirits" (Jolles 1989, 18). Again, I am struck by certain parallels between the two villages (Gambell and Hooper Bay) in relation to this unspoken understanding. In her discussion of contemporary worldview, Jolles writes:

> Spirits were and are still believed to be unpredictable and difficult to control. Although shamans no longer practice openly, the involuntary acquisition of a spirit assistant (*tunneghaq*) remains an unwanted legacy of the descendants of some powerful shamans. Even conversion to Christianity does not wholly protect those marked by destiny to inherit their ancestors' spiritual power and they may be pursued relentlessly by potential spirit helpers. (Jolles 1989, 21)

There are good reasons for reluctance to speak about shamans and the preference for guarding knowledge about them. The reasons are probably twofold: the fearsome power long ascribed to shamans and, more recently, the attitudes introduced by Christianity. In keeping with the missionaries' perceptions of shamans, this role is often associated with "bad" or harmful people even today. Shamans were central to the Yup'ik way of life prior to contact. Before missionaries there were shamans. They served as culture-bearers, healers, and community leaders. A shaman was a special person, man or woman, who was bestowed with the gift of deep awareness or ella, sensitivity, and the ability to communicate effectively with those of the spirit world. This included not only the many spirit beings, but also the dead, including one's ancestors. They had a greater connection to and awareness of the spirit world.

Shamans and Ellam Yua

In the past, shamans routinely served as a bridge between the human world and that of spirits. Contacting and appealing to the spirit world was practiced on a day-to-day basis. Hooper Bay shamans could transform themselves into whatever form they wished to take. Sometimes they appeared as an animal, other times they became a plant or feature upon the land. The previous narratives speak of shamans who travel in the form of a seal, swimming about in the hopes of not being detected. One community member in Hooper Bay said that

> one shaman that tried different animals, plants, etc.. said that the loneliest plant he ever tried being was blackberries. Being a blackberry was lonely, dark, and so immobile. This shaman tried a blackberry plant and almost got eaten by a goose who was foraging at the same time for food.

Likewise, the weather could be influenced in favor of human action. Negeqvaq can make the land a very dangerous place. People go out and never return. A shaman's ability to appeal to spirits, especially those who controlled the weather, meant the difference between a safe return and never being seen or heard from again.

Eliza Cingarkaq Orr and Ben Orr documented a contemporary tale in which a shaman "conjured" or summoned the weather. This tale was told by George Kanrilak of Tununak. The story begins:

> I once observed an *angalkuq*, a shaman, during the winter when it was very cold and the ground was hard to travel, thick with snow. Even if they wanted to go someplace, they couldn't. They also wanted to fetch some people over there for a festival, but since the trail they needed to go by was bad, they hesitated because of the bad trail. As I observed them, they started to get ready; they asked that shaman to prepare to *luumaq*[i] that evening in order to induce the weather to rain. The weather outside was especially cold at that time of the year. Very cold! (Orr and Orr 1995, 307)

In the endnote after the word *luumaq* above, the authors further state that "according to Alphonse Menegak of Tununak, *luumar-* (or *elumar*) refers to that part of the ritual consequent to the binding, when the shaman flies through the atmosphere" (Orr and Orr 1995, 374).

"They Used To Use Their Own Power": Healers and Political Leaders

Over time, shamans and those associated with shamanic ability have played a major role in community leadership. Prior to missionary influence, shamans were called upon in times of sickness. One Hooper Bay elder said that "people long ago weren't like white people the way they are today. They used to use their own power" (Miller 1982, 16). In a previous chapter I discussed the devastation brought about by ship-borne diseases. Following Napoleon, Wolfe, and Fortuine, I examined the vital role that shamans played in both combating the forces of illness as well as treating those who were suffering and dying. "In treating disease the most common method is for the shamans to perform certain incantations" (Nelson 1983 [1899], 309). Shamans also played an important role in assuring the proper treatment and burial of the dead. "The shaman was in constant demand for curing their many illnesses. There were respiratory ailments, eye diseases, and skin disorders to rectify. . . . Very little information is actually recorded during these years about the Eskimos' health except for the busy shaman, the smallpox epidemic, and a few other scattered observations" (Ray 1975, 178).

Shamans played yet another important role as an intermediary between the land of the living and that of the spirit world. This was especially important during the Yup'ik ceremonial cycle. The ability to appeal to the spirit world was and is of primary concern to those who wished for a successful hunt. Especially before the coming of missionaries, shamans used their powers to influence the natural spirit world in favor of the living. Game was certain to be more plentiful if, and when, shamans made an appeal to the spirits (Jolles 2002). This assistance assured hunters that they would be able to provide for their families. A successful appeal could mean the difference between survival and starvation. This important role of the shaman was described by Ernest Hawkes:

> Then the shaman donned an *ińua mask*, and began running around the entrance hole in ever lessening circles. He finally tumbled over and lay in a trance, the while he was communing with spirit-guests (so the Eskimo told me) in the fire-place below. After a time he came to and informed the hunters that the *ińua* had been pleased with the dances and promised their further protection for a successful season. (Hawkes 1913, 17)

Eskimo shamans assumed political leadership roles in their communities. I have demonstrated how shamans played a key role in both identifying the enemy and in making war against those enemy groups. These same people were clearly significant members of society since they not only held the powers to heal the sick but the leadership skills needed to resolve conflict. There is some ethnohistorical evidence to suggest that these dual roles often seemed incompatible to early explorers and missionaries. At the time of contact, outsiders arrived on Alaska's shores with a preconceived notion of what constituted leadership. In the European tradition, of course, there were political leaders, spiritual leaders, and healers (physicians). These were distinct roles in society.

Vasilii S. Khromchenko was sent by ship from Sitka in 1821 by the Russian-American Company. He was to explore "the Bering Sea and coast northward to ascertain native trade routes" (Ray 1975, 66). Khromchenko addressed this confusion over existing Eskimo leadership, concluding that "people took advice from shamans, who [also] treated their various ailments." He reached this conclusion because "he did not see a single chief" (Ray 1975, 73). Edward Nelson noted that "the Alaskan Eskimo, so far as I observed, have no recognized chiefs except such as gain a certain influence over their fellow-villagers through superior shrewdness, wisdom, age, wealth, or shamanism" (Nelson 1983 [1899], 304).

Scant historical accounts exist for the early contact period, and Dorothy Jean Ray states that "the presence of shamans was acknowledged but not discussed by any explorer" (Ray 1975, 97). Historical records may not tell us much about the importance of shamans, but the oral tradition speaks strongly to the importance of shamans before and after the kass'aqs arrived. As I will show in later chapters, Hooper Bay missionaries at the turn of the century would begin to recognize the true leadership qualities and power of the shamans. And once identified as both important healers and spiritual-political leaders, they became direct targets for elimination. These deeply rooted historical tensions would have lasting impact that would survive in the discourse and narratives of Hooper Bay.

The various tales of Hooper Bay shamans do indicate that there were times when shamans presented real danger for people and times when they were especially sought for guidance and leadership such as during wars. The tales also demonstrate how central the role of the shaman was in everyday life, both before and after the coming of outsiders to this region. It is also very significant to note that long after the missionaries declared an end to the practice of shamanism, their continuance is evidenced in the tales and personal narratives. The account recorded by Woodbury at neighboring Chevak, for example, was recorded in the region during the 1980s. The teller is not recalling a tale that was shared with him as a boy but recounting an actual encounter with Nunivak shamans during his lifetime. This continuity is important to understanding historical encounters as well as contemporary events.

Richard Nelson's work *Make Prayers to the Raven* (1983) explores the complex relationship that the Koyukon Athabascans maintain with the natural-spirit world around them. In his discussion of contemporary Koyukon views of shamanism, he states that "although shamanism apparently is seldom, if ever, practiced today, most adult Koyukon have seen and experienced it many times in their lives" (Nelson 1983, 29). He hints at the fact that there is something of these shamanic powers still operating in Koyukon communities. Nelson is somewhat cautious, but leaves room for the possibility that shamanism may exist even if it appears that it "is probably not practiced today" (Nelson 1983, 29). In the summer of 1950, a young man from Hooper Bay said that "one man was [a] medicine man, maybe still is" (Oswalt 1951). The open practice of shamanism certainly does not exist in Alaskan villages, but certain understandings and related knowledge does for many people in many places.

As previously stated, not all shamans were considered to exercise bad or evil powers. Many were community leaders and healers. Hooper Bay shamans, with the onslaught of missionization, faced a direct challenge to their leadership positions in the community. Hooper Bay shamans, as elsewhere, were a direct target for those missionaries who came to convert souls. One missionary, in summarizing the accomplishments of the Jesuit order, said that "the medicine men spread such stories about the diabolical work of those intruding white people that the Eskimos avoided the Missionaries. In 1900, an epidemic decimated the whole region. Entire villages disappeared. The bulk of the elderly and more aggressive medicine men died" (John P. Fox Collection 2017, 484). He then goes on to say that, having these people out of the way, the Jesuit missionaries' job of conversion was now much easier. This was just the beginning of the tensions between Yupiit and white people. This point will be revisited in a later chapter as I trace contemporary tales and their meanings.

Implicit in these various stories is the understanding that these shamans are strongly associated with particular places. When people talk about these shamans they invariably refer to them as a "shaman from" a specific place. Shamans are, as community leaders and healers, place-based. The tale recorded by Woodbury refers to shamans from Chevak and Nunivak Island, and Oswalt's earlier account begins "a shaman from Mt. Village." Enemies are also place-based. These enemy shamans represent that "other village" and as such, when defeated, "we" have defeated that other place. Our place has defeated their place.

The Shaman's Grave: An Important Place on the Land

In chapter 2, I demonstrated the way that a community member expressed her fears and pain through use of metaphoric discourse about a particular shaman's grave at Hooper Bay. One might ask *why* this place is so significant. The answer is complex and multifaceted. It is important because it represents beliefs and practices that are still highly valued, respected, and observed by Yupiit. At the same time, it is a place that serves as an indicator of the health and well-being of the contemporary community. It is also an important place because it anchors memory: the shaman's grave has become a tangible symbol for the tensions and conflicts of the past.

The Same Old Story as of Old

To understand these tensions we must consider the attitudes of those who sought to replace Yup'ik culture and beliefs. Hooper Bay missionary Father John Fox expressed the core ideas that missionaries held in relation to shamans.

> We are just now at a critical point in the Christianizing of the Eskimo. They have renounced the devil and all his works and pomps [*sic*]. But there is quite a difference between doing this in word at baptism and doing it in reality when the time comes. . . . For the older folks, it is a hard struggle to part with some of their superstitious practices, especially those regarding their dead and the calling of the medicine man in case of serious illness. Fear is an awful thing. The old medicine men have drilled into the minds of these poor natives for years that unless their prescriptions are obeyed, terrible chastisements will befall them.
>
> I never quite understood the reason why natives cling to their foolish superstitions until my coming into contact with the people of this district [Hooper Bay]. It is the same old story as of old. What the Scribes and Pharisees were to the poor Jews, and the bonzes to the Orientals, that the medicine man is to the Eskimo. Mainly for his own emporal [*sic*] advantage, he lays on his poor fellow-native all sorts of tabus [*sic*] and prescibes [*sic*] a lot of practices that have to be carried out to keep the bad spirit from doing harm. (John P. Fox Collection 2017, 1110)

"The Last of His Tribe": The Death of a Shaman

Gobernach . . . had just moved to his spring camp, where he intended to hunt ducks, geese, and muskrats. His fish-traps were left behind at his winter camp, and so after he had moved his family and his few belongings, he started back for his traps. The day was somewhat stormy, but not bad; and he got his traps out from the ice without too much trouble. The following day he started back to his spring camp. The day was perfect with snow spreading; white as a sheet in every direction till it was lost in the distant horizon. The glare of the sun reflected from the snow was excessive, as it always is at this season, so that the Eskimos almost turn black, with the exception of a white circle around the eyes protected by the sun-glasses [snow goggles] they wear. But Gobernach had neglected to take his along when he started from home the day preceding, which happened to be a dull one. So he pinched his eyes shut so as scarcely to be peering out through his bushy eyelashes. Still the light was too strong. He had not gone far when he was snow-blind, and found himself wandering around haphazardly in search of his home.

The above is, of course, a bit of theory to explain one accident. For dead men can't speak. However, the day after Gobernach left home, folks saw at a distance a lone man pushing his hunting sled ahead of him. But, due to the glare and the distance they did not recognize the figure. When, however, five days had elapsed and Gobernach was not yet home, the family grew anxious. He would hardly hunt that long, and the weather too had now cleared up again. For it had been snowing and blowing a good deal the five days intervening between his departure and the present. As they were wondering why he had not yet returned, someone mentioned the lone hunter and sled that he had noticed five days ago, without recognizing him. Going on the clue that this was the missing man, and that he was lost somewhere, a searching party went out. For several days no sign of Gobernach was found, but after five days one of the men found a shovel sticking up from the snow, and near it the top of a sled was protruding above the drift. On closer

> examination he found the frozen body of Gobernach in a sitting position and practically covered with snow not far from the sled.
>
> The poor family, like so many others here, was in destitution especially for the past four months. The man was in no condition to meet the demands made on his physical endurance. He was starved and poorly clothed, and so fell an easy victim to the cold weather, though it was already the last week of April. With their bread-winner gone, the destitute family is in a still more hopeless condition. I have offered to take the three small children if the mother will part with them. She might be able to support herself; but she certainly could not support her family. It is but another of the many similar cases we have here. As the people live mostly hand to mouth, an accident of any kind to the hunter, leaves all in utter destitution.
>
> But there is another aggravating circumstance in this particular instance. Gobernach was a medicine-man, and as such, heartily disliked by the people. For that reason he generally lived in a camp by himself, and in the present need, the people are less inclined to help his family than they would usually be under such circumstances. He is the last of his tribe in this district, and few tears were shed over his accident. However we hope God was merciful to his soul and will do for his family what we can. (AM Collection 14, 527)

This description is a painful one in many regards. It is a sad account because it describes, with some callousness, the death of this Yup'ik man. The "aggravating circumstance in this particular instance" is that this man was a known shaman. "He is the last of his tribe in this district." It is haunting because the writer, a Hooper Bay missionary, believes that this last "medicine man's" death signals the death of a central aspect of Yup'ik culture and belief. This culture and belief is something that Father Fox had overtly sought to eliminate from his very first days in the village.

There is a clear and deliberate "moral" to this missionary's tale as he lays out the probable demise of the shaman's "destitute" family. His response is an offer to "take the three small children" from their mother, rather than helping her with what is necessary to survive. Fox seems to imply that this family will suffer for their father's actions (sins). This kind of attitude is indicative of the ways that outsiders often viewed Yup'ik cultural belief and practice. Fox cast this tragic event as an inevitable outcome of practicing the old ways. There is almost a sense of relief on Fox's part since he will now face less opposition in the effort toward conversion.

Fox's tone reflects the deep resentment that many missionaries felt toward Yupiit. Any sign of following the old ways was seen as a direct challenge to the authority of the missionary, and by extension, a direct challenge to the word of God. Years of this ill-treatment resulted in tensions that can still be seen and felt today. Kass'aq attitudes and behaviors are anticipated and often expected to follow a pattern of condemnation even today. It is important to know this history if we are to gain a deeper understanding of contemporary folklore as it exists in the Yup'ik region today. The next several chapters speak directly to the issue of kass'aq attitudes and cross-cultural conflicts that find expression in narratives set in places that represent contact points between Yupiit and outsiders.

7

The Tale of the Teakettle Ghost

PERFORMATIVE ASPECTS OF DISCOURSE

> "He stepped on the whirling ground and smoothed it with his foot. When it stopped he felt relieved. Then he asked the white man to go out with him, saying the ghost would not bother them again." (Tennant and Bitar 1981, 11)

Among the places that Yupiit are instructed from an early age to avoid are graves, abandoned villages, and old campsites. The landscape of the Yukon Kuskokwim Delta region is heavily marked with the tangible signs of such places. As previously noted, some of these places are said to be the result of warfare. In his travel notes, Edward Nelson wrote that "along the Lower Yukon are many indications of villages destroyed by war parties." He goes on to say that "according to the old men these parties came from Askinuk and Kushunuk, near the Kuskokwim, as there was almost constant warfare between the people of these two sections before the advent of the Russians" (Nelson 1983 [1899], 264). Others were created by epidemics, though villages were also abandoned due to erosion, the desire to relocate nearer to a mission or school, or some other practical cause. Campsites, too, are frequently abandoned for a variety of reasons. These kinds of places are associated with a particular genre of story simply known in English as "ghost stories." It is largely through such narratives that Yupiit learn to avoid these places.

The Yupiit of southwestern Alaska recognize two categories of stories. *Qulirat* are stories told about events and characters of the distant past, and *qanemciit* are told about people and places in more recent times (Morrow 1984; Fienup-Riordan 1990 and 2017; Woodbury 1992; Fienup-Riordan 2017). Both categories of stories may be shaped differently from one telling to the next. In the case of Yup'ik ghost stories, the telling differs as the audience shifts. The question, then, is why these stories and the emphasis placed on various elements in them change. What is being said indirectly through the telling of the story? That is, how is it told or used in ways that convey meaning to the listeners? How are the listeners coparticipants in the construction of meaning? What have we tended to miss in the interpretation of both oral and written contexts?

These themes are central in understanding what the stories mean to the Yupiit. Since the mid-1970s, cultural anthropologists and folklorists alike have paid closer attention to the importance of context (Briggs 1988; Cruikshank 1995; Darnell 1974; Finnegan 1992; Hymes 1971). In her examination of oral traditions and the verbal arts, Ruth Finnegan reminds us that "the context of the performance (including the organisation of the event and the participants within it) may be central rather than peripheral to its meaning" (Finnegan 1992, 94).

No one has better demonstrated this point than anthropologist Julie Cruikshank and the late elder Mrs. Angela Sydney. More than two decades ago, Mrs. Sydney presented a story to a large and diverse audience at the opening ceremonies for the local college in Whitehorse, Yukon Territory. Both Cruikshank and Mrs. Sydney came to the realization that this broad audience would understand the telling of the story to varying degrees and in different ways. This awareness led to a decision to publish it accompanied by a brief explanation of the narrative itself, which allowed Mrs. Sydney the opportunity to ensure that her listeners—past, present, and future—would understand why she had chosen this particular tale for the occasion and how she had hoped to use the tale to convey her meaning.

What Cruikshank has also shown, in a subsequent work, is that Mrs. Sydney used oral narratives in general "as a kind of cultural scaffolding on which to construct the story of her life" (Cruikshank 1995, 70). After many years of work with Mrs. Sydney, Cruikshank came to realize that "you have to learn what the story says. Then you learn what the story can do when it is engaged as a strategy of communication" (Cruikshank 1995, 71). Mrs. Sydney employed the same story differently in various settings for distinctly different reasons. Meaning could only truly be understood if one was aware of the context and what Mrs. Sydney hoped to convey in a given setting, with a specific audience in mind.

What does Cruikshank's analysis of the ways that Mrs. Sydney used this Tlingit tale have to do with gaining a better understanding of Yup'ik ghost stories and their usage? The answer is that it calls for us to pay attention to rather than negate variations in the telling of a story. In my own work with Native American and Alaska Native stories, which began more than two decades ago, there is a growing recognition that variation, once considered problematic or indicative of "culture loss," is key to situational meaning. Like scholars working in other parts of the world (Narayan 1989), I am reanalyzing why stories were told to me, as the audience, in the way that they were told. Who I was as an outside researcher, at what stage I was at in my life, and how the various tellers saw me had everything to do with the way that a given story would be told. This interaction between myself as a listener and the storytellers was, and is, a crucial key to meaning.

Teakettles, Ghosts, and Graves

The story of "The Teakettle Ghost" is a case in point. I have chosen here variants of this story. The first variant considered is one that was recorded and transcribed into a written text in the early 1980s as part of a collection published by the Lower Kuskokwim School District (LKSD) in southwest Alaska. Those stories were originally collected by high school students as a part of a cultural heritage project, and the tales were used to enhance the local curriculum.

"The Teakettle Ghost," as it was titled in the LKSD version and shall be referred to herein, was told by Yup'ik elder Minnie Carter of Eek. Her story tells of two men traveling from Eek to Bethel by dog team when either bad weather or weariness causes them to stop and make camp for the night.

The common elements of the tale are as follows. There is a Yup'ik man accompanied by a white man. They seek shelter in an old, abandoned village that is located next to a graveyard. In each version of the story the white man takes a teakettle from one of the graves so that he and his companion can make tea. The Yup'ik man warns the *kass'aq* (white man) to return the teakettle to the grave, but the kass'aq ignores his warnings. That evening, as the men sleep, they are visited by an angry ghost. Again, the Yup'ik man instructs the other to return the teakettle to the grave site. After this terrifying experience and/or becoming very ill, the white man returns the teakettle to the grave where he had found it. Specific details vary, but this description outlines the important, underlying elements present in this stock story.

In Mrs. Carter's telling, the white man appears to symbolize the ignorance of outsiders. This is an important theme that I will return to again later in this work. The emphasis of Carter's version is on Yup'ik knowledge about ghosts; that is, how they appear and what one should do when one encounters a ghost. Throughout her telling she keeps her intended audience, Yup'ik students, in mind; Mrs. Carter clearly uses the story to transmit her knowledge to the next generation. She says: "Then the Eskimo remembered what his mother used to say. She said that if you stayed still when you saw a ghost, it would turn the house inside out and kill you. The Eskimo told the white man to stand facing him[1] and to move backwards very slowly toward the ghost. . . . Once outside, they walked around the house according to the custom, then went back inside" (Tennant and Bitar 1981, 11). Carter's telling contains several such allusions to the importance of recalling Yup'ik knowledge.

> The Eskimo told him that the person who sees the ghost is supposed to touch the ghost's skin, then put a hand on its head and push down with the weight of the arm. The white man started walking backwards toward the ghost. The Eskimo moved facing him and the ghost. There was something covering the ghost's face. When they came near, the Eskimo, although it was repulsive to him, reached under the ghost's collar to touch its skin. He kept in mind what he was supposed to do in this kind of situation. When his hand touched the skin, it felt like sand.

> It was very cold. His hand felt as though it were burning because the ghost was so cold. After that he asked the white man to move to one side, and putting his hand on the ghost's head, he gently pushed it with the weight of his arm. The ghost was facing away from them. As he pushed the ghost, it started to go down into the ground, even though the ground was frozen.
>
> Then he thought to himself, "To make it go down faster, I'll push a little harder."
>
> When he did that, the ghost came back up. So he just let the weight of his arm push it down. Then the ghost disappeared completely into the ground. The spot where it went through was going around like a whirlpool. Then, as he had heard it said, he stepped on the whirling ground and smoothed it with his foot. When it stopped he felt relieved. Then he asked the white man to go out with him, saying the ghost would not bother them again. (Tennant and Bitar 1981, 11)

Mrs. Carter concludes her tale with several more instructional comments regarding ghosts and specific ways to ward them off. She adds that "he remembered that he had also heard that ghosts are afraid of knives or weapons" (Tennant and Bitar 1981, 13).

In the mid-nineties, the Alaska Native Language Center, in conjunction with the Lower Kuskokwim School District, published a collection of traditional narratives told by elders from Tununak, Alaska. This collection, edited by Ben and Eliza Orr, was recorded between 1983 and 1990 as part of a different classroom project in which students recorded the stories of their elders. Another variant of "The Teakettle Ghost" was embedded in a longer tale the compilers entitled "The Time the Evil Spirit Almost Came In." This story was told by Yup'ik elder Madina Flynn, and like Mrs. Carter's earlier telling, it emphasized Yup'ik understandings about ghosts and how one should behave if a ghost is encountered. Mrs. Flynn's version is told within a longer story about a ghost or an "evil spirit" that tries in vain to enter the *qasqiq*. The longer story tells of the way that a shaman is asked to send the ghost back into the ground. This story is also very specific in the way the teller instructs her listeners to behave if they were to have a similar experience.

> Then he placed his hand palm down on the top of the head of that person [the ghost] who was sitting and continued to leave it there, just using the weight of his arm. When it started to go down, it kept going down, going down, going down, very slowly. He continued to leave his hand there, using just the weight of his arm. When he intentionally put pressure on it, it is said, it would rise up a little. So he just let [the weight of his arm] bring it down. (Orr and Orr 1995, 191)

Mrs. Flynn goes on to comment about those who discount ghost stories and the importance of the knowledge that she is sharing with her audience. It is at this point that she shares with her listeners an incident similar to the story of "The Teakettle Ghost," in which a Yup'ik and a white man had an encounter with a ghost.

> Then too there was this *kass'aq*, this white man here, and because they were haunted by a ghost, his companion tried to tell him about it. They were spending the night in an old winter camp; the Yup'ik tried to tell him that a frightening thing was entering. The *kass'aq* said that he would shoot it when it enters. So when the ghost came in, he kept on shooting, but nothing happened to it. Having tried various things without any results, they quickly made a line to hang down from up there. They climbed up and out, he, the Yup'ik, going first, tearing the window—this was when they used to have seal-gut windows, when they had none of these glass windows—he tore the intestine cover.
>
> While he was helping his companion out, the ghost grabbed his companion by the ankles. When it grabbed him—it is said that ghosts are very strong—the Yup'ik tried to pull him up, and, after tying the line to the window rim, he quickly entered through the door. When he entered, he grabbed the ghost. The ghost held on to his ankles but nothing happened; the Yup'ik was unable to move it at all.
>
> Then, turning his back on it, he farted real hard. Then instantly, it is said, that ghost vanished into thin air. Then the

> Yup'ik said to him, "See that! And you thought it was simple!" This was when they traveled to villages together, selling items, and they had stopped at an old winter camp to sleep there. They were going to spend the night. The poor man's leg, it was said, was swollen all the way up. The people back then used to say that ghosts were afraid of humans farting. (Orr and Orr 1995, 205–9)

Clearly the emphasis of this telling is on the specific details regarding proper actions when dealing with a ghost, but it also reinforces the cultural knowledge about these kinds of places. This abandoned camp, once belonging to the living, is now inhabited by those of the spirit world. Flynn's audience, young Yup'ik students, are getting lessons that have been transmitted orally for many generations. In a previous chapter I discussed the many ways that Yupiit maintain boundaries between the human and spirit world. I said that various substances serve to protect people from dangerous spirits.

Water serves to protect, and oily soot ashes and food scraps keep people safe as they bridge worlds. I discussed how various bodily fluids held powerful potential in protecting or in harming others (Morrow 2002). In the above narrative the "ghost vanished in thin air" when the Yup'ik man "farted real hard." It seems, in some contexts, then, that flatulence also serves to protect from danger and maintain the boundary between worlds. This human action sends the ghost back to the land of the dead.

The image of struggle between the humans and the spirit world is powerful. The places where such encounters occur is equally important. As previously discussed, windows play a very significant part in many Yup'ik narratives. In this tale the Yup'ik man "quickly made a line to hang down from up there"[2] (the window or smoke hole of the old sod house made, as was typical, from gut skin) and "they climbed up and out . . . tearing the window" (Orr and Orr 1995, 207). The Yup'ik man "tore the intestine cover," literally tearing at the boundary between worlds to escape and exiting in the manner in which a corpse would be removed from the land of the living. The Yup'ik then has to tie a line to the kass'aq in order to pull him back into the land of the living. When this fails, the Yup'ik man resorts to another tactic that sends the ghost back. The kass'aq is only saved because his Yup'ik companion knew how to act.

Shaping the Tale

In these tellings, the white man's ignorance is a vehicle; it provides an opportunity for the teller to instruct listeners. It is not, however, a prominent theme. The emphasis of this story changes, however, when the audience is no longer made up of Yup'ik listeners. In these cases, "The Teakettle Ghost" seems to be used by Yup'ik tellers to transmit other important information to those outside their cultural tradition. One clear example comes from my own research on Yup'ik ghost stories. When I asked a young Yup'ik woman in 1996 to tell me about ghosts and ghost stories, she began with "The Teakettle Ghost." She fondly recalled having heard the story not only from her grandparents, but also from a favorite classroom teacher, also a Yup'ik. This teller said that she believed this event took place sometime during the 1950s or 1960s. She went on to say that it was one of the first stories that she remembers hearing about ghosts.

> Two men [were] traveling from Eek, Alaska, to . . . Bethel I guess by dog team. One of them was a white guy and the other was Native. And they stopped at a sod house, and before they had got to the sod house they had passed an old village. And nobody lived there anymore, but there was a "grave" site there. And um, there, on the graves, you know in the old tradition . . . where they used to put people's stuff [funerary objects] on there like old tea pots or, old masks.

The teller went on to explain that the two men were out on the tundra without many of the items needed to make camp. The white man had decided to return to the grave site for the teakettle so that he and his companion could make tea. As in the versions recorded in 1981 and 1995, the white man is warned by his Yup'ik partner not to take the teakettle from the grave.

> And so he was interested in one of the teapots, at the grave sites [she laughs nervously]. And so the one guy says "No you can't do that. My, our elders always told us never to," you know, "mess with graves or touch them, because they're sacred." And he didn't listen, so he just brought up a tea pot and some other cups and what not.

Figure 7.1 A Yup'ik Eskimo grave. Jesuit Oregon Province Archives

In this version the two men are later awakened by a cold smoke that enters their room from a crack under the door. The Yup'ik man immediately recognizes what is causing their discomfort, while the white man is both startled and confused. She described the ghost as "a dark figure." She went on to say:

> The Native guy knew what it was you know. You're not supposed to bother graves or, [pause] or you will pay for it, and you will be bothered, by the spirits. . . . I don't know, a period of time it was there and it left, and when it left, that guy told that guy to put that stuff back to where it belonged.

This telling differs greatly in both content and form from the aforementioned versions of "The Teakettle Ghost," and it suggests an important distinction; that is, that it was told to a white person with a different emphasis. Finnegan states that "meaning and artistry emerge in performance; this means attention not just to words but also to how they are delivered: such elements as intonation, speed, rhythm, tone dramatization, [and] rhetorical devices" (Finnegan 1992, 93). With these elements of performance in mind, listening to this version one can hear a strong emphasis on the word "grave," and a clear message, *graves* are places to avoid!

This teller shaped the story for a white listener. She not only considered her audience, but took the background and experience of her listener into account. Yupiit know that most outsiders do not understand or believe in ghosts. The other two storytellers alluded to this point when speaking to their Yup'ik audiences. Madina Flynn told her listeners that "when some people are told about these things they do not believe them or scoff at them; those are the ones who see ghosts" (Orr and Orr 1995, 205). They know that their knowledge, shared so freely with Yup'ik listeners, would probably fall on deaf ears if told to a white listener. This fact is one that elders and other Yup'ik community members have learned from many years of experience and interaction with outsiders, beginning with missionaries and traders who came to the Yup'ik region to gain souls or profit. Contemporary experiences in dealing with outsiders are not always that different than those of the past. When she told me the story of the teakettle ghost, she, too, was aware of her audience. She emphasized how very wrong things can go when outsiders disturb ancestral graves. Similarly, Yup'ik elders explicitly state again and again that, in the context of ghost stories, white people are unable or unwilling to understand their important cultural elements, simply dismissing them as nonsense. For example, in the telling by Minnie Carter of Eek, the white man emphatically defies all warnings: "He told him not to do that, but the white man insisted. 'No! There are no ghosts! The people are dead! They won't come back'" (Tennant and Bitar 1981, 7). Interestingly enough, this is the statement that immediately precedes her embedded telling of the story in which a Yup'ik man rescues his white companion from a ghost.

The Haunting of a Teacher's Daughter

Graves and abandoned villages are not the only kinds of places that are routinely avoided. Yupiit are also particularly wary of houses recently unoccupied due to the death of an occupant. I remember once walking through the village with a friend as we made our way to steam. I turned to cut between two houses and was quickly warned to stay on the road. The house where I had chosen to take my short cut, I later learned, had only recently been abandoned by the family following a tragic death. After that I always went around. It was some time before the house was again occupied in spite of the shortage of housing in the village.

In 1996, I had the opportunity to record the following story. The teller is a Yup'ik woman, from another village upriver from Bethel. We had been talking about people who have disappeared on the tundra or have had strange things happen to them when they are out on the land. Like the previous tale, this narrative seems to highlight the ignorance of white newcomers and reinforce the message that kass'aqs, although expected not to, *should* believe in the existence of ghosts and spirits. Like the previous stories, this encounter takes place in an abandoned house. She began:

> I guess one of the winters . . . throughout that summer there were two deaths, two drownings. And, later that, later that summer an old person (also) died. And so, the first freeze up came and there was this young high school couple who

just wanted to get away from town and so they went on a snow machine ride. It's just not even right outside of town, it's probably half a mile to a mile away from town. And they went to the man's house, this guy, one of the people that died, he was an elder and one of the people that went on the ride, the guy . . . that was his Grandpa [who died] and the other girl was a teacher's daughter, you know, it was just, probably her first year there, you know.

And they went on a ride and, so they came to the house and they walked in there, you know, at first nothing was, you know, I don't know if everything was still there (the dead person's belongings), but I guess they were sitting down and the TV was still there. I think they were watching TV. And right when they were gonna go out, you know, get out of the house, and I guess he [he was Yup'ik] walked outside to start the snow machine and the girl [she was kass'aq] was still in there and she, she was about to walk out.

There were three figures, you know, like greenish ghostly figures, um [pause] blocking the door. And she immediately got really sick, and was really scared. So, she couldn't even move, I mean—He ran inside and grabbed, I mean, he was walking inside and saw what was going on and he just grabbed her. And I guess they left on the snow machine and they never went back again. And they say those three figures were the same people that died throughout that summer.

And, I guess she was sick for about a week, you know, because she wasn't, she never had seen anything like that. . . . It's kind of like, well people in my area (Yup'ik region), for instance, they kind of always know that, you know, they could be haunted. They could be, you know, it's [pause] expected, you know? If, if it happens it happens, you know?

Villains and Fools

The fact that the girl was white is significant in this telling. It is even more relevant that she was the teacher's daughter because teachers, like missionaries, represent the outside world and imposed change.

She became ill because she did not know what proper actions to take when one encounters a ghost. She found herself in an encounter with "three figures . . . greenish ghostly figures" who blocked the door. And, as the teller reveals, "she immediately got really sick." She continued to be ill, in fact, for "about a week." Clearly the young Yup'ik man in this tale recognized the danger and at least knew they needed to get out of that situation quickly and so "he grabbed her" before the situation got worse. We get the sense that she not only lacked the knowledge to get out of this encounter, but that she physically was unable to help herself at that point.

People are instructed time and time again not only to avoid such places, but also that when one encounters a ghost, to always tell others about it. If you don't then you will be ill and, sometimes it is said, vomit greenish matter. Outsiders are explicitly warned of the dangers associated with dismissing this lightly. In 1981 I was warned by the people in Akiak to stay away from an abandoned village because of the ghosts. I'm not the only anthropologist to get such warnings:

> [An] Alaskan anthropologist . . . in 1982 visited a "haunted" place after being warned that those who went there became ill and vomited "a green thing." After his return to Russian Mission . . . [he] was very sick for four days. (Hansen 1985, 65)

In the previous narrative, the teacher's daughter also became very ill for several days. While we are not told if she vomited, we are told that her attackers had a "greenish" appearance.

Another story from Hooper Bay includes some of the same elements and cultural understandings about ghosts. Hooper Bay elder George Bunyan told Helen Oswalt, in 1950, of an encounter that his brother had with a ghost at trapping camp. Oswalt writes:

> His brother (informant's) [was] once out at trapping camp, [he] expected [another] man that night so [he] left lamp on when [he] went to bed. Heard footsteps to door, then two big white hands with big knuckles and long fingers at [the] door. He tried to move but couldn't. He knew if it looked at him he would die. All of a sudden something went bang, then [the] lamp went out, and he could scream. [He] Never knew what it was, but writing left by ghost is still on [the] door post. (Oswalt 1951, 11b)

In the particular case of the teacher's daughter, she faced the ghosts and became immobilized with fear. The Hooper Bay hunter also "tried to move but couldn't." Unlike the teacher's daughter, however, he "knew if it looked at him he would die."

Thus, by following his own cultural teachings about ghosts, he was able to escape unharmed. It is also significant that in both these tellings the ghosts appeared in and blocked the entryways at such places, thus preventing people from escaping. In essence the living are trapped between worlds (at doorways) and only through proper behavior do they escape the dead. Like the Hooper Bay hunter, the young Yup'ik man, knowing the teachings and proper conduct, "saw [understood] what was going on and he just grabbed her." Unlike the young man, the teacher's daughter is not expected to act appropriately. Nor is she expected, even when explicitly told, to act upon instruction in a culturally appropriate way.

This expectation of white disbelief and ignorance is common in Native American cultural traditions. I recall a fieldwork experience in 1988 in which I was interviewing an Anishinaabe (Ojibway/Odawa) elder on the Wikwemikong First Nations Reserve at Manitoulin Island, Canada. The first story that he ever shared with me began: "That's something that the white people don't believe too. I don't know what kind of white people they are, they don't believe that" (Cusack-McVeigh 1993, 28). This statement was made in relation to Anishinaabe teachings and stories surrounding the animal and spirit world. A particular genre of narratives in this Anishinaabe community emphasizes the ignorance of white disbelievers and the terrible results of this ignorance—illness or even death (Cusack-McVeigh 1993).

Other researchers and writers have noted the ways in which white characters are used in Native stories. Jarold Ramsey argues that a depiction of Anglos as "villains and fools" can be traced to the time of contact:

> More commonly, Indian anxieties about and resentment of Anglos and their ways expresses themselves directly in stories featuring whites as villains and fools. . . . A Northern Paiute twisting of Genesis declares that Eden was made for the Indians, but a white man in the form of a rattlesnake got into the apple tree and has kept Indians out of Paradise ever since. And

> in a latter-day Kiowa tale, Saynday the Trickster meets "Smallpox," in the form of a tall, skinny, pock-marked Anglo Preacher who asks for directions to the Kiowas. (Wiget 1994, 141)

This depiction of white people can be found in other forms of Native discourse. Keith Basso describes how white characters are used as models for inappropriate behavior in Western Apache discourse. In that setting the meaning is conveyed through a complex form of joking.

> By making of "the Whiteman" an improbable buffoon, Apache jokers isolate and accentuate significant contrasts between their own cultural practices and those of Anglo-Americans. And by presenting the behavior of Anglo-Americans as something laughable and "wrong," by displaying with the help of butts how and why it violates the rights of others, they denounce these standards as morally deficient and unworthy of emulation. In sum, joking performances make it emphatically clear that Whitemen and Western Apaches come to social encounters with conflicting ideas of what constitutes deferential comportment—ideas that are ultimately grounded in conflicting conceptions of what it means to be a person and the kinds of actions that can discredit a person's worth in public situations. (Basso 1979, 64)

A Yup'ik audience already knows that these places should be avoided and that the desecration of a grave constitutes behavior socially marked as inappropriate. A Yup'ik audience already knows that this can be a dangerous behavior on the part of the living. This lesson, however, is reinforced for the Yup'ik audience by inclusion of the white man in the various tellings of "The Teakettle Ghost." The white character not only serves as a vehicle for defining inappropriate behavior but also allows for the teller to comment on, and accentuate the differences between, Yupiit and non-Yup'ik people. One effect is to reinforce a sense of group identity by contrasting Yup'ik beliefs and ways with those of the outsider or "the other."

After this teller finished her story, she linked it to NAGPRA (the Native American Graves Protection and Repatriation Act), emphasizing that white people shouldn't steal from and loot Native graves. The following excerpt is taken from the recording:

> Teller: I think I used it ["The Teakettle Ghost"] in one of my papers about NAGPRA.
> Holly: Did you?
> Teller: Yeah.
> Holly: I'll bet that was a neat connection to make.
> Teller: Yeah. (pause) That was one of the examples, of ghost stories that I like because there's that (connection)....
> Teller: And, um, the other thing is that it also reminds me of my parents telling you, you know, you know proper procedures and stuff. You're supposed to, when a person dies you're supposed to gather their stuff and, um, distribute it to the village, or you can burn it.
> Teller: You know, you're not supposed to keep any of their things in the house.... [she laughs uncomfortably]

We, teller and listener, found common ground through her telling of this story as we learned that we had both had previous involvement with the federal NAGPRA law and the issues surrounding it. What she had done with "The Teakettle Ghost" was to create meaning in the story in a way that she felt I, her outside listener, would understand. Perhaps more importantly, this message was one that she felt all outsiders should hear and understand about the disturbance of Yup'ik graves.

Performance and Meaning

Meaning is not a fossilized relic from some distant past. Meaning-making is a dynamic feature of culture. Through the analysis of narrative and discourse we can see how all people negotiate their place in this world. Stories, both oral tellings and written texts, can tell us something about the context, the teller, and the listener. They can tell us something about the complex relationship, always changing, between the teller of a tale and the listeners (the intended audience). This understanding has broad implications for all those involved in the process of ethnographic research.

In sum, "The Teakettle Ghost" was told differently in all three cases, but the emphasis of each telling was determined by the audience. Three important themes are, to varying degrees, present in all three versions. First, all three versions contained Yup'ik cultural knowledge and beliefs about the places where ghosts are most often encountered and the proper actions needed to counter such attacks. Second, each contained important lessons about the disturbance of these places (graves and abandoned villages). Third, lessons are learned through the inappropriate behavior of a white man. The key difference between the first two tellings and the last one is on the emphasis of the performance. The meaning conveyed by the first two tellers is on the transmission of cultural knowledge: what the elders emphasize is Yup'ik culture, Yup'ik belief. What my teller, thinking about the impetus for NAGPRA, emphasized in her telling was that graves should not be disturbed. Graves are important places that need protection from the living, especially from those outsiders who do not believe in and respect the ways of the Yupiit. Graves, then, become tangible markers for the kinds of tensions that have existed since the time of contact. Graves have become places that connect people to their past, present, and future. The shaman's grave at Hooper Bay, for example, remains an important place not only because it is a symbol of the past, but because it is a commentary on the present. The shaman's grave is a barometer of the current social and physical health of the community and world at large.

The version of the Teakettle Ghost shared with me was about the need to respect these tundra graves, but it was specifically shaped for an external audience. The situational meaning of a narrative, then, can be understood by considering the emphasis placed on the various elements of the story. Stories do not contain a single message or a single meaning, but rather allow tellers to express a wide range of meanings in a wide range of settings. Listeners—including anthropologists and folklorists—need to consider how a narrative is being used before they can begin to comprehend what the story means.

A New Mark on the Land: Internal and External Control

I've shown that not only the "natural" landscape but also human-made places are "barometers," or indicators of the relationship between people and the land/universe. With the coming of outsiders came a new "mark" on the land in the form of church buildings, school buildings, and other structures that represented a new system. Human-human relationships and human-land tensions that derive from crosscultural histories are, as I will demonstrate, evident in the ghost stories that are told in Hooper Bay. Many of these ghost stories take place in the school buildings and the church, buildings that most directly symbolize those conflicted histories.

I have been particularly struck by the use of ghost stories in Hooper Bay and what they reflect in relation to particular places and kass'aqs. Several stories depict the familiar theme of a white person as the one who ignores Yup'ik knowledge of proper conduct and pays a price for having disregarded this cultural wisdom. It does not escape me that I qualify as a kass'aq audience and that many tellers, with that in mind, instruct me about proper conduct and inform me about past histories of kass'aq transgressions in these tellings.

Examples from other parts of the region will further demonstrate my point in relation to situational meaning and the repeated themes in narratives of specific kinds of places. Several stories, some recorded, show how a story is shaped for its particular audience. Much of my research (recorded data and field notes) particularly points at the telling of ghost stories in relation to the outside world and the places that represent outsiders. These stories essentially reflect the "ghosts" of tensions and conflicts that Yupiit have experienced since the time of contact. In sharing them, Yupiit find empowerment on both a personal and political, group level. My examples will illustrate the ways that narrative is used to establish and maintain personal and group empowerment in the face of external control.

8

Anchoring Memory in Place

TALES OF BROTHER OSCAR AND THE OLD CHURCH

September 11, 2002, marked the one-year anniversary of the terrorist attack on the Pentagon Building in Washington, D.C. Over thirteen thousand people gathered on the grounds of this place. They came together to remember and to mourn those who were lost. From this gathering people found strength. That very same morning, only miles from the Pentagon, another gathering was taking place. This gathering lacked all of the pageantry that characterized the Pentagon ceremony, but it too was a time of remembrance, a time to mourn. As mentioned in chapter 4, delegates representing the Native Village of Hooper Bay had traveled to Washington, D.C., to begin the long process of repatriating their ancestors to their homeland.

No one had anticipated that this day would be such a painful one. The human remains of Yup'ik men, women, and children were laid out on lab tables and covered with white sheets. A brief prayer was offered in the Yup'ik language. When the sheets were removed, the Hooper Bay delegates found themselves face-to-face with their ancestors. Many of them had handwritten notations on their skulls. One read "Hooper Bay Eskimo, Female," along with an upside-down female symbol. Another read "Eskimo/Hooper Bay/Alaska" along with the symbol for "male" written in black ink. One skull had an older label that read "property of" across the frontal lobe. Nearby a faded, handwritten note in pencil read "Father Fox/Hooper Bay, Alaska." One of the community members remarked that it is a difficult thing to see their ancestors so far from home, but even more difficult to see them written on and labeled like objects.

All agreed that it must be a very good thing for the ancestors, after so many years, to hear their own Native language spoken again. All agreed that this had provided, perhaps, some measure of comfort to both the living and the dead. In the small room, time suddenly collapsed as tears were shed not only for those of the past but for those who have recently departed. They too are victims. Remembering that the Pentagon ceremony was taking place that very day, one community member remarked that it was truly a day of mourning.

The story of how those ancestors got to the Smithsonian's National Museum of Natural History is also a painful one for community members. In 1936, Father John P. Fox, of the Little Flower Mission in Hooper Bay, had become very interested in "scientific" endeavors. He began to collect human remains for the well-known physical anthropologist Ales Hrdlička. Hrdlička, who was trained in medicine, had himself become interested in physical anthropology in the mid-1890s (Montgomery 1996). Hrdlička's aim was to promote physical anthropology as "a distinct and important field" (Montgomery 1996, 1). One means by which this was achieved was through public lectures, nontechnical anthropology articles, and popular radio talk shows (Montgomery 1996).

It is unclear how Father Fox became so interested in anthropological endeavors, but his letters to Hrdlička clearly establish his desire to please and impress this well-known scientist. Father Fox, in closing his letters to Hrdlička, would simply write, "With An Expression of Respect I Remain, Yours Sincerely, John P. Fox" (NMNH Collection 1936, 142374). A letter, dated September 23, 1936, to Fox from Hrdlička, suggests that Father Fox was following in the footsteps of his predecessor, Father Philip Delon, who was stationed at Kashunuk in the late 1920s. In 1927, Delon had also written to the famed Hrdlička, claiming that "the country about the village is literally strewn with graves, skulls, bones etc. . . . You would revel in these for some of the graves are very old" (NMNH Collection 1927, 99599).

Historical records demonstrate that this "collecting" spanned several years. Father Fox freely wrote about his grave-digging activities, while at the same time serving as a spiritual leader to the community. On

July 8, 1936, he wrote, "I have dug out and packed a shipment of material for you. . . . I doubted as to whether such things were mailable. But I found no mention made of bones in the list of unmailable matter, and so proceed to send the boxes" (NMNH Collection 1936, 142374). The discovery of these archival documents brought a great deal of pain to the Hooper Bay community members who were learning, for the first time, that this man had committed such acts of disrespect.

There is substantial documentation pointing to the fact that Father Fox received not only recognition for his efforts by the scientific community, but also financial compensation. One of Hrdlička's accession records from the then U.S. National Museum simply notes that "four Eskimo skeletons from Hooper Bay, Alaska" were "purchased by the donor [Hrdlička] from Father John P. Fox with private funds" (NMNH Collection 1936, 142374).

So important was this undertaking to Father Fox that he once traveled to the Mountain Village post office to mail the ancestral remains. He tells Hrdlička, "I have to haul the boxes to another post office 200 miles one way from here, at my own personal expense. Were I to charge you for that transportation you could get very few bones for $100 from Hooper Bay. I have paid as much as $110 per ton for freight, and that is not a slip of the pen either" (NMNH Collection 1936, 142374).

That letter, dated July 8, 1936, also describes in detail Father Fox's various attempts to remove the remains from their gravesites. Fox informs Hrdlička that he "had a good deal of trouble to segregate the bones from the dirt and other foreign matter with which they were mixed." Again, he closes his letter with the words, "With an expression of respect I remain, Yours sincerely, John P. Fox" (NMNH Collection 1936, 142374).

Perhaps it is the folklorist in me that finds irony in the fact that it was exactly sixty-one years to the day after Father Fox wrote this letter from the Little Flower Mission Church that I found myself sitting in the old church.[1] This building, I was about to discover, was haunted by a ghost whose story embodied the tense history of relations between the people of Hooper Bay and representatives of the Church, and by extension, other "outsiders" who knowingly and unknowingly violated Yup'ik sensibilities. A tangible symbol for social frustrations and the subject of innumerable stories, the old church is a human-made site that anchors the collective memory of experiences with such outsiders.

When I first found myself there, it was July 8, 1997. I had come to Hooper Bay to teach an introductory folklore course for the University of Alaska Fairbanks's Summer Sessions. Unfortunately, all but a few of my registered students had decided to drop the course when an opportunity to fight forest fires near Red Devil presented itself. I decided to volunteer my time and teach the folklore class as planned. Keep in mind that, at this time, I had no knowledge of Father Fox and his activities in the village. The Little Flower Mission, known locally as "the old church," seemed like the perfect place to hold class as it was much quieter than the busy traditional council office. The building made an impression on me from the first moment I entered it. It was a strange mix of the past and the present.

While waiting for my students to arrive, I looked around. On one wall an old pair of sealskin mukluks hung from a rusted nail. On the opposite wall was a painting of a child gazing up at the heavens. The title simply read "Eskimo Saint." This work continues to intrigue me to this day, but its creator remains a mystery. That night I wrote in my field notes that "the painting shows the 'Eskimo' in a sealskin parka looking up to the heavens and crossing herself with the sign of peace. She has blond curls and baby-blue eyes." Obviously this painting has been around for a long time, probably dating to the same period as the old, Catholic iconic objects stored in the basement of the old church. These life-sized religious statues (almost five feet tall) stood covered in dust and cobwebs, peering out from dark corners of the basement where they had been stored for many years. I would later remark to a friend who reluctantly gave me a tour of the old church that this building was straight out of a horror movie. Had I known, at the time, the local folklore surrounding this old church, I never would have made such a seemingly careless statement.

When my students arrived that day in July, we sat down and began to go over my three-page syllabus and the course materials. We had not been in the building for more than half an hour when the interior door suddenly and abruptly slammed shut! Looking at each other in surprise, we sat silently for a moment before one woman said to me, "Do you know about this old church?" I suddenly recalled my friend's reaction earlier that morning when she learned that I would be teaching in the old church. She had simply said, "There are a lot of stories about that place." We later agreed that, had it been an exterior door, we might have been able to blame the wind. Nothing more was said about this occurrence the rest of the class period. In the days and weeks to follow I would learn more about folklore than I had ever planned for in my syllabus. My field experiences in southwest Alaska over the past several years had taught me that when you are not looking for stories, stories find you.

It did not take long for people to establish who was responsible for the slamming door. Everyone, unequivocally, knew that Brother Oscar was responsible. My friends often teased me about the fact that my students and I would be keeping old Brother Oscar company. There are so many stories about hauntings by Brother Oscar's ghost that it would be impossible to include them all in this book. Each time I travel to the village I learn new ones. The transcript of one Brother Oscar story that I would later record is over fifty pages in length. The old church is clearly a place of great significance.

Brother Oscar's Place

The story goes that Brother Oscar was a young man who had been sent by the Catholic Church to serve as a spiritual leader in the village. One teller states that he "came into Hooper Bay as a missionary hoping to convert some of the local people here." She added that this was no great feat, since most were already converted to Christianity. For a time masses were held and all seemed normal. One day when some of the locals came to the old church to bring him food, as they routinely did, they got no answer when they knocked. They decided to simply leave the food at the door, but over time they became increasingly concerned about the priest. According to one community member, "Nobody really expected a priest to come here and, and not go to mass and miss mass and . . . they thought it was a very peculiar attitude that he had." The following excerpt is taken directly from one teller's account of a Brother Oscar tale:

> But there came a time when [pause] the Brother, he would act very strange among the community members. Um, the community members would talk among themselves, but they'd never . . . you

> know, ask him what was wrong with him. They did know that something was definitely wrong with the man though.

Brother Oscar was eventually found by some concerned local people inside the old church. "They found Brother Oscar laying there dead!" they told me. They could not bury him because he had died in the winter when the tundra is frozen solid, and so they placed his body in the basement of the old church. Early spring arrived and a replacement for Brother Oscar was sent to the village. The body remained in the basement of the old church. The new priest, who was living upstairs in Brother Oscar's old quarters, was eventually led to the basement by a series of strange noises and events. One teller described, in detail, what the priest found when he went down to inspect these occurrences:

> Eventually time passed on and they got a new priest, for the Catholic Church. They needed a priest to carry out the, uh, the masses and [pause] the Catholicism. So, I'm not sure what the priest's name was, but I [pause]. . . . The priest, he lived in the same confinements that Brother Oscar did. And, I'm pretty sure, he did know of the, the body in the basement, but it hardly bothered him. So, it was just another dead, lifeless body down in the basement. He didn't really think anything of it. So, he was living there for about, um, quite some time. And um, the uh, the members of the community would often tell him their beliefs of, you know, the spirits and, and ghosts and other . . . things, but he would say "oh, oh that's, that's nothing!" You know, "God takes his people up to heaven after they have died and, and there aren't souls that are left on this earth to walk among us."[2]
>
> So, he didn't, didn't really believe in ghosts or spirits, or any of the beliefs that the community members did. And um, he was lying there in bed one evening, it was about, so they say, about midnight when he heard [pause] somebody, in the basement walking up the stairs. It was very slow, but the [steps], the footsteps were indeed heavy. You could hear them. It, it was very, very slow. It came up the stairs and, he had thought that somebody had broken in there, and messed with the body. Somebody, you know, who, some crazy person, some

crazy community member had broken into the basement because there is another entrance into the basement, right underneath the stairwell to the, the upstairs area which was then the rec.-room. . . .

He thought somebody had managed to break in there and vandalize the basement with the body in there, and was coming up the stairs as quietly as he possibly could in order not to wake the priest. So, the priest got out his knife, and, he walked to the basement, the entrance to the basement. He heard these [foot]steps, walking up slowly, slowly [pause] he opens the door and he starts to, he didn't have his lantern, something was wrong with his lantern. I don't think there was much light, so he couldn't see who or what was down there. So, he walks down and, um, as he's walking down, it's very, very cold. Extremely, much, much colder than it should have been.

He's walking down the stairs and [pause], all of a sudden something reaches up and grabs the priest's leg. And he's, he can't move. It's an extremely cold, cold hand. Not [pause], it didn't feel like any, any human. Human hands are usually warm and, and hot, they're warm blooded and so, of course, it's going to be, it's not going to be as cold as this hand was. This hand was icy, icy cold.

He couldn't see anything, but he took out his knife, he did have a knife. And he pulled up his leg, pulled it up real hard so that the, the body of the person would . . . jerk and, you know, he could get a better chance of hitting this person.

He hits the person and, I believe it landed on the person's head. The guy [priest] runs up the stairs, locks the door and he wakes up some of the members of the community. Now, they go down. They all go down, the priest with the members of the community, to see exactly who this person is. They have the lantern and everything. They go down there and, at first, they didn't see anything. But, then they took a look at the coffin. The coffin, was open. The body was taken out [pause], the body wasn't in the coffin. They looked around for the body, and underneath the coffin, the coffin sat on a table, was laid out on a table and underneath this table, there was the body of Brother Oscar with . . . the knife stuck in his head.

Um, the members of the community thought that this was very, very wrong. The priest just, you know, he was extremely reluctant to believe any of what they were saying. He thought that somebody . . . had escaped. He didn't strike the person's [Brother Oscar's] head. The person [an intruder] had just stuck it into the, the body of this brother Oscar. But, as time went on the priest continued to live there, [and] strange occurrences kept on happening.

It got to the point where, this body was just, it was so eerie that they had chained up the, uh, coffin and the next day when . . . the night after they had chained up the coffin, the priest was still in his house and they, as night drew closer and closer it soon became dark. It was the middle of the night, he heard some chains, chains rattling in the basement and, and he heard this big, big old bang down there. Like some, some door had slammed or something.

Then he heard the footsteps again. The notorious footsteps that kept bothering him [long pause]. The basement door was locked. Now, this priest was pretty much fed up by this point, with what was happening, you know. He thought that some community member was trying to scare him. Just scare him off [laughing out loud], you know? This poor old priest [laughs again]. He still didn't believe any of it! So, he goes over, he takes his lantern, he goes over to the door, opens it [pause]. And, whatever's down there isn't as brave as it was before. It, it shies off and, and it stumbles down the stairs. Except it didn't sound like anybody running down the stairs.

It sounded like a drum roll. Like a drum, a gasoline drum had fell and was falling down these stairs. It was extremely loud. So he's wondering, you know, what the heck is going on here. So, he takes his lantern, he starts going down into the basement [lowers voice] hoping to find whoever keeps bothering him there. And he looks around, and he looks around, he sees nobody! The coffin is, open and the body isn't there. But he can't find anybody.

He [the new priest] looks in one of the corners and he sees this, this figure. It was, it was placed in a position that the, that the

> old Yup'ik people, before the missionaries came and, and showed them how to bury, a proper Christian burial under the ground and everything. It was placed as they [the ancestors] used to place the dead bodies. It was sitting in the corner and it was very dark. So the priest he, he quietly and slowly . . . there was this one figure just sitting there, placed in this, this position. It was sitting down, but its head was placed between its, its knees. And that, the hands were crossed, uh, holding, the hands were placed, um, around the knees holding each other as they used to do.

This same mortuary practice was described by Edward Nelson as observed on the lower Yukon in the late 1870s and early 1880s. "After death," Nelson wrote, "the body is placed in a sitting posture on the floor; the knees are drawn up and the feet back, so that the knees rest against the chest and the heels against the hips; then the head is forced down between the knees until the back of the neck is on a line with the tops of the knees; the arms are drawn around encircling the legs above the ankles and just under the forehead" (Nelson 1983 [1899], 314). Nelson documented a similar "sitting posture" at St. Michael (311).

Father Fox, in the aforementioned letter, wrote to Hrdlička:

> You may not be aware of the fact that our people here don't know what a coffin is and if the corpse has anything at all by way of a container it is a rough board box that will soon be rotted away. For the same reason it is hard to get solid bones. (NMNH Collection 1936, 142374)

In a second letter written two months later, in August of 1936, Father Fox further informs Hrdlička that "it is very hard to get good ones (complete human skeletons) as they do not bury in coffins but simply double up the corpse before it is cold" (NMNH Collection 1936, 142374). In this same letter Fox indicates his preference for more recent remains because the flesh helps keep the skeletal structure together, thus making his job of removal from the grave and shipment easier.

"A Few Graves . . . Scattered Around the Place: A Good Place to Build"

Some community members have told me that the changes in Brother Oscar began when he attempted to dig a well at the site of the old church. Father Fox writes at length about his own dislike for pond water and his attempts to dig wells at the site. Church records indicate a lot of activity surrounding well-digging. In 1932, we are told that "Brother started to dig the well around the 9th or 10th of November" (AM Collection 14, 582). In December of that same year the "well is about 12 feet deep" (AM Collection 14, 583). In February of 1933 "digging stops on well . . . 32 ft. & no water" (AM Collection 14, 592). Later that same year, in a "History of the Hooper Bay District" for 1932–1933, someone frustratingly wrote that they ceased all digging—reverting back to collecting water from the church roof.

Others contend that it was the building of the old church at that particular site that brought trouble. The site is well known as an ancient burial place. Yupiit had always chosen high ground, when available, to bury their dead. The missionaries also valued this high ground for the building of their churches and consistently disregarded the fact that such spots had already been designated for burials. These tensions were immediate and lasting. Father Keyes, who was stationed at Holy Cross in 1900 and Mountain Village during the 1920s (Carriker et al. 1980), had selected the place where the Hooper Bay mission would be built. Church documents recall:

> Our troubles with the government Mission school started even before our mission was started. Father Keyes picked a good place to build, right in the center of the village, the only available high ground close by. Immediately there was a howl from the school teacher, Misha Ivanoff [a Protestant]. Father had instructed the workmen to move a few graves that were scattered around the place. According to native custom, the log boxes that contained the remains had been set on top of the ground. Mostly very old . . . skeletons and other bones lay all around. These were reverently gathered, put into a box, and buried on a small hill close to the village. Father Keyes faced the charge

> of desecrating graves, stealing another's ground, etc. But he let the teacher talk and went ahead with the building. (John P. Fox Collection 2017, 192)

At the old village of Kashunuk, Father Delon wrote, "I picked up these skulls where I built a church and school" (NMNH Collection 1927, 99599). It is thus little surprise that such places should be haunted. In fact, Father Fox himself wrote to his superiors of "a few unusual occurrences" at Kashunuk in 1931. Fox had been stationed at Kashunuk before his transfer to Hooper Bay. Readers will recall that Fox, annoyed by constant spitting in the church building, had placed cans of ashes in every corner. I have noted that this action made sense from the missionary's world-view, recalling that among Euro-Americans of this time, spittoons or cuspidors were frequently used for purposes of spitting indoors. Yupiit, both in the past and today, spit for a variety of reasons. Chewing tobacco (*iqmiq*) is common among both Yup'ik men and women. So, spitting would have been a practical habit, but it also served another function that missionaries probably never understood, one that may have been marked by Yup'ik parishioners as apropos in connection with the church.

Spittle, as previously mentioned, seems to form some kind of protective barrier in much the same way that water does. This behavior also fit the cultural logic of the Yupiit at Kashunuk since both spittle and ashes help to form a protective barrier against the human and the spirit worlds. Apparently there was good reason for establishing a protective barrier at this place. Fox himself reports that several churchgoers saw a "figure" or "apparition" in the Kashunuk church building that, when approached from the side, suddenly vanished.

The Ghost at Kashunuk Mission

Fox wrote to his superiors of this encounter at the Kashunuk Mission in great detail, stating:

> It may not be amiss to narrate here a few unusual occurrences without offering any explanations or comments. They were dictated to me by those to whom they occurred. Nor do I recall of ever having spoken to the people about these extraordinary

things, except perhaps by way of an occasional illustration during sermon. On the feast of the Translation of the Holy House of Loretto, December 10, 1931, Patricia Pakarkalrea, Agatha Kayutak, Agnes Naparkalrea and Lucy Kónkushin stayed in the chapel (at Sacred Heart Mission, Kashunuk, Alaska) for confession after the usual daily evening prayers. Everybody else had gone home.

Patricia was the first to finish her confession. As she reentered the chapel (for here our confessional is in the Father's room, not in the chapel) to say her penance she noticed someone dressed in white, with a white veil over her head and shoulders, kneeling with her hands clasped in prayer on the top of a low bench along the wall on the right hand side of the chapel towards the back. She thought it was my catechist, though she wondered at the strange kind of dress. Paying no farther attention to the praying figure she went up to the altar steps and knelt down for her prayers. When finished she went out passing the same apparition again, looking at it while passing, but paying no farther attention to it.

Patricia's sister, Agatha, came next. She saw the figure but also went by to say her penance at the foot of the altar. But on leaving the chapel she approached the figure as she passed. There was no light in the chapel except that given by the sanctuary lamp, which happened to be a small lantern. She putting her hand to her forehead to shade her eyes went up to within four feet from the figure. When she got that far it suddenly vanished and all she saw was the bare wall.

Next came Agnes Naparkalrea for her little thanksgiving and penance after confession. She saw the same as the other two, and like Patricia, simply noticed the figure, and thinking it was my catechist, passed without farther investigation. When Lucy Konkushin came for her prayers after confession and saw the same figure kneeling there with hands clasped in fervent prayer she said her prayers as the other three, and then approached the figure as Agatha Kayutak had done. As she came within three feet of it, partly stooping over and with her hand to her forehead to see better in the dark, the figure vanished.

> Naturally the girls compared notes when they met the next time which was the following morning, and as all saw exactly the same thing they came to tell me.
>
> I questioned every one of them separately as to the exact spot where the figure knelt, the exact posture and position of the hands, the color of the dress and veil, and whatever else I could think of to see if they agreed in everything. Their story was identical in every respect as regards to description. When I asked about the color of the hair, the shape of the face etc. all answered that the veil prevented them from seeing as they approached from the side. (Hooper Bay Collection Part 1, 4)

To establish the authenticity of the stories, Fox assures his superiors that he questioned each teller separately and, in his words, "their story was identical in every respect."

Some Yupiit contend that, perhaps, it is the Church's (outsiders) lack of respect and concern for the ancestors that results in hauntings such as this as well as those more recently recounted.

In 1932, Fox wrote about another experience that he captioned "Some interesting incidents from the Missions of Kashunuk and Hooper Bay Alaska." He described an incident in which two Yup'ik boys witnessed an apparition in the church.

He noted that they saw an "apparition [that] looked like the common picture of the Sacred heart," but goes on to say that "this last detail is different from anything the writer [Fox] has seen in this line. The figure was exceedingly bright so that the boys could hardly bear to look at it, and from the belt down the figure was wrapped in what looked like smoke" (AM Collection 30, 1185).

Two important cultural themes are present in the above narratives. First, the way that all four girls approach the "apparition" is standard Yup'ik knowledge about how one should approach a ghost. Approaching a ghost directly and hastily will have dangerous consequences. Agnes Henry and Mary Black of Kongiganak said that "when people saw a ghost, even if they ran away from it, it would always end up in front of them" (Tennant and Bitar 1981, 247). The Yup'ik girls at the Kashunuk Mission did not look directly at the ghost's face because "the veil prevented them from seeing [the face of the ghost] as they approached from the side" (AM Collection 13, 22). Henry and Black also said of ghosts that "they never faced the person" (Tennant and Bitar 1981, 247).

The other significant detail, in relation to ghost encounters, is the fact that the figure witnessed by the boys was "wrapped in what looked like smoke" (AM Collection 30, 1185). Anyone familiar with Yup'ik ghost encounters will recognize this element of the tale, similar to the cold smoke that awakens the men in the teakettle ghost account, after the white man removes the kettle from the grave.

Anchoring Memory: Collective-Community Memory and Place

The fact that so many stories are circulated about the place known as the "old church" is telling. A strong sense of collective or community memory exists in relation to it, a sense that involves a sharing of knowledge. The stories of this particular place in Hooper Bay include "accounts which are deemed important enough to pass on in the collective memory" (Schneider 1995, 189). The "old church" serves as an anchor for the community's collective memory. Paul Connerton demonstrates that memory can be treated as a cultural, rather than individual, faculty: "Groups provide individuals with frameworks within which their memories are localized and memories are localized by a kind of mapping. We situate what we recollect within mental spaces provided by the group" (Connerton 1989, 37).

Connerton, following Halbwachs, states that these mental spaces "always receive support from and refer back to the material spaces that particular social groups occupy" (Connerton 1989, 37). In other words, place anchors community, collective memory.

In this case, the old church is the anchor to which memory is attached, in much the same way that the Pentagon building holds a newly found significance for many Americans.

The Pentagon memorial not only allowed for mourning the dead but also celebrated this place, permanently marking its significance as a shared symbol. The president, quoted by the *Washington Post*, declared that "within one year, this great building has been made whole once again" (Vogel and Kunkle 2002). The chairman of the Joint Chiefs of

Staff referred to the construction workers as "the hard-hat patriots of the Phoenix Project," and the Pentagon renovation program manager told the crowds, "America, we give you back your Pentagon" (Vogel and Kunkle 2002, A25). From statements such as these one gets a strong sense that, perhaps for a time, someone else had laid claim to this place of great significance and people were anxious to reclaim it. This, of course, is also true of the place where the twin towers once stood, now revered by many as hallowed ground.

One gets the strong sense that the old Catholic church was a place that, for a time, belonged to someone other than the community members in Hooper Bay. Like the Pentagon building, the old church was reclaimed by the people, although, significantly (as we shall see), it remained church property for a long time. The succeeding priest, Father O'Connor, would pen an entry in the church house diary noting the speed with which community members "reformed" the old church into a community hall. He writes that "the former mission building has been turned over to the novices." One room was fixed up as a carpenter shop; others were converted to office space.

A Men's Meeting Room

More important is what became of Father Fox's room. Father Fox's living quarters became, in the words of the new priest, "a men's meeting room" (Hooper Bay Collection Part 1, 23). The irony here is striking. In the past the men's community house was known as a *qasgiq*. It was a place where men lived and worked. It was a place for sweatbaths, dancing, and feasting. Upon their arrival, missionaries had aggressively sought to replace these important cultural activities with church events. The missionaries discouraged men's houses in favor of nuclear family residences. Community members quickly reclaimed this place and made a strong statement in doing so.

Stories are often primed in such moments, when others make claims to places. Attempts to reclaim places and the relational tensions implied in such efforts also perpetuate such stories.

It is not just this place that was reclaimed. It is very significant to note that Brother Oscar himself, when finally found, had assumed the posture of those ancestors buried before missionary influence. This

FIGURE 8.1. The old church, 1960 (at right). Archives and Special Collections, Consortium Library, University of Alaska Anchorage

is a strong, symbolic reversal and it leaves a strong message: clearly, Brother Oscar no longer belonged to the world of the Jesuit Order. It holds significance beyond its symbolic import in that each telling of Brother Oscar's demise allows for a sense of empowerment on the part of the teller and listeners. It is in essence an active part of social life in Hooper Bay.

As for Father Fox? Well, Father O'Connor describes his final departure from Hooper Bay in the following way: "When he finally pulled out, practically the whole village was sitting on the bank. Not a word was spoken. What terrible apathy on the part of a people for whom he sacrificed so much!" (Hooper Bay Collection Part 1, 26). The story of this power struggle, however, did not end with Father Fox's final departure. As I will demonstrate in the next chapter, the old church building would continue to be the center of tension and turmoil.

9

Haunted Places and Their Symbolic Import

NARRATIVES FROM THROUGHOUT THE YUP'IK REGION

Ghosts in the School

Churches and school buildings, not only in Hooper Bay but throughout the Yup'ik region, must have transformed the Yup'ik landscape in profound ways, especially when one considers how traditional semisubterranean homes and the qasgiq with its underground passageways blended seamlessly into the natural setting of the surrounding tundra landscape. Constructed of imported materials with Euro-American architectural designs, the newly erected structures would have dominated a village skyline and signaled dramatic change. No wonder these places also became a focal point for the tensions between community members and outsiders.

In my field notes from November and December of 1999, I wrote of an exchange that I had with a woman regarding the school in Hooper Bay. This young mother was in her mid-thirties. I had just met her for the first time. She was curious about my reasons for coming to Hooper Bay and assumed that I was working for the school. I had an hour before someone would arrive to take me by snow machine up to the school. As we sat drinking our tea, I explained to her that I was there to begin a grant-funded project with the council and was supposed to go up to the school and discuss it with the staff later that morning. In part, I told her, we hoped to explore options for developing a locally relevant history curriculum for use in the schools.

She immediately looked concerned and asked me if I was aware of the fact that a man had died at the school when it was being built. I said no. When my ride pulled up at the door she said to me, "Those stories are true, so be careful up at that school." I did not see her again, but I never forgot her words. I was curious about this assertion because both the school and the church fulfill such important roles in the daily lives of community members.

In chapter 7, I presented a story about the haunting of the school teacher's daughter, a kass'aq whose encounter with a ghost made her very ill. She did not demonstrate appropriate actions and "was sick for about a week" because "she'd never seen anything like that." The implied message here is that, regardless of how "educated" this white family may have been, they were ignorant in the ways of the Yupiit. In this case, the haunting occurred elsewhere but schools are often the focus of ghost stories. As I will show, this reflects a great deal about the relationships between whites and Yupiit, in terms of both the historic tensions that have played out in the region and how cross-cultural relationships are shaped in contemporary settings.

A white elementary school teacher in Hooper Bay once told me that she often heard stories of the school being haunted. She had been teaching there for over three years; this was to be her final year in the village. When I asked her, she replied that she had "heard [ghost stories] from the kids themselves and that they had warned her that because there were ghosts in the school you would never want to be in there at night."

I recalled that, five years earlier, I had recorded a tale with a Yup'ik woman from a village upriver from Bethel. She too had talked about the school in her own village being haunted. She explained that this was a widely known and accepted fact in her village. She told me the following story.

"These Planes Are Flying!"

> My Grandpa was a maintenance man for our school, when the school was a BIA [Bureau of Indian Affairs] School, and um [pause], a principal of ours, he was a pilot and he liked flying planes and he always made models and, and he hung them up

> in his room and everything, you know, his principal's office and stuff. He hung them up all over and, I guess right before spring breakup he got into a, a plane wreck and died.
>
> And my Grandpa was supposed to go into his room and clean up and, um [pause] get rid of stuff, and all that kind of thing. And so he walks in and these planes are flying, I mean just literally, you know, like they, they were on strings, but they were flying — yeah, they were just flying. So, I've always grown up, you know, knowing that other spirits existed and I've always learned to respect that.

Churches and schools have particular resonance because they are specific places associated with contact, but they are not the only places that may be haunted in association with cultural change. Houses also bear that association. Colonization involved a long period of forcible change aimed at not only beliefs and practices, but also how Yupiit lived. Older-style housing was viewed as an impediment to progress and efforts to Christianize the people in Yup'ik communities. At Hooper Bay, as elsewhere in the Yup'ik region, men and boys historically lived in a qasgiq (the men's house). Women traditionally lived in separate housing, but regularly brought food to and attended ceremonies in the qasgiq which also served as a community ceremonial center. This unfamiliar residence pattern horrified missionaries who believed that husbands and wives should live together in a nuclear family. The traditional semisubterranean and the somewhat later log-plank-style houses were condemned not for their lack of function as much as for their representation of the old ways.

In Hooper Bay people have explicitly told me that houses should not be left unoccupied. When a house sits empty, people become very concerned. Even when a place is abandoned as a result of a person's death, elders warn community members not to leave the house unoccupied for too long. In chapter 7 I described such an abandonment after a tragic incident. It is not only old houses, however, that can be inhabited by spirits or ghosts. New houses also seem to be vulnerable, perhaps because new housing projects, although much needed, are also projects introduced by representatives of the outside world.

FIGURE 9.1. Little Flower Mission. Jesuit Oregon Province Archives

The following narrative, told to me in 1996, demonstrates that discomfort may be associated with new housing.

> It was four years ago, these friends of ours, of our family, I guess this woman was sleeping with her children in her house and they each had their separate rooms and, and in the middle of the night, ya know, it was, what, four o'clock in the morning or so. The door was locked and, and there was nobody that could come in there. Their father was in Bethel for a conference and, and I don't know where he was [which conference], but, they were sleeping and all of a sudden they started hearing, you know, like a big thud, you know. And they kept hearing big thuds, so the kids ran into their mother's room [teller laughs nervously] and like, jumped on top of her and they were all scared for a moment and the mother was all "that's probably somebody."
>
> So she walked out there and, and all she saw were like footprints, you know, um in the house. And those houses were new. And it's weird that, I think it was my mom who told me that story and she kind of connected it to, you know, I mean just

> immediately she connected it to, you know, one of the people that built these houses, [he] had died the week before. So she, you know, she kind of connected it to that situation.

She told me that "every once in a while, I mean, well every time, not every single time after a death, but you know, people kind of expect hauntings. Or not hauntings, but encounters with these people, in a ghost form or some sort."

Empty houses create unease, but the reasons for the abandonment are also significant in understanding why such places are haunted. The kinds of deaths that lead to hauntings are very often violent deaths. Of course, this can be said of Euro-American ghost stories, too, but in the case of Yup'ik hauntings, violent deaths are a result of social problems rooted in postcolonial conditions.

The First Post Office at Hooper Bay

I have already described the community building known as "the old church," but what I have not discussed is the building's subsequent history as a post office. Some say that the community got the name Hooper Bay when the post office was established and recognized by the United States Postal Service. Years after Brother Oscar, some time after Father Fox left Hooper Bay, the old church building was still used as a post office. So it should come as no surprise to learn that the post office was also haunted. One woman told me the following story about the post office at Hooper Bay. Apparently this incident occurred when a friend was filling in for the postmaster.

> Soon after the new Catholic church was built, they in turn, um, didn't want to tear the [old] building down because it was, it was big you know. It's nice and they could use it for many purposes, such as a rec.-room or, or you know, certain activities that the Catholic church wanted to, maybe hold a community meeting or something [presumably the building remained "church property" although it was transitioning to more secular uses]. So, they didn't tear the old Catholic church down.

They figured that later on, they'd find, you know, some pretty good uses for it, since it was, you know, fairly new. . . . They decided to use the rec.-room as the, um, the post office. And, this was the community post office for a few years. . . .

She [community member] was down there and, it was in the middle of winter, it was a very stormy day. Nobody was coming into the post office, nobody [laughs] wanted to come into the post office. She was working there, sorting out some mail and everything, and she heard . . . after a while, you know, she was busy with her work. It was very quiet. She didn't have a radio, you know, she didn't have anything. It was extremely quiet. The only sound was her and the rustling of the mail that she was, uh, taking care of. And then she heard it. She heard these footsteps, from the basement, again.

And she heard the creaking of the stairs and everything. Going up, and up, and up. And she didn't want to leave . . . to leave the church, so she just went real close to the door there . . . Just in case, you know, it came to the point where it got so bad that she could just open the door and run out. So she's sitting there and she's listening to these stairs and she's wondering what, what is this. . . .

She's standing there listening to this [pause] to these footsteps coming up these stairs. And they're very, very slow. Slowly they move up. And she heard some . . . she knew that this place wasn't [good], it was kinda haunted. As everybody, everybody in this community knows. But she'd never experienced anything before. She, she just heard these footsteps climbing up and up and up. Getting closer to this door. The door that led to the post office from the basement.

It got closer and closer to the door. Pretty soon, it was right by the door itself. Right by the door. And she could hear something grabbing the knob and she was, at this point, she couldn't move. She heard somebody, about to open this door and all of a sudden "bam!" She heard this door slam right open and she just screamed, she was so scared. She, um [pause] felt somebody um, trying to, you know, shake her. Asking her

> "what's wrong, what's wrong?" "What's wrong?" She looks up and sees . . . somebody had opened the door to the post office . . . but while he [the man who had come into the post office] was doing this [coming inside], and they were both in the post office, they heard the drum roll [sound] again. As soon as that happened they heard this big ole drum roll, extremely loud, falling down these stairs again.
>
> And [laughs nervously] she knew, you know, she wasn't hearing things, or going crazy or anything, because this person [the man who came in], in fact, did hear it too. So she . . . closed up and, you know, it was a stormy day anyway.
>
> Nobody was coming to the post office.

She concluded this telling by stating to me that some community members "did see it [strange light in the window] again about three, four, five days ago." It was important to her that I understand how recent this last sighting had been and she stressed this point. Several people explained to me that the strange light often seen in the old church building windows is the light that is seen when "a ghost is beginning to take formation," and when "it takes its formation it is then free to move about in any way it possibly can."

After the old church was no longer a community post office it served various purposes. Sometimes the old quarters would be used to house outside visitors (figure 9.1). In fact, this building had a long history of housing outside visitors, even during the time that it served as a church. Visitors, it seems, that were in need of room and board routinely contacted the church or government school to make such arrangements. In July of 1934, for example, church records note that a visiting doctor "wishes to have a living place here for 1 month in summer" (AM Collection 14, 616). When the Disney team came to Hooper Bay in 1946, they made their housing arrangements through the Bureau of Indian Affairs, rather than contacting community members. "In Hooper Bay the couple moved into the old and drafty teachers' quarters" (Fienup-Riordan 1995, 140). In August of 1960, visiting nurses "held clinic daily" and lived at the Catholic Mission (APRD, Alaska Nurses Association Collection 45).

During my second summer of work in Hooper Bay I decided that I myself would need to find a place to stay on a long-term basis. I loved living with a family but did not want to become a burden to my friends. One community member told me about an apartment that was available in the old church building. This, of course, was before I had begun teaching in the old church and learning about its history. I was very excited about the idea of having a place to myself that was close to the store and other families I had come to know well. The following narrative was shared with me only days after my summer sessions course had begun. It would have a direct and immediate impact on my housing plans. I was told that a kass'aq woman had come to Hooper Bay in the 1970s and had lived in this place that I was interested in renting. The narrator told me the following story about the old church building and the woman who lived there.

> It [the old church/post office building] was a lot more modernized [than it had been when Brother Oscar lived there], they had changed it around just a little bit. And the old church is a very secure building. They lock, make sure all the doors are locked and, so that nobody can break in, um, and vandalize or mess with, you know, the property. She's [the white woman], she's down there and she spent about a couple of months here. . . . It would be in the middle of the night and she would lock her bedroom door. . . .
>
> She was hired by the Catholic Church, um, just to help out with mass, or paperwork, or filing or whatever they needed to have done. She wasn't a nun, but . . . she was white, Caucasian. She was living down there and, at first, nothing seemed to bother her, it was just fine to her. But, um, as time went on she would live there and, you know, she [pause] she was afraid of somebody breaking in too.
>
> So, she would lock her bedroom door every night. But, in the middle of the night, all of a sudden she'd hear this knocking. This knocking on her bedroom door. And she was wondering . . . "all the doors are locked, who could get in here?" She, she'd leave it alone and, after a while it wouldn't stop knocking so she was forced to get up and open up this door and, she

didn't find anything. She found nothing. Nobody was there. It was empty.

She'd go back into her bedroom, and a couple of minutes later the knocking would continue . . . and once in a while this dog [the woman's dog] would have frantic, it would act panicky. It would act extremely uncomfortable, its hair, its fur would be risen and, you know, as a dog does when something isn't right. She thought the dog was acting extremely strange due to the fact that it needed to go out . . . she opens the door for the dog and goes into the porch. And, it's a nice night. There's, you know, no wind, nothing like that. It's a nice calm night.

And the dog runs out, as if it was extremely thankful to be out of the building. She goes after the dog, and as she goes after the dog the door [she nervously laughs] slams shut on her. And she's locked out of the building. Now she had to go over [to a neighboring house]. It's cold outside, it was in the middle of the winter . . . [they] called public safety to have them come down and open the door for her. They did, and, and, again [nervously laughing] she goes out for some silly reason in the middle of the night and, is locked out again. The door slams shut on her. . . .

By this point she's fed up . . . she can't handle what's going on. You know, the dog is acting extremely weird, she can't get any sleep. Every time she walks out the door, not that far from the door, it slams shut on her. And she knows that there is no wind, there's nobody in there, but it's as if somebody was in there slamming the door shut on her, this woman. And you know, she knew something wasn't right with the building. So, she in turn had it blessed, and [pause] I guess the occurrences were a little bit more vague, but they did, they did occur every once in a while. That's just one of the stories that she [her mother] had to tell me. . . . But yeah, she, she did know that something wasn't right in the building and it was something phenomenal, not human. Not of this, [pause] this realm . . . it's said to be the spirit of Brother Oscar, but, but a lot of people have different stories.

The Bishop Was Irritated

Needless to say, my housing problems weren't solved. It did not escape my attention that this narrative was being shared with me while I was considering a move. Later, while doing archival research, I discovered church documents that talked about the "Old Church Property Sale." The Hooper Bay post office was originally run and owned by the Catholic Church. Church records dating to the mid-1940s describe the community post office as "church property" and document the profit made by the church through this activity.

Even more interesting is the fact that Father Fox himself served as the postmaster. O'Connor wrote that "Fr. Fox had a multiplicity of jobs, postmaster, Reindeer Supervisor, quasi trader, doctor, and whatnot" (Hooper Bay Collection Part 1, 26). As with so many aspects of life in Hooper Bay, Fox had attempted to exercise control over the community by exercising control over the incoming and outgoing mail. The church also controlled the income that was generated by this business. It would be years before community members would take over the business of running the community post office.

As noted earlier, the tension and conflict did not end when Father Fox pulled out of town. Historic records document the sale of the old church. The transaction was not a smooth one. The church, in fact, attempted to control this building for many years. The village council and Father O'Connor had drawn up a contract to purchase the old church in October of 1948, just two years after Father Fox had left Hooper Bay (AM Collection 14, 82). Letters written in the late 1940s and early 1950s show that a dispute arose over ownership and control of the building. Boyle, the secretary of the Catholic Society of Alaska, wrote that "the difference of opinion arose from the payment of the three installments" (AM Collection 14, 85). Boyle's letter, written in February of 1949, was followed six months later by a letter from Father James U. Conwell, S.J., at the Bishop's Residence in Juneau to Father O'Connor at Hooper Bay. It addressed the conflict and confusion "about your old church building" (AM Collection 14, 83).

Another half a year passed before Conwell wrote to O'Connor again. On December 5, a letter arrived in Hooper Bay saying "that business about the old church moves along slowly" (AM Collection 14, 82). In

January of 1950, Conwell once again informed Father O'Connor that "matters are plodding along very slowly regarding that deal of the sale of the old church." He went on to say that "the bishop was irritated that they [the Hooper Bay Village Council] still demand a deed and bill of sale before completion of payment" (AM Collection 14, 80).

Conwell wrote that the "bill of sale [will] be held in escrow by a bank" until the village completed all of the payments to the Catholic Church. He also mentioned a "reservation clause," which he credits Father O'Connor for suggesting: "according to which the land would revert to us if the Village disposed of the building" (AM Collection 14, 80).

That same month Father O'Connor responded to Conwell's January letter regarding the sale of the old church. He wrote: "My what a lot of fuss this is with the government. . . . The natives have taken over the building completely since the day we signed my original contract [October 1948]. They believe that they already own the building" (AM Collection 14, 79). The community, as I discussed in chapter 8, had begun to reclaim the old church back in 1946 after Father Fox moved out. This action of reclaiming place predated any formal, written agreement by two years.

In May of that same year (1950), Conwell wrote again to Father O'Connor and enclosed the agreement "to be signed by the bishop regarding that business of your old church." He declared, in this letter, that the "stalemate [was] between the bishop and the ANS [Alaska Native Services] and that the entire matter was not as diabolical as you imply" (AM Collection 14, 78). However, only two weeks later, on June 9, 1950, Conwell sent another letter to Father O'Connor saying that "the state of the question on that business of selling your old church building is still a bit fuzzy" (AM Collection 14, 77).

In the same letter Conwell explained to Father O'Connor that they had "typed up a new deed to be signed by the bishop, incorporating the suggestions made by you and the Village Council, and sent it to Hooper Bay." He then declared "where that deed is now seems to be a mystery . . . this deed was sent to Hooper Bay even before this agreement was. Where is it? . . . there is nothing in the file indicating whether you and the Village Council approved the wording of the bill of sale." He ended the letter by stating:

> The deed and bill of sale will not at that time [after receipt of the first payment to the Catholic church] be delivered to the Village Council, but they will be placed in escrow with Behrends Bank, Juneau (in order to safeguard our interests, as required by the bishop), until such time as the other two payments of $1,500.00 each have been made. When full payment has been made, the deed and bill of sale will be delivered to the Village Council. (AM Collection 14, 77)

Clearly, the bishop was not the only one who was irritated. The Village Council and community members probably expected these kinds of blunders and delays on the part of outsiders. The Yupiit of Hooper Bay had come to expect this kind of ignorance and imposed control. This incident was just another example of the kinds of relational tensions that characterize outside, historic control. The most significant point here, however, is that community members reclaimed the building completely. Regardless of what was taking place between the church and the government, "they believe[ed] that they already own[ed] the building." Father O'Connor went on to say that "the Eskimos are mere pons [*sic*]" (AM Collection 14, 79), but he failed to recognize the years of control the community exercised over this building, irrespective of a deed of sale. Perhaps it was the bishop who played the role of pawn.

The following month Father O'Connor himself would establish who was truly in control of this place as he wrote a letter to Reinhold Brust, acting area director for the Bureau of Indian Affairs. O'Connor informed Brust about the status of the old church by declaring:

> Incidentally, the village took over the building completely after they signed the original contract in Oct. 1948. They have already been in complete possession of the building since that date. I was even forced to take out some of my stuff that I had in storage there. (AM Collection 14, 87)

Anthropologist Ann Fienup-Riordan noted a similar example when she was given sleeping quarters in the pottery workshop building at the village of Toksook Bay on Nelson Island during the mid-1970s. Like the old church/post office building at Hooper Bay, the building at Toksook was used to house outside visitors. "Incapable of housing Western industry as a design school," the building had quickly been claimed by the men of the community and used as a communal gathering place (Fienup-Riordan 1990, 38–39).

In 1955, the Little Flower Mission of Hooper Bay once again welcomed a new priest. Father Hargreaves entitles his account of coming to Hooper Bay "In the Midst of Things" as he describes his new living quarters. "Alexis showed me my quarters—or should I say 'two bits' worth? For, there's a bit of a social hall, and a bit of sleeping quarters, my room. Pace it: four steps long, and two strides wide. Talk about compact!" (AM Collection 14, 26). Clearly this place was no longer controlled by the church. It belonged to the community members. The new priest was given a space, but it was defined and limited. The old church's status as a "living quarters" was now secondary to its purpose as a community space.

As noted in the aforementioned narrative about the kass'aq woman who kept getting locked out of the old building at night, church workers and visiting priests continued to be housed in the old church building. In the early 1970s a visiting priest, Father Ambrose, described his arrival in Hooper Bay (Ambrose 1971):

> Our journey ended beside the Alaska Native Store, a few paces from the building which housed the Church, rectory, and post office, a relic of the days when the priest had been postmaster. Many hands helped me with my luggage, and [the] Postmistress opened my quarters for me. (AM Collection 14, 393)

Like the continuous flow of outside visitors, the reports of strange and unusual occurrences have continued through time. Several community members have told me that dogs, in particular, often seem nervous or uncomfortable around the old church building. Sometime after the visiting church worker and her dog left the community, another dog was seen barking at this place.

"Something Wasn't Right"

The same teller who told me the story about the white woman and her dog getting locked out of the old church, also described the following incident said to have happened sometime in the 1980s.

> So, it was tied up right, right outside the old church. And, one evening . . . I remember it very well. We all looked out the window and were wondering what the heck this dog was barking at, because it would not stop barking. It was [pause], it looked as if, as the woman had explained [refers to previous tale of the white woman and her dog], its hair was all risen, it knew [he laughs nervously] something wasn't right.
>
> It, it looked very eerie like it, like it was very uncomfortable. Um, it was barking up at one of the windows at the old church. In the upstairs room, in an old office. The dog was, it was just barking there and [pause] we could see where it was barking at, but it wasn't until the next day when the old man [a community elder] told us exactly what he was barking at. And it was . . . the eerie red light . . . And he, that was when he explained to us, um, what the red represents and what exactly it was.

The light (see chapter 5), I have been told, represents something bad (*assiituq*). Others have used the word "evil" to describe this manifestation. Dogs, in particular, seem to be sensitive to its presence. More than once I was told about dogs seen barking nervously at the "old church." I recorded the above story of the old church in 2001, but only discovered a historic church record regarding dogs several years later. In September of 1934 a member of the Sisters of Our Lady of Snows wrote the following account of Father Fox's "order" regarding stray dogs in Hooper Bay:

> As village dogs continue doing much damage by breaking into igloos of absent people, and even into our Mission [building] during night. Order is issued by Father Fox with backing of teacher that henceforth any loose dog is to be shot, if not loose accidentally. Father gives out 15 chains on credit and not a loose dog left in village by bedtime. What a blessing! (AM Collection 14, 620)

We can only speculate as to how the actions of this priest were understood by Yupiit at this time, but it is compelling to think about the ways that some community dogs did (and do) react to "the old church." No one has ever explicitly explained to me why dogs are so sensitive to the events surrounding this particular place. It is interesting to note, however, that Lantis recorded at Nunivak Island specific beliefs surrounding dogs and their particular abilities. She states that "the spirits who became helpers of angakok [shamans] were varied. Some that were specifically mentioned by shamans were dogs" (Lantis 1946, 200).

I recall the words of a woman in Hooper Bay some years ago and her warning about dogs. She never explicitly said that there was any particular association between dogs and the powers of shamans. She did, however, talk about bad signs in relation to dogs. Her elders had become very uneasy when this one particular dog "cried like a human being." This dog had been taken out and shot. Ethnographic description from the Koyukon region bears some similarity in relation to dogs. There, I was told about a dog that was obtained from one of the Yukon River villages. The owner, unaware of the dog's origin, had noticed that the animal was hostile towards him. Eventually he inquired as to which village and which family the dog had originated from. He soon learned that the dog had come from a woman who was known to have bad powers. Their families had long been rivals. Upon learning this, he immediately destroyed the dangerous dog (pers. comm. 2004).

In my discussion of shamanism, I presented two very distinct narratives about Yupiit who were attacked by dogs. There is probably a strong connection here between dogs that "cried like a human being" and those that have "human heads." Dogs seem to both hold the potential of being a dangerous threat and have the appropriate awareness to sense present dangers. Readers may recall, for example, the narrative about places "where nobody camps." As the Yup'ik travelers began to sense some kind of danger, they noticed that their dogs were already extremely agitated by their present surroundings. The teller states that "then during that period they [the Yup'ik hunters] could feel that spirit, you know, someplace around them. Their dogs also were scared, you know. They were down on the ground, scared and barking a little."

Readers may also recall that the *ircinrraq* sitting on the steps was spotted because of all the "ruckus" caused by the dogs at Hooper Bay that particular night. In 1950 a man from Hooper Bay told Helen Oswalt that "when dogs howl at night, if you get down and look 'through' their eyes, you can see the ghosts they see" (Oswalt 1951, 11). Stories and statements such as these point to the notion that dogs have some kind of deeper awareness or insight that sets them apart from other creatures. If dogs can sense the presence of spirits, then we know why Hooper Bay dogs are incessantly barking at that old church. Something isn't right!

Clearly there is an ongoing concern over the place known as the "old church." One day in 2003 when we were working on a budget for an upcoming proposal, a young man came into the office. I had never met this community member before and I was a complete stranger to him. We all started talking about office space, and the subject of the "old church" was once again raised. Without any knowledge of my background or experience there, he made it clear that it was not a place where he would want to work.

He told me that the place really scared him and that "they had kept bones in there." I asked, "Who put bones down there?" This young man abruptly stated that he did not know. His discomfort was obvious. At that moment someone else passing by the doorway jokingly told him that "maybe it was Brother Oscar" who had put those bones in there. He looked at me and I shook my head, saying, "I know those stories." He whispered to me that the religious statues were "scary," and without hesitation, I agreed. He added that one of them had "talked or something" and that (he whispered) they had thrown it away. He then laughed nervously as he described to me all of the strange noises that had been heard at that old church. Another person walked in the room and we turned back to our work.

In 2004, another man from Hooper Bay told me that a lay volunteer who had been living in the "rec. room" noticed her dog was uneasy. She began to hear noises and, thinking that someone had broken into the "old church," went down to the basement to inspect. This teller then explained that there was a "large statue of the Blessed Virgin" stored in the basement and that her dog went crazy upon seeing it. "His [the dog's] hair was standing up, it was just growling and looking at that statue!" It was determined that there was "a spirit in that statue" and the church volunteer "made the maintenance people get rid of it at the dump."

When I returned to Hooper Bay in July of 2015, after several years away, I was surprised to learn that the old teacher housing, where I had once stayed with the school principal and his wife in the mid-nineties, was now owned and operated by the Sea Lion Native Corporation as the new hotel. Even more ironic, I ended up sleeping in the same room where I had first stayed almost two decades earlier. This time I shared the room with a Yup'ik elder who was visiting from another village far to the north near St. Michael. As I lay in bed that first night back in Hooper Bay, I thought about the old school which had been located only a stone's throw from my window. The old school and many buildings around it were completely destroyed by fire in August of 2006. This devastating fire destroyed not only the K–12 school, but also over a dozen homes and other outbuildings. When community members finally extinguished the flames, this section of the teacher housing was one of the few nearby structures that remained. The other was the old church. Father Gregg D. Wood, S.J., in a 2008 interview with the *Juneau Empire*, said that "the fire stopped about 400 feet short of the church thanks to providential weather." (DeMarban 2008).

Still wide awake, I recalled how during my first stay in this building (then teacher housing), I'd complained to a friend in Hooper Bay that the outdoor security light went on and off all night long, alternately lighting up my bedroom and making it nearly impossible to sleep. In the weeks that followed, more stories about this place found me.

Local knowledge is reinforced through regular tellings of narratives about encounters with ghosts. These narratives, shared with me numerous times over many years, taught me something important about how people relate to places, but also how places relate to people. My "roommate," clearly still awake, turned in her bed and whispered to me, "You can't sleep either?" I replied that I could not, at which point she whispered, "Ya know the locals told us this place is *really* haunted. It used to be where the teachers lived." I whispered back, "Yes, I know."

10

What Haunts These Places?

CULTURAL ENCOUNTERS AND NARRATIVES OF RESISTANCE

> "The past makes itself felt in the present, even while the present may react back against the past." (Giddens 1979, 70)

> An Elder from my community once told me a story she heard from her grandfather about the arrival of the first priest and changes [that] began to happen. The first thing they did was to cut off the long hair, from the men and throw it into the water. I think about this often, this was the beginning of taking our traditions and our beliefs and throwing it out, as if it had no meaning. I don't know how people might have coped with this change; they were giving up one set of beliefs for another. People were forced to suppress their own beliefs for another. How does one heal from something like this?

An Alaska Native woman recently shared this sentiment with me as she reflected on cultural encounters and the "replacement" efforts of missionaries in her village. With the arrival of such outsiders came the establishment of new kinds of places that represented the outside world and inevitable change, some of it undoubtedly painful. Morrow and Schneider remind readers that "oral traditions are only meaningful when they connect people, places, and events in changing relationships" (Morrow and Schneider 1995, 224–25).

This long history of cultural encounters is embodied in the oral traditions of Hooper Bay, particularly the narratives about contested places, which reflect these events and the changing relationships that characterized them. The narratives remain resonant because the tensions remain. The new places, particularly the "old church" and school building, became tangible representations of the tensions and historical conflict that characterized the early years of missionization in Hooper Bay. Hooper Bay was a particularly contentious place. Several historical factors and conflicts led to this contentiousness.

In chapter 3 I described a conversation with a Hooper Bay community member about a young girl's sudden death and the fear expressed by village elders (see discussion about health and disease in that chapter). A few days after that discussion, I found myself in another, about the recent outbreak of influenza in Alaska (winter of 2004). This time, a non-Native man in his mid-fifties explained to me that his friends had just returned from the village of Hooper Bay. They had been out in the village to do missionary work for their church. He spoke with authority as he explained why the recent influenza outbreak was such a problem in the villages. This man had never set foot in Hooper Bay himself, nor did he have any idea that I had spent a great deal of time in the community. But he stated to me that "they live in tiny, cramped houses and never go outside." This was his explanation to me about why cases of influenza had occurred in southwestern villages again.

I was struck by the similarities between this outsider's fairly recent remarks and those of the Jesuit missionary, Father Keyes, in April of 1920. In a letter to John Kilbuck, Keyes argues for the merit of eliminating *Elriq*, known as "The Ceremony of the Dead" (Fienup-Riordan 1990; Lantis 1947; Mather 1985; Morrow 1984), also referred to as "*Aithûkatûkhtûk*, the Great Feast of the Dead" (Hawkes 1913, 1). Among his many arguments, Keyes states that this ceremony leads to a "health loss." He goes on to say that "the people gather in cabins or kashims [men's house, also known as a qasgiq, also used as a community ceremonial space] for hours and hours consumedly infecting each other while they relax. They live in dirty houses all packed indecently" (Kamerling and Elder 1989; AM Collection 23, 0743).

What outsiders say about the impact of disease reflects a superficial understanding of the ways that Yupiit maintain health and wellness.

Such discourse is very telling, however, in understanding a history of tension with the outside world. The kass'aq who attributed the recent outbreak to housing conditions displayed an ignorance that is both deeply rooted in history and still expected by Yupiit. Although eighty years have passed since Keyes wrote to Kilbuck, there is a startling continuity in these two statements about the causal effects of epidemics in Alaska Native villages. It directly contradicts the Yup'ik sense that it is better to stay indoors until one is fully recovered. These missionaries' pejorative attitudes served as a justification for actively changing the existing social structure.

Two Tiers of Historic Conflict and Tension

The archival collections from the Jesuit Oregon Province Archives at Gonzaga University, which I have researched, point out two major tiers of conflict in Hooper Bay. The first, and most obvious, tension arose from the contact between Yupiit and non-Yupiit. This was characterized by an active campaign on the part of missionaries, both Catholic and Protestant, to wipe out and replace Yup'ik cultural beliefs, customs, and language. In chapter 6, for example, I discussed the struggle between missionaries and Yup'ik shamans, who became targets for elimination. They were blamed for circulating "stories about the diabolical work of those intruding white people" (John P. Fox Collection 2017, 484).

Another tier of conflict at Hooper Bay involved the battle between the Catholics and the Protestants to convert the people of Hooper Bay. This struggle tore at the very fiber of the community, also leaving a lasting mark on places like the school and church.

Early missionaries working in the Yup'ik region were probably unaware of just how much they upset people. They often assumed that Yupiit were compliant and willingly accepting of Christian conversion. They were then puzzled when a Yup'ik person seemed to act in a contradictory manner. Yupiit whose actions did not match their compliant words were then viewed as noncompliant and cast as incapable of making choices in the matter of "true" conversion. Fienup-Riordan has stated that "the [Yup'ik] value placed on the appearance of agreement partly explains the verbal assent missionaries sometimes received to their proposed reforms, followed by no real change in a person's behavior" (Fienup-Riordan 1990, 74).[1] She goes on to say that "Yupiit probably deeply resented (though they did not say so) the rude intervention of the missionaries, which ran counter to their own highly refined system of indirect, yet nonetheless effective, interaction" (Fienup-Riordan 1990, 74). In addition, these missionaries would not have seen how their own beliefs and practices fit into the existing worldview of Yupiit; recall, for example, how the act of spitting was understood very differently by the two parties.

A Spirit of Resistance: Words and Stories Empower People

Folklore often serves as a form of personal and political power in settings where people have endured a history of domination. The Yup'ik narratives about human-made places that represent the intrusion of outside forces serve this function, as well. The following description of the dominating forces that brought change to Hooper Bay will help to set the stage for understanding how such place-based stories empower Yupiit.

A Teakettle at Hooper Bay: The Past Makes Itself Felt in the Present

As Morrow reminds us, "implicit differences in cultural logic make explicit differences in the way people are treated" (Morrow 1992, 69). The effects of interactions between missionaries and Yupiit came from both implicit and explicit differences in attitudes and actions. In chapter 7 we saw how narratives highlighted kass'aq ignorance and disrespect for the ways of Yupiit. Readers won't be surprised to learn that Father Fox himself once took a teakettle from a Yup'ik Eskimo grave at Hooper Bay and then boasted of his actions. Fox did so explicitly to demonstrate for Yupiit that their beliefs and cultural practices (proper treatment of the dead) were nothing more than "old superstitions" that needed to be replaced. In 1942, Fox described a Hooper Bay grave on the tundra, writing that among the funerary objects, there was "an old net, [and] a tea kettle" (AM Collection 14, 455). Fox went on to say, "I cleaned up the scattered articles [funerary objects] and took them home. Eventually somebody got them. Nor did any spooks come to bother them" (AM Collection 14, 455).

An overt and complete disrespect for Yup'ik culture was part of the missionaries' plan. Very public displays such as Fox's collection of funerary objects commonly characterized missionization efforts throughout Alaska. Jesuit missionary Father Lonneux, like Fox, bragged about his ability to make a fool of a "medicine man," writing, "with a thermos bottle of hot tea I once fooled an Eskimo medicine man. He had never seen a thermos. Making magic passes while quickly concealing the top and cork, I poured into the cup of an onlooker who quaffed loudly" (AM Collection 37, 350). During a 1990 conference session on the spirituality of Alaska Native peoples, Phyllis Morrow recounted a similar tactic by Father Segundo Llorente (1990):

> In the 1930's, Spanish priest Segundo Llorente regaled students at Akulurak, the Catholic mission, with classically horrific European ghost stories given a local twist, some concerning "medicine men who felt that they were losing their power, so they would go to a graveyard on moon-lit nights to dig up some bones, crush them with a hammer, and eat them; whereupon they regained their power to make incantations." (1990, 49)

Christian missionary Sheldon Jackson's "replacement theory" (which later became an official policy of the United States government in Alaska after 1884) was based on the idea that "while we throw down, we also rebuild; while we dispossess, we replace a hundred fold; while we remove weakness, disease, deformity, we confer wealth, strength, and beauty" (Cox 1991, 30). This "policy" reflected a broader attitude that had accompanied missionaries from the start: "white" culture was seen as superior. These acts of disrespect for a way of life hurt people then and this pain has been passed on from one generation to the next.

One writer described how, in this kind of alleged "rebuilding" process, cultures become "economically marginalized, lose access and control of natural resources, lose traditional culture and languages, are designated as deviant, and are criminalized by the dominant society" (Lee 2000, 2).

Such actions and attitudes have indeed had a lasting and ongoing impact on Native communities. Harold Napoleon writes about the devastation brought about by exposure to outside diseases and forced change. Following Napoleon's discussion, Walter Soboloff reminds us that people continue to suffer "another wave of destruction due to alcoholism and drug abuse" (Soboloff 1991, 37). Napoleon also writes about the white people who were present at the time of the "Great Death." He states that they (kass'aqs) were few in number, but that they "took advantage of the demoralized condition of the survivors to change them, to civilize them, to attempt to remake them" (Napoleon 1991, 17–18).

As past injustices are revealed, Yupiit experience new pain. Upon learning of Father Fox's grave-digging endeavors, one well-respected elder in the village told me, "To find out what the priests have done in the past is shocking and appalling. If our ancestors, at that time, knew what underhanded activities the 'trusted' priests were doing . . . how devoted and sincere would our ancestors have been? In my view, our ancestors would have beheaded and cast out the Catholic faith" (pers. comm. 2003). This is a very direct and forceful statement. In many regards, it is uncharacteristic of the speaker's usual manner of discourse, but it reflects the deep anger and betrayal that so many feel in this region and beyond.[2]

Another Face: Defining Power and Power Relations

An overt attempt to achieve "compliance" is one face of power, what Giddens described as "the capability of actors to secure desired outcomes in interactions with others" (Giddens 1979, 89), but the second face of power is what characterized the initial contact and missionization period in Hooper Bay. This is what Bachrach, Baratz, and Giddens call "the 'mobilisation of bias' built into institutions." This is a sphere of "'non-decision-making': of implicitly accepted and undisputed practices" (Giddens 1979, 89). Such practices exemplify the kind of power that was exercised by the church throughout the Yup'ik region at the time of contact. Time and time again I have asked myself how a priest like Father Fox could have acted in the way he did. Understanding these two faces of power helps explain how and why the Jesuit efforts were so strong and why they had such a lasting impact in the community. The practices that comprised the conversion process were "implicitly accepted and undisputed" for those who dedicated their lives to this campaign.

Candy, Bullets, and Medicine: The Control of Community Resources and Unseen Advantages

Missionaries exercised control not only over the church, but also in relation to goods and resources. In Hooper Bay a single priest could exercise control over many because he controlled certain resources. As Giddens points out, "the exercise of power is not a type of act; rather power is instantiated in action, as a regular and routine phenomenon. It is mistaken moreover to treat power *itself* as a resource as many theorists of power do. Resources are the media through which power is exercised, and structures of domination reproduced" (Giddens 1979, 91). The control of resources was explicit in Hooper Bay: at the Little Flower Mission, Fox wrote of "rationing rations" and the "restricted use of necessities of life" (AM Collection 14, 412). In October of 1933 it was recorded in the Hooper Bay church diary that "Fr. Fox [was] working and directing the work at the igloos: all are anxious to help in order to get some tobacco or some tea" (AM Collection 14, 603).

Part of the question of how so few could dominate so many comes from understanding historical events of the time and the control over limited resources in Hooper Bay. As previously stated, disease took a heavy toll on community members during this time period. Harold Napoleon reminds us that "famine, starvation, and disease resulting from the epidemic [the influenza epidemic of 1918 referred to as the "Great Death"] continued to plague them through the 1950s, and many more perished" (Napoleon 1991, 11). In 1941, a priest at the Little Flower Mission wrote that "in the past two years we have had so many epidemics around here, (measles, Diphtheria, German measles, and some other infectious diseases that so far doctors here [at Hooper Bay] have not been able to diagnose)" (AM Collection 14, 434).

Birth and death records for Hooper Bay clearly demonstrate the vast and widespread impact of disease. Tuberculosis and measles spared no one. Some families lost several members within a matter of a few days. This became an unseen, accepted advantage for the missionaries since they controlled the distribution of medicines. Medicine was apparently a resource that tipped the scales in the power balance during the 1920s, 1930s, and 1940s at Hooper Bay. Missionaries like Father Fox manipulated community members through the control and limited distribution of much-needed medicines.

The church sought to maintain social control through the allocation of other resources in Hooper Bay, as well. These included, besides the much-needed medicines, food and ammunition. On July 4, 1936, the mission even withheld promised prizes and candy for the Fourth of July children's races. The "mission did not contribute due to friction with chief" (AM Collection 14, 633). More seriously, missionaries controlled access to much-needed food and clothing. Both the Jesuits and the Protestants played this game. Long lists of names tell the story of individuals and families who were known to have "gone over" to the Protestants lured by gifts and promises.

In January of 1936, Hooper Bay individual community members are named as having "turn[ed] back to [the] Protestants, [because] the preacher [was] making clothes for his congregation." The Catholics asserted that "the arguments of the [Protestant] preacher are addressed to the belly or the skin." As a result, Father Fox angrily announced that he was "cutting down on [his own] giving of any kind in proportion to the [Protestant] preacher's increased giving" (AM Collection 14, 630). This, in spite of (or, perhaps, because of) the fact that he had acknowledged "the people are terribly hungry" (AM Collection 14, 593). Fox's actions were in direct contrast to Yup'ik values and beliefs about sharing food. A few weeks later, in the spring of 1933, an entry in the church diary disapprovingly reported that a Yup'ik man, "an ex-catholic caught two seals [and] thought it would be a good idea to spend Easter by giving a share to those poor hungry people" who were "short of food" (AM Collection 14, 594).

"Don't Know If Fox Scalps Are Any Good or Not": Catholics vs. Protestants at Hooper Bay

Although the Russian Orthodox presence was indirect and intermittent in parts of the Yup'ik region, it was the only active mission group in southwest Alaska until 1884. It wasn't until after Sheldon Jackson, the general agent for education in Alaska, invited Protestant churches to open missions and schools around Alaska that the region saw a steady influence. He appealed to the Moravians to consider mission work in the Nushagak and Kuskokwim River areas. Farther to the north, on the Yukon River delta, the Roman Catholic church opened a mission at Kanelik in 1891. Two years later, they moved to Akularak. When a boarding school was built at the mission in 1896, students came from as far as St. Michael and Nelson Island to enroll.

Hooper Bay was first visited by Catholic missionaries sometime around 1890. The United States government established a school there staffed by Lutheran (Swedish Covenant) teachers in the early 1900s. For many years, therefore, the Jesuit missionaries urged that a Catholic mission, with a school, be established in Hooper Bay. According to the *Alaska Shepherd* newsletter, the mission was finally established in 1928.

At Hooper Bay, conflict and tension arose from the struggle between the Catholic and Protestant churches as they were constantly pitting community members against one another. "Very stormy and cold. Rest as usual," wrote a sister at the Hooper Bay mission (AM Collection 14, 593). The "rest" entailed account after account of the stormy relations between the competing missionaries at Hooper Bay. This community conflict permeated every aspect of life. According to one sister, the "Protestant gossip [was] terrible" (AM Collection 14, 631).

Even the weather was seemingly controlled by these battling religious factions.[3] In March of 1933 the Protestants held a conference at Hooper Bay. Father Fox, announcing the Protestant conference, had told his church goers "it might be a good idea for you to pray for bad weather during that time" (AM Collection 14, 593). According to the Jesuits, the "Protestants here boast: 'Brave Protestant!' you Catholics prayed for bad weather, but they [converted Yupiit] came anyhow." Even the aforementioned Catholic church bell at Hooper Bay had to compete with the presence of a Protestant bell. A Catholic wrote in the church diary that the "entire village attends [their event] in spite of Protestant bell" (AM Collection 14, 634). These tensions tore families apart as people felt external pressure to conform to the rigid doctrine of one group or the other. Fox described one woman's struggle at Hooper Bay in 1934, stating that "she proved herself a good staunch Catholic, though during her long illness living in a Protestant family, and cared for by her Protestant parents, always resisted their invitations and prayers" (AM Collection 14, 609). In the eyes of the missionaries it was an all-or-nothing proposition. You were either with them or you were against them.

In the village of Hooper Bay, it seems that this tension began to surface in the late 1920s when the Catholic Church raced to establish a mission in the village before the Protestants laid claim to the community of "about 130 souls." "Opposing religious forces are coming into my district very fast . . . can we hold the ground won?" (John P. Fox Collection 2017, 1110). One Hooper Bay missionary wrote that "when our mission here was founded in 1928 the work before us was to win back from the Lutheran mission our 'Baptized pagans.' With the Protestant poison already in their veins, the work has been incomparably harder here than in other parts of the district where people were merely ignorant, but not prejudiced" (John P. Fox Collection, 507).

The village of Hooper Bay served as the Catholic district's headquarters. The Jesuits referred to this region as "the Hooper Bay District" and it encompassed the smaller villages of Chevak, Scammon Bay, Paimute, and Mountain Village. The church also considered the many seasonal fish and berry camps as a part of their domain. Records indicate early frustration on the part of missionaries who sat virtually alone in Yup'ik villages as people dispersed for their important seasonal hunting and fishing activities. Eventually obtaining boats and dog teams, Jesuit priests followed their flock to these seasonal subsistence camps to administer the word of God. The Jesuit missionaries made sure that they made it to fish camp before the Protestants got there!

These bitter contests between the Jesuit and Protestant forces lasted for many years in Hooper Bay. Father Fox, writing about the conflict in the community, said, "Don't know if Fox scalps are any good or not, and so don't just see what they hope to gain, except that the teachers [Protestants] came here to grind an ax, which they hope to use on my scalp" (AM Collection 14, 445).

Fox goes on to complain of his continual trouble with the Protestants giving away Bibles, and of "Protestant boys pulling away some of the Catholic girls" at Hooper Bay (AM Collection 14, 624). According to the Catholics, the "Protestants [were] particularly active [in] lying in an attempt to draw away people from the mission" (AM Collection

14, 631). "I do not think," Fox wrote, "that any amount of labor at the mission is going to keep a lot of them from drifting away from the church due to almost constant collusion between the government school and the Protestant mission here" (AM Collection 14, 430). The tension between Catholic and Protestant forces persisted as late as the mid-1950s, when a Jesuit priest wrote that "the Protestant don't cause any trouble but they remain Protestant" (Hooper Bay Collection Part 1, 36).

Community Control and Empowerment at Hooper Bay

Native peoples who have experienced dramatic and devastating cultural change are often portrayed as passive players in the game of conversion. It is often assumed that there is no agency on their part; that they merely endure cultural and spiritual loss. In Hooper Bay, I believe there is ample evidence to suggest that Yupiit were neither unaware of this power struggle nor completely powerless in what was a complex, two-way relationship. I argue that at least some of the stories not only express tension but also result in individual and/or group action. One question that this raises is the notion of what constitutes action. I will argue that people don't need to take up arms or incite a riot to be identified as actors. In fact, people exercise agency in a multitude of behaviors that are informed by their particular worldviews. I propose that nonparticipation (or partial or limited participation), for example, is as much an action as participation. Both behaviors signal agency on the part of the actors. When Yupiit chose not to participate, their action did not go unnoticed. A frustrated priest wrote that "many children miss mass today; they are lazy and the parents irresponsible" (AM Collection 14, 652). Following Giddens's argument, we must recognize that

> power relations . . . are always two-way, even if the power of one actor or party in a social relation is minimal compared to another. Power relations are relations of autonomy and dependence, but even the most autonomous agent is in some degree dependent, and the most dependent actor or party in a relationship retains some autonomy. (Giddens 1979, 93)

Church records clearly document that the Hooper Bay community members exercised autonomy and group-level power, in spite of the church. In 1934, several related disputes erupted between Hooper Bay community members and the Catholic Church. This was an ongoing dispute in which community members insisted, among other things, that they receive some financial compensation for their labor. The church position was that they should willingly do this work "unpaid and for the Lord." In August of 1934, a member of the Sisters of Our Lady of Snows wrote the following in the convent diary of "Big and Small Happenings" at the Little Flower Mission of Hooper Bay: "11th Sat. Calm weather. We begin tearing siding off north wall of chapel to prepare for new addition to [building]. Some of the boys volunteer to help unpaid and for the Lord" (AM Collection 14, 619). That same month another entry began.

"Working Only for the Love of God"

> Thursday. Great stir among our men; a long meeting [to] protest again against "working only for the love of god," as they say, pay <u>must</u> be given. Father Fox gives a good piece of his mind by Ivan's interpretation, bringing home somewhat to their thick brains that we do work for them without pay, that is only for their help that we have the main part of supplies, even if they give us lots of bother and no gain whatever; that is only to help them that we buy mukluq sealskins, though we have hard time to dispose of them etc. etc. They seem to understand and promise to work gratis <u>next year</u>. Father Fox answers that if things continue as at present, there will be no need of their helping, he himself will bring up what we need in one hour. The afternoon . . . meeting showed that the lesson was learned. [Named "chief" in the village] confessed that he did wrong etc. etc. A good many privately come to state their <u>innocence</u> etc. (AM Collection 14,618)

This is the same "chief" (community leader) who had reportedly already "broken his promise" to the church in spite of the fact that he had been "spoken to several times." "He . . . had promised not to go to the Protestants, but also this promise he broke" (Sisters of Our Lady of the Snows Diary May 1934). Another sister, in September of that same year, writes of yet another conflict in which the community members want to charge the mission for unloading goods at their dock. In the convent diary, the sister pens the following account.

Doing to the Mission as They Expect the Mission to Do to Them

> Several meetings in kazoo [the qasgiq] to settle dispute about unloading our freight; people finally agree that "one good turn deserves another" and that they should at least do to the mission as they expect the mission to do to them. (AM Collection 14, 620)

Historian Victoria Wyatt, in her discussion of Alaska Native wage earners in nineteenth-century Alaska, argues that "Alaskan Indians [and Eskimo groups] who worked in canneries, mines, and other Caucasian industries used their wages to perpetuate and participate more actively in their old customs" (Wyatt 1987, 47). Hooper Bay community members by this time had begun to enter the wage economy and may have seen the mission's expectations of nonwage labor unreasonable, but more importantly this was an effective means of exercising control in the ongoing power struggle. Demanding pay may have been one way to exert local control.

The chief and other community leaders at Hooper Bay developed other strategies for establishing and maintaining control as well, in spite of the efforts by the church. The following incidents illustrate forms of resistance in which Hooper Bay community leaders matched the actions of the missionaries.

Driftwood on the Beach: Another Battle at Hooper Bay

In October of 1939, the "chief" (a community leader) at Hooper Bay went to the mission with community concerns over the dwindling supply of driftwood, the only source of wood, critical in this treeless region. Fox himself documented the event, writing that "we still had a little pile [of driftwood] or two left and were hauling that in when the chief, and I guess some men came: 'Father, he began, didn't you finish your wood yet?' 'Why do you ask?' I replied. 'Well, if you want wood you should buy it from the people.'" Fox responded in the following way to these Hooper Bay community members:

> How come? Doesn't the lord send that wood there for anybody that is not too lazy to go out and pile it and bring it in later? You know that out of consideration for you folks I have never used any of the wood from the beach except a bit for fish rails and kindling. But I have not relinquished my right to it. I buy my coal at Seattle for $18 a ton, and by the time it is delivered here at Hooper Bay it cost me $59 a ton. And what for? To warm the skins of you folks. . . . No . . . you are wrong when you claim all the wood on the beach belongs to the village. . . .
>
> And I guess you understand to what extent I can depend on wood from the beach. It is there, but generally in small amounts. And though I have a right to use it as much as anyone in the village, perhaps more, still I could easily burn all [the driftwood on the beach] by myself, all the wood that is there. (AM Collection 14, 513)

Fox's attitude here reflects his assumed position of a "superior" to a "subordinate." Essentially he has the power to use all the resources, but refrains out of benevolence.

The "chief" at Hooper Bay based his argument on his own cultural logic relating to resource use and Yup'ik notions of "ownership." Driftwood has always been a particularly valuable resource at Hooper Bay. At Nunivak, Lantis reported that "driftwood was bartered within the village, particularly when it was requested for a sweat bath to be given as a celebration, since then a man would pay well for the wood" (Lantis 1946, 169). This "battle" over a single resource exemplifies the kinds of ongoing tensions that existed between local leaders and the missionaries of this time period. Missionaries knew that local emerging leadership threatened their stronghold. Exercising control over any resource was a public demonstration of power on the part of the missionary.

The Yup'ik community leader's response was an overt "expression of resistance" directed at the church.

Jean Comaroff wrote, "As has occurred elsewhere in the Third World, the submission to authority celebrated by the Christian faith was transformed into a biblically validated defiance. . . . Yet such defiance had, of necessity, to remain concealed and coded" (Comaroff 1985, 2). Comaroff goes on to say that an understanding of these processes requires an understanding of both the cultural logic behind it as well as the "long-term historical significance" (Comaroff 1985, 2):

> But the coming of Christianity was merely the edge of the colonial wedge; its effects were not to prove containable by such chiefly strategy. To be sure, the mission was an essential medium of, and forerunner to, colonial articulation; it was *the* significant agent of ideological innovation, a first instance in the confrontation between the local system and the global forces of international capitalism. The coherent cultural scheme of the mission—its concepts of civilization, person, property, work, and time—was made up of categories which anticipated and laid the ground for the process of proletarianization. In time, these categories would also provide the basis for expression of resistance. (Comaroff 1985, 27)

Only One Foot in the Church: Exploring Nonparticipation as a Form of Resistance

Numerous entries in the church diaries take aim at the same "chief" in the village. Throughout the 1930s and 1940s, a new form of political leadership was taking shape in Hooper Bay. A traditional council was formed and assumed many of the leadership roles that, in precontact times, would have been left to respected elders and shamans. Like Native villages throughout Alaska, the tribal council was emerging as the governing body. These governing bodies, variously identified as the "traditional council" (most people in Hooper Bay simply refer to it as the TC), "Native council," "tribal council," "IRA council," or "village council," adopted constitutions under the IRA (Indian Reorganization Act) or through their own tribal authority to organize their government. The Indian Reorganization Act of 1934 (alternatively known as the Wheeler-Howard Act), was federal legislation central to what many called the "Indian New Deal." It was defined as "an Act to conserve and develop Indian lands and resources; to extend to Indians the right to form business and other organizations; to establish a credit system for Indians; to grant certain rights of home rule to Indians; to provide for vocational education for Indians; and for other purposes" (IRA 1934).

Those within the church clearly recognized this new political mobilization as a threat. In September of 1935 the church diary notes a "men's sodality organized in the shape of a chief and councillors [*sic*]" where mission records spoke of the newly emerging Hooper Bay leadership as guided "by a chief more Protestant than Catholic, and seven Protestant counselors . . . not one Catholic!" (AM Collection 14, 618). An ongoing attempt to discredit this new "chief" is well documented in the historical writings of Hooper Bay church personnel. In January of 1936, a member of the Sisters of Our Lady of the Snows wrote that the priest at Hooper Bay "repudiates [the] authority of the chief" (AM Collection 14, 631).

The Jesuit missionaries believed that if they were to maintain absolute control, they must win over those who had leadership roles in the community of Hooper Bay. They wrote at length about this chief and his lack of true, devout commitment to the Catholic faith. The chief was blamed for an all-time low in the "general attendance." A Holy Hour was "offered up especially for our fallen-away Catholics and negligent Christians of Hooper Bay . . . [attendance had] never been so poor. Cause? Don't know any special one beyond ordinary laziness. . . . Fr. has begun calling absentees of children at end of service" (AM Collection 14, 653). The chief continued to demonstrate flexible membership in the church, and this greatly annoyed the Catholic missionaries. Fox became so frustrated with this leader that he made an "announcement to the effect that no one going to [the] Protestant church again will receive absolution" (AM Collection 14, 622). Fox knew that this leadership was a direct threat to his own ability to control the community.

An interesting parallel is noted by Jean Comaroff as she examines social and political tensions of the Barolong boo Ratshidi (known as the Tshidi) people of South Africa. Of the Tshidi chief, Comaroff writes:

> But acceptance of Christianity by a chief would be tantamount to his voluntarily renouncing some of the highest political functions, his abdication of authority as king and priest at tribal ceremonies and festivals. . . . The best that a chief could do . . . was to put only one foot in the church, and keep the other outside; to listen to the missionary with one ear and tradition with the other. (Comaroff 1985, 27)

I think this well summarizes the kinds of decisions this Hooper Bay community leader was making during this period of forceful missionization. In fact, I would argue that many people in Hooper Bay during this period kept only one foot in the church while keeping "the other outside; to listen to the missionary with one ear" (Comaroff 1985, 27) and their Yup'ik traditions with the other. Hooper Bay missionary Father Fox wrote of his concerns:

> The chief of the village, [named], had been growing very careless in the practice of his religion. On Trinity Sunday, in spite of a previous warning that the Paschal Season was closing, [the chief] did not come to the Sacraments with the rest of the village. As this was the first case of the kind we had here so far, naturally all noticed it . . . but nothing more was said. (AM Collection 14, 461)

The Present May React Back Against the Past

One can clearly see the cross-cultural tension that characterizes life in Hooper Bay today as much as in the past if we diverge from our traditional sense of what it means to "resist" another, outside force and recognize that resistance is not always achieved through physical, overt means. We see this when, in 1946, Disney came to Hooper Bay to film. A nurse at Hooper Bay wrote that "shortly after their arrival the local Catholic priest, Father John Fox, gave the villagers permission to have a masked dance for the benefit of the picture" (APRD, Alaska Nurses Association Collection 45, 30). Masked dancing and Yup'ik ceremony had not been openly practiced in over two decades. These activities had been disallowed within the first days of establishing the Little Flower Mission at Hooper Bay. The Milottes later wrote:

> There seemed to be an undercurrent of unseen activity. We learned that the older men were busy in the Kasga [qasgiq] carving masks and learning songs. In the evening from 8 to 10 they taught the dancers the motions to interpret the songs. Everyone seemed happy and excited over the coming event. (APRD, Milotte Collection, 31; Fienup-Riordan 1995, 140)

This journal entry suggests that Hooper Bay community members saw this event as an opportunity to gain control over important activities that were in danger of becoming lost forever. The "undercurrent of unseen activity" was real and absolutely necessary to escape the watchful eye of Father Fox, who had spent the better part of two decades trying to extinguish the very practices to which he now gave his blessing. I have often wondered why the dancing took place at Kashunuk instead of being held in Hooper Bay.[4] I think it is quite possible that this place was chosen not only because it was an ancestral homeland for surrounding villages but because of its distance from Fox himself. Perhaps Hooper Bay community members could exercise better control over the masked dancing if they put some miles between themselves and Father Fox. Selecting Kashunuk for rehearsals, then, was yet another purposeful strategy for excluding outsiders and maintaining boundaries.

Returning to the issue of narrative discourse in Hooper Bay, such as the stories of the haunted church, we have seen that it too serves as a strategy for defining and excluding outsiders. Indirect forms of expression allow for communication between Yup'ik community members while at the same time often excluding those who inadvertently represent the tensions, frustrations, and conflicts of the past.

The ability to communicate indirectly through informal discourse can be an especially strong form of local empowerment. At Hooper Bay, the use of informal discourse was one of two such strategies. The second was simply speaking the Yup'ik language, which provided a forum for communication and another means of excluding the "other." This "code-switching," alternating between the Yup'ik language and English in the context of a conversation, served as a highly effective way to maintain boundaries between locals and outsiders.

Between the Devil and the Deep Sea: Speaking the Yup'ik Language

Missionaries struggled to learn the Yup'ik Eskimo language, not to better understand Yup'ik culture, but rather to gain access to those things which they sought to destroy. Language, then, was seen as a tool for the systematic destruction of Yup'ik culture. On April 7, 1948, Father Tennelly wrote: "This is confidential, but I am sure that [the Yup'ik Eskimo language is] just about impossible to learn. . . . My personal conclusion has been for a number of years that the sooner we get the Eskimos away from their impossible language, the sooner we will be able to work among them effectively" (AM Collection 37).

On January 30, 1929, Father Fox wrote the following in regards to learning the language at Hooper Bay:

> I must confess that I have not been making wonderful progress, and I am afraid that I shall have to sit on a hot rock in the next world for not learning the language faster, as much good will necessarily be left undone here until I can handle the language. I am sort of puzzled, I am more or less between the devil and the deep sea. (John P. Fox Collection, 63)

"I Somehow Believed and Did Not Believe": In the Underground Hiding Place

Speaking the Yup'ik Eskimo language was not the only way that Hooper Bay community members were able to protect certain forms of knowledge and belief. In chapter 6, I made the point that certain words and narratives are "guarded" in relation to shamanism. In the wake of missionization, shamanism was forced to go underground. There is reason to believe that Yupiit learned to guard those beliefs and practices that missionaries explicitly sought to eliminate. Historical records, however, point to the fact that missionaries were somewhat aware that such secret practices had not been completely eliminated. Referring to the shaman whose death was celebrated as "the last of his tribe" (see chapter 6), the following 1939–1940 Hooper Bay house diary entry hints at this:

> He was our last medicine man, and all feared him for some reason or another. He went to the sacraments when living at Kashunuk last year, but people say he secretly practiced his old superstitions. He had gone to his fish traps and was found dead sitting on the snow next to his hunting sled. (Hooper Bay Collection Part 2, 526–27)

Shamanism was cast as "the work of the devil" and, as such, singled out by missionaries as a cultural system of belief and practice that must be eliminated. Jesuit priest Menager said, "Yup'iks believed that 'God is far away in His heaven, and the devils are all around us'" (Morrow 1991, 3). The "devils" he refers to are the many spirit beings that inhabit the Yup'ik world.

One missionary wrote, sometime in the 1940s, "We are just now at a critical point in the Christianizing of the Eskimos. They have renounced the devil and all his works and pomps [*sic*]. But there is quite a difference between doing this in word at Baptism and doing it in reality when the time comes" (John P. Fox Collection, 1110). What this missionary did not understand, nor would he have approved of, were all of the strategies that people employ when something important needs protection. Much of Yup'ik cultural practice and belief, in order to survive missionization, had to go underground. Over one hundred years ago, Edward Nelson wrote:

> Services have been conducted irregularly in the small Greek Catholic [i.e., Russian Orthodox] churches at the places named, as well as at one or two points farther southward, but the influence on the Eskimo has been very slight. So far as could be observed, the sole effect of the priestly efforts have been to cause the Eskimo to become more secretive than formerly about practicing their religious rites when in the vicinity of white men. (Nelson 1983 [1899], 421)

Similarly, Lantis wrote about the existence of Yup'ik "secret societies." Concerning these secretive groups, Lantis wrote that "society members might have been putting on a show [ritual performance] for the public, without any element of secrecy being apparent to an outside observer" (Lantis 1947, 27). While certain practices were no doubt secretive, it is likely that things became more so after contact. The difference is the type of secrecy, why things went underground and who was being kept from this cultural knowledge. Taking important cultural practices and beliefs, including the existence of shamans, "underground" is a form of resistance. Elsie Mather, in working with her own Yup'ik elders today, states:

> Our religious feelings and the traditions and customs related to them are usually not talked about openly. What compounded my apprehension [about researching ceremonial practices] was that I had previously ventured to ask some questions about our old beliefs and shamans. I knew many of our customs came from those old beliefs about our origins; what we thought about the dead or how we looked at our world in general. (Mather 1995, 16)

I recently asked some Hooper Bay men about shamanism and if this was something that was talked about when they were growing up in the 1940s and 1950s. One man responded by stating that "people knew" (who the shamans were). "If everybody knows [that they exist and who they are] then *why* is it secretive?" he asked his grandmother when he was young. She never gave him an answer, and he admits that, to this day, he does not really understand why there was this need for secrecy.

Shamanism may have gone underground as a direct response to the attacks of missionaries. Consider the following words written by a Hooper Bay priest, which explicitly acknowledge his attempts to eradicate cultural beliefs and practices:

> One sees at a glance that many of these and similar prohibitions interfere with the proper performance of our religious duties, according to which we have to go to church on Sundays and feast days and do other things that clash with these superstitions. The native who happens to fall under any of these tabus [*sic*] has to choose one of two things: either disregard superstitious practices and incur the displeasure of the medicine man and all the hunters, who will blame that native for

> their bad luck, or carry out the prescribed superstitions and violate the commandments of God. But I get after them pretty hard. As I am a more tangible thing to them than the devil, they can not afford to incur my displeasure. I know the guilty individuals will be very careful not to repeat their superstitions, at least publicly or before any one that might tell me about them. With this I must be satisfied for this keeps at least the children safe from perversion. And missionaries have to be satisfied if in the beginning of a mission among pagans they can stop the progress of superstition. The old folks are hard to change and if the children are well protected, superstition will die with their elders. (John P. Fox Collection, 1110)

"Going underground" is a form of defiance and it is also a brilliant survival strategy. The oppressor cannot attack and destroy what he does not see.

It is true that the Yupiit of Hooper Bay could "not afford to incur [the priest's] displeasure." By limiting access to certain resources, this missionary exercised a certain power over community members. Much-needed medicines, which were, incidentally, kept in the basement of the church, are an important example. If the medicine of their shamans failed to cure the sick, then people were forced to turn to the church. Rather than viewing this as an "all or nothing" form of conversion, however, I would argue that this was a strategy of accommodation. Fox himself acknowledged this when he confessed, "I write 'converting' with quotation marks. For a conversion here, in the ordinary sense of the word, is a rare bird indeed" (John P. Fox Collection 2017, 1101). The employment of this strategy of partial or limited participation is not unique to the Yup'ik people of southwestern Alaska.[5]

A case for this kind of response can be made for contact situations throughout the state of Alaska and well beyond its borders. In fact, a Russian Orthodox priest who questioned one of his Athabascan "converts" described the following exchange: "Then I asked him, 'Do you believe that God is all powerful?' The Kenaitze responded 'Until now I somehow believed and did not believe at the same time, but now I believe'" (Znamenski 2003, 91). We can't know for certain what this Kenaitze man "now" believes or doesn't believe, only that the missionary's confrontation, as was commonly the case, was met with seeming compliance.

Compare an incident recorded by Father Menager in 1927 in which he gathered twenty Yup'ik adults together for an "examination." One Yup'ik man, Chungalrea, "an old seal hunter," was asked if there is a God. He simply responded "*Nau mike*" [I don't know].[6] This answer angered the priest who then proceeded to throw the man out of the church (Morrow 1991, 3). Menager then writes that "this [incident] made a deep impression on all and I never got that answer again" (Menager 1962, 82; Morrow 1991, 3). Phyllis Morrow reminds us that "whether Chungalrea felt more certain of the nature of God after this encounter is unknown; what is clear is that he (and everyone else) quickly learned that priests would not accept indefinite answers to such questions" (Morrow 1991, 3).

What seemed like compliance may simply have been the less confrontational way of maintaining and guarding one's own beliefs, keeping them hidden away and out of sight, in the face of conversion attempts. Yupiit, like many groups throughout the world, placed those things that they value underground. Like the ancestors at the Battle of Hooper Bay, who literally "put the children in the underground hiding place" (Lantis 1946, 307) to keep them safe, so too did the people of Hooper Bay protect their cultural traditions by figuratively placing them underground and away from further harm. What did not go underground were the stories. Some specifically speak to the historical underpinnings of place, but they can be coded. Stories express, at an implicit level, things that otherwise are suppressed.

Ghost Stories and Place: Cautionary Tales and Resistance

I have shown throughout that ghost stories set in contested places serve as a strong form of empowerment. In the case of such stories, told to and about kass'aqs, this empowerment arises from the very action of telling the tales. This action, in being especially aimed at the institutions that symbolize the outside world, constitutes a form of resistance. Various scholars have highlighted the ways in which oral traditions can be shaped for a specific purpose; they may, in particular, reinforce connections to the past while at the same time express current political or social tensions. That is because oral tradition may be "recurrent in form and content, but changeable in performance" and thus in emphasis and effect (Schneider 1995, 189; Toelken 1979, 32).

William Schneider noted a similar theme in contemporary South African tales. Like the Yupiit of Hooper Bay, African peoples have a long history of tension and conflict with outsiders. As in Hooper Bay, the African folklore reflects a sense of place that is intertwined with a history of conflict. Schneider examines a story from the Northern province, in the Giyani region of South Africa, in which white people are said to have caused a drought. The white people, playing the "probable buffoons," steal a baby snake. The mother snake is angered by their careless actions and withholds water. Much like the Yup'ik ghost stories previously discussed, "white people . . . suffered most" as a result of their own foolish, disrespectful actions (Schneider 2002, 131). "The disasters are expressed in terms of White people's wrong actions or bad influence" (Schneider 2002, 132).

Schneider notes another story from the Western Cape that blames severe weather on a white person's actions. In this instance, a "white fisherman caught the mermaid Momlambo and took it out of the water" (Schneider 2002, 131). This caused great rainstorms and flooding conditions. In a third narrative, which is said to have taken place in Venda, the son of a deceased king begins to mix "the traditions" of his people with "Western ways." The ancestors become angered and cause drought and war. The elders of this tribe advise "the king to go back to his traditions and not to follow Western ways. The king returned to tradition, the stream was replenished, and there was peace" (Schneider 2002, 132).

> In each story, White people are blamed for disrupting the natural order, and there are ramifications that affect everyone. Thus, in all cases, the stories provide a somewhat indirect way to talk about Black South Africans' anger with actions of White South Africans. (Schneider 2002, 133)

In July of 1986, Robert Drozda conducted interviews with elder Jack U. Williams Sr. of Mekoryuk (Nunivak Island) (Williams 1986). This Yup'ik elder tells a story in which the constant "hollering" of the *irci*[7] (half-human/half-animal beings) drove the white schoolteacher (Mr. Bird) crazy. Eventually this kass'aq teacher goes out to the tundra, finds the entry passageway of the irci, and pours iodine down into the tunnel where they live, silencing the irci. This partial excerpt is from that interview. Williams is explaining why the irci don't live in the village.

Miriam: But there are no *irciqs* [*sic*] that live in the village!

Jack: No, not now, because of too many loud and too many kind of poison things.

Drozda: What kind of poison things?

Jack: These kind of tin [metal containers], sickness, or something. Something like that. They [irci] used to get loud over there in Nash Harbor. My school teacher is Mr. Bird. In the evening all the time, they holler and holler across the high mountain. They, way no magicians [shamans] cannot stop 'em either. The Mr. Bird he said he gonna be stop it. He take a little bottle, this much high and this much round, iodine. You know iodine? That kind. He was walking alone, make my heart beating! He just cross in the evening, direct to those noisy rocks over there. You can completely see they're getting rocks noise. But inside of that ground [earlier Williams says, "another world under the ground"], there's *irciq's* in there. Half way up he poured that bottle. ["Thud," Jack pounds his fist on table] Automatically noise stopped. From after that [until] now, no more hearing.

That quarters where they lived down there, long old schoolhouse, used to be getting noise all the time too. Just like [demonstrates noise by pounding rapidly on table.] Like this, here's a sound [repeats rhythmic pounding], like this. Sometimes "Aah, waow, waow, waow, waow," you can hear.

Drozda: Were you afraid of that sound?

Jack: Dangerous! They will be scare you. When it's in the night, it will be mountain open underneath, just like electric lights all over. I did walk one time too. Dangerous! Awful dangerous!

Miriam: So they can be dangerous?

Jack: When I remember that, it's like to me I'm gonna came to death. But I'm still alive. If I go to sleep right there, when I get sleepy, I might be gone.
Miriam: You could carry iodine though.
Jack: [Laughter] I don't have any iodine! I carry the leaf tobacco.

Yupiit know that irci are to be respected and, sometimes, feared. What is upsetting here is that this teacher actually poisoned them. When the interviewer jokingly suggested that Jack could also carry iodine, he instead states that he carries tobacco, a sign of respect in many indigenous communities today. Too much noise and "many kind[s] of poison" have brought about change in the world. Like the whites who are responsible for drought and flooding in Africa, whites at Nunivak are responsible for upsetting the natural harmony and balance of the human-spirit world.

In the above narrative Williams also says locals have heard some kind of disturbance at the "old schoolhouse" and that such things are "dangerous! Awful dangerous!" As I have shown, the ghost stories of Hooper Bay also indicate the ongoing presence of danger in the old church and school buildings. These tellings warn people of these potential dangers, but they also, in a sense, "attack" the very tangible/physical representations of the outside world. Churches, school buildings, post offices, and housing developments are not the only places where people see and experience ghosts, but they are very common locations in Hooper Bay and other Yup'ik communities. In a variant of the above baby/mother snake tale, Schneider tells us that when the white people take the baby snake it causes thunderstorms. These "storms are so strong that they even destroy government buildings" (Schneider 2002, 132).

The physical structures at Hooper Bay, which are relatively new marks on the land, are places that serve as a symbolic representation of the outside world, tangible reminders of the dramatic and often devastating cultural change that the community has endured. The fact that these are ghost stories is also significant. When Margaret Lantis recorded Yup'ik narratives in 1946, she noted that "the human ghost (or soul spirit) was not prominent in religion or folk tale" (Lantis 1946, 198). She offers various explanations as to why she found little evidence of human ghosts. She states that "perhaps [this was] because the other world destination of the soul was well known to the survivors and promptly reached by the dead, perhaps because of the belief in reincarnation, the human ghost was not prominent. . . . Of fifty-odd myths collected, only one dealt with ghosts. Although ghosts may not have been an ever-present menace, they were very dangerous when they did appear" (Lantis 1946, 198).

In contrast, ghost stories are certainly common among Yupiit today. A clue to why this may be so rests in an understanding of which places are haunted and which places are not haunted. Few, if any, Yup'ik ghost stories are centered around the traditional qasgiq, perhaps in part because this traditional setting no longer plays a central role in Yup'ik life, but also because the spirits of the dead routinely visited the qasgiq. Spirits were welcomed, invited guests during times of ceremonies and Yup'ik beliefs and practices regulated and maintained the boundaries between the living and the dead. We just don't find stories about ghosts who, uninvited, appear in the qasgiq and wreak havoc on the place.

It seems, from the narratives that have been shared with me, that what haunts the sites of ghost stories are the tensions, conflicts, and pain of both the past and the present. Are there more ghost stories circulating today than in the past? Much more consideration of this aspect of ghost stories is needed before we can say with any certainty that hauntings of place are more common today than in the past. Perhaps these ghost stories began circulating around the time that outsiders first began to gain greater and greater political and economic control in the Yup'ik region. It is worth noting that ghost stories are extremely common in Euro-American folklore. Are Yup'ik tellers also recruiting Euro-American beliefs and traditions against Euro-American tellers? Is this, in itself, a form of active resistance?

What is for sure is that these stories continue to be told on a regular basis. Anthropologist and folklorist William Schneider reminds us that we should pay greater attention to "the reason stories continue to be told," rather than "how long they have to be told to be part of the oral tradition" (Schneider 1995, 189). I will argue here that these ghost stories, which form a local "genre," remain significant as a form of resistance in Hooper Bay. By warning people away, they control and limit the participation and interaction that takes place in these outside institutions. Their persistence is significant and warrants further investigation.

A Contemporary Setting

Many years have passed since "Calamity John" Fox (a nickname given to him by the succeeding priest) sailed away from Hooper Bay (John P. Fox Collection, 554). Yet, the pain and the tensions of the missionary past continue to make themselves known in the present—and they live in places, reflected in the discourse and narratives of the village. These tell us not only about past tensions, however, but also present ones. Narratives about place continue to express strong feelings about outsiders.

Today Hooper Bay community members belong to many radically different religious groups, some simultaneously. This flexible membership does not present conflict for those who choose to attend the Catholic church one week and another church the next. As I have argued in the past, participation seems to vary from individual to individual and, as in the past, the social dynamics are complex (perhaps more so today given that those who proselytize are sometimes Native themselves). Morrow reminds us that "wherever there is more local control, there is a tendency towards tolerance of multiple viewpoints: people attend services and functions of more than one church, for example" (Morrow 1991, 5). If there is tension with this fluid membership in a contemporary setting, I am guessing those who still take issue are the ones who have come to gain converts. Whether they go by the title of missionary, priest, reverend, or something else, the end game is still to win souls.

Formal religion works well in the lives of many today. It serves as a guide and reinforces "right" ways of living. It does not, however, simply replace or preclude culturally Yup'ik understandings of the world. As in the time of Father Fox, participation in any church is never an "all or nothing" proposition. Many Yupiit are devout Christians today, but that has not made them any less distinctly Yup'ik.

I have argued throughout that to understand sense of place in the Yup'ik region, we must know something about the relationships people have with specific kinds of places. Within the context of historic buildings such as the church or the school, deeply held beliefs and understandings about place easily carried over to the historical period and its associated structures. In that sense, they were not unlike the hidden dwellings of spirit beings (at hills or volcanoes) or the abandoned villages with gravesites. Like sites that mark the tundra, churches and schools were also often perceived as places either to avoid or to approach with caution as is evidenced by the associated narratives. These understandings, informed by narrative (and experience), were also transmitted and reified through narrative. Places like the giant footprints, the volcano mountains, and human-made structures are tangible representations of Yup'ik understandings of place, but they are also active and responsive to human actions thus reinforcing those understandings.

Cultural encounters between Yupiit and kass'aqs played out in specific places that became contentious. I demonstrated in chapter 2 how people relate to one another through places. The places where these encounters occurred were new, but multiple narratives about them reflect cultural continuities. As new places emerged, a Yup'ik sense of place gave them meaning. Like their ancestors before them, Yupiit interact with these man-made places, and through their narratives make powerful statements about the health or illness of the world.

11

Sentient Places in a Sentient World

Feld and Basso point us to the necessary links between discourse, power, and place. They remind us that "people don't just dwell in comfort or misery, in centers or margins, in place or out of place, empowered or disempowered. People everywhere act on the integrity of their dwelling. . . . Whether they are embedded in discourses of sensuous beauty or ugliness, in discourses of morality and theft, or in discourses of nostalgia and longing, struggles arising from loss and desires for control are always placed" (Feld and Basso 1996, 11).

A Hooper Bay community member said it best when she told me that "the old church has lots of bad memories in it. Different people have different experiences and once a place has all these, these past experiences that aren't good, then, you know, it just sticks with it. And, so be it. The Catholic Church is haunted. The place that is haunted with all these bad memories and bad, experiences of the past. And, you know, it . . . well, they're both linked. You can't [she laughs], you can't escape that fact."

The old church is a place that has long been invested with significance. This physical place serves to anchor a collective, community memory. This human-made structure serves as a tangible reminder of the social tensions and frustrations of the past as well as the present. As observers of culture, we should always consider how and why places are lived out and experienced in meaningful ways, remembering that stories of places often tell us as much about the present as they do about the past.

In 2015 I was shocked to learn that the old church had been demolished. I'd been back in the village for several days already, but hadn't ventured to that part of town. Standing next to his snow machine, my friend sternly raised his brow when I loudly replied to this news, "*Really, they tore it down*?" Knowing my familiarity with this place and my keen interest in Brother Oscar, he then laughed uncomfortably. I pressed him for further details, "What does this *mean*?" I asked. He said nothing and, sensing his genuine discomfort, I dropped the subject.

A reporter for the *Juneau Empire* wrote of the impending demise of the old church, stating, "A rotting Catholic church built around the time FDR was president is coming down in Hooper Bay, but its storied history won't soon be forgotten. . . . Built above an ancient Yup'ik grave where bones still surface, the two-story church might be the oldest building in the Western Alaska village of Hooper Bay, residents say" (*Juneau Empire*, 2008).

The old church with its distinctive weathered siding no longer stands against the elements, but I strongly suspect that its physical removal is not the end of the story. Archaeologist Paul Mullins, in his discussion of postwar urbanization (the dismantling of American cities), argues that landscape *absences* "provide potentially compelling places to illuminate, interrogate, and acknowledge contested dimensions of the very recent past." Understanding something now about how Yupiit respond to places and how these places respond to people, I can't help but wonder about the future of this site and the narratives that have yet to be told.

A Place Where the Earth Used to Be Much Thinner

The same year I first began working in the village of Hooper Bay, Keith Basso wrote that "time will tell what other cultural constructions await the ethnographer bent on an interest in place" (Basso 1996, 147). It is my hope that I have in this work, at least partially, answered that call. By centering my discussion around the folklore of a particular community and progressively illustrating the relationship between stories and the kinds of places with which they are associated, I hope that I have revealed for my readers new understandings of place. I began with a discussion of places that are general features on the land in areas beyond the village (the volcano mountains and hills). I moved next to a consideration of those kinds of places that are not simply natural features on the land, but rather the kinds of places that have originated from human activity, but since moved more into the realm of the natural-spirit world (graves, abandoned villages, old camps, etc.). Lastly, I asked my readers to see human-made structures in a new light, to see how Yup'ik worldview is extended to these kinds of places as well.

The encounters that happen in these various kinds of places clearly illustrate that Yup'ik sense of place continues to be shaped by a complex and deeply meaningful sense that Ellam Yua, personification of the physical and spiritual world, is everywhere and in everything. Places don't simply remind Yupiit of story. Places in southwestern Alaska are social actors in an ongoing story. Places are imbued with a spiritual quality that enables them to be sentient. Place responds to human thought and human actions.

As I have shown through numerous tellings and multiple narratives, painful realities and human fears are more than mere reflections on the land and in specific places. They are afflictions that places on the land feel and respond to directly. The shaman's grave gets lower because human suffering is felt by the natural-spirit world. The grave is a place of awareness or ella, always listening and always watching. Many times I have been told that the "earth used to be much thinner" than it is today, but why is this so? This sense of place describes a dramatic change in the world, one that serves as almost a call to action. Yupiit are not just describing some kind of physical change in the land, although concerns over topics such as climate change are certainly informed by this important cultural understanding. This particular discourse also makes strong statements about changes in the relationship that Yupiit have with the spirit world.

The ongoing reciprocity between the human and spirit world is in jeopardy when the windows between worlds are no longer open as they once were. Many things have contributed to this sense that their place is changing. Social and cultural ways have been disrupted, so the spirit world and human relationship to that world has been upset.

As people suffer, the land and specific places on the land reflect that suffering. Contaminants seep into the earth and into watersheds along the coast, graves are looted, and, as these things transpire, the spirit world is further disrupted. The narratives of places in Hooper Bay make powerful statements about these disruptions.

> And always these people are thinking—thinking of place-centered narratives, thinking of the ancestors who first gave them voice, and thinking of how to apply them to circumstances in their own lives. . . . [T]hese people now consult the stories as guides for what to do and what not to do in specific situations. (Basso 1996, 140)

Yup'ik narratives of place, like those told by the Apache with whom Basso worked, do remind people about appropriate and inappropriate action and as such often serve as cautionary tales. "The Giant Footprints" continue to be an important place on the land because they speak to people of the importance of following the words of their elders. The Volcano Mountains also speak to Yupiit in this way. Place narratives serve to guide people and minimize ill effects on people, but they also minimize potential ill effects on the land. Throughout, I have argued that what is unique here is the way that Yup'ik places are consulted as guides. The land and specific places are, in essence, beings among beings, and particularly powerful and sensitive ones.

A better understanding of informal storytelling will lead to a greater understanding of Yup'ik culture as it exists today. A deeper understanding of narrative discourse will shed further light on the complex relationship that Yupiit have with the places around them and the outside world. It will enable us to better understand the complexity of cross-cultural communication and the various scenarios that are repeatedly played out in the region. For Yupiit in Hooper Bay, stories are not simply symbolic expressions but, as Elsie Mather says, "Storytelling is part of the action of living" (Morrow 1995, 33).

> Yupiit have long felt the failure of outsiders to understand their traditional ways. This includes our language and traditional stories, which are still very much a part of our everyday lives. In hunting and other subsistence pursuits and even in our

> everyday social activities, the ideas and values which underlie our ancient worldview are always near the surface, still operating to guide us in our behavior and way of life.
>
> Stories are often told spontaneously during daily activities when similar situations are recalled from the past. Admonishments and rules for living are part of the stories. Even when the older people tell about events in modern day, they use references and allusions to old Yup'ik beliefs and their worldview. (Mather 1995, 14–15)

In Hooper Bay, narratives of place empower in ways that go largely unnoticed by the outside world. Outsiders may see a community suffering, but they don't see the ways in which people establish and maintain personal empowerment through a connection to these places. They fail to see the forms of resistance that have empowered the community on a political group level. They may not see the ways that meaning is established and maintained over time, nor do they see how Yupiit continue to find strength in their cultural beliefs and worldview. People in Hooper Bay have always found great strength in their own cultural heritage. Community members today, like those of the past, find hope in the ways of their ancestors. In the introduction to Edward Nelson's *The Eskimo About Bering Strait*, William Fitzhugh wrote:

> The history of Eskimo contact with white society in the North is replete with examples of cultural devastation and its side effects—despondency and alcoholism—caused in part by the loss of traditional values and their replacement by foreign ones forced upon societies by conditions of modern life. Fortunately, to a large degree, Bering Sea Eskimo people have an opportunity to mitigate this loss through their continued retention of traditional life and customs. (Nelson 1983 [1899], 9)

Each March the village of Hooper Bay hosts the Louie Bunyan Festival. Known locally as "LBF," the village festival was named in memory of a respected village elder who fought to protect area fisheries and the Yup'ik subsistence way of life. People from surrounding villages look forward to this festive occasion. *Yuraq* (Eskimo dancing) remains a central aspect of Yup'ik life. Dance groups prepare months in advance and skillfully perform their dances, each unique to their group.Dance leaders lead their dancers to the floor with great pride, often explaining for the audience the cultural significance of the dance moves. Food, as always, plays an important part in this social celebration. Gatherings such as this are characterized by a social atmosphere that reinforces important community bonds, strengthens kinship ties, and affirms the importance of Yup'ik stories.

The old songs and dances of the Yup'ik culture are reinforced and reinvented simultaneously. These are the songs and dances that Father Fox, per Disney's request, had "allowed" people in Hooper Bay to perform. Today people openly express and celebrate their rich cultural heritage once again. Older songs and dance moves are performed alongside newly created ones that express contemporary Yup'ik experience.[1] Since the time of contact, Yupiit have sought ways to retain expressions of traditional life. People in Hooper Bay have always turned to their own culture—their own stories—in order to survive.

Greg Sarris once wrote of Pomo oral tradition that "words and stories poison the healthy, heal the sick, empower lovers, [and] transform the world" (Sarris 1994, 127). In Hooper Bay, narratives of place empower people in the face of fear, hardship, and pain. Many of these narratives are deeply rooted in Yup'ik tradition, yet remain relevant to contemporary lives and issues. The stories guide people and temper emotion. The stories, like the land and certain kinds of places, have a life essence of their own. Like the land upon which they are told, the stories play an active role in the social lives of Hooper Bay community members, still operating to guide behavior and perpetuate a way of life in their place.

In the preface I described how, at the invitation of the Hooper Bay Traditional Council, I returned to give a community presentation on my research findings relating to Hooper Bay objects still housed at the Smithsonian Institution's National Museum of Natural History. This was the very museum Hooper Bay community members and I had visited so many years before and from where, after waiting decades on museum collections storage shelves, the Hooper Bay ancestors had finally departed on their journey home.

FIGURE 11.1. *Yuraq* (Yup'ik dance). Courtesy of James H. Barker 2002

Once again, I found myself boarding a Hageland plane at the Bethel airport with four other passengers: three community members from the neighboring village of Chevak and another from Scammon Bay. From the air I once again observed the vibrant green colors of the tundra and beach grass, the tiny shimmering kettle ponds too numerous to count, and the long stretch of sandy beach that borders the Bering Sea. I strained to locate the old abandoned village I once carelessly explored with friends. Scarcely visible under the long grasses of July, I spied it only for a moment as we passed overhead, the plane casting a brief shadow on that place that was once an active, thriving village. Beyond, I could see the old Quonset huts that marked the community airport and the tiny four-wheelers racing down the narrow road.

Our flight's arrival was greeted, as I had witnessed on my first trip to the village so many years ago, with four-wheelers, pick-up trucks, and dogs chasing behind. Some welcomed home loved ones, others patiently waited as the pilot unloaded their cargo. Here I was, all these years later, awkwardly waiting for someone to claim and deliver me to the Sea Lion Hotel (now located in the center of town near the location of the old school) where I would stay with other visitors to the village. Just about the time I began to give up hope, someone I didn't happen to know asked, "Do you need a ride?" And, just like my first arrival years before, I found myself bumping down the airport road explaining that I was not a nurse or a schoolteacher. As we made our way towards town, I provided the details of my purpose for coming to Hooper Bay. It occurred to me that, despite my close connections and involvement in ongoing community-based projects, I was met on my return in some respects as though I was a newcomer. Although I was soon reunited with old friends, this greeting as yet another itinerant says something meaningful about community expectations, and perhaps the need to reinforce the understanding that most kass'aqs are transient in Yup'ik community life.

When we got to the Sea Lion Hotel, I thanked them for the ride and we parted ways. As I described in chapter 9, upon entering this "new" Sea Lion office building and adjacent hotel, I realized immediately that this very building was the old teacher housing building where I had once stayed with the school principal and his wife.

I sat on a hard bench along the far wall of the office entry, waiting for someone to check me in and show me the way to my room. A man in his late thirties, maybe early forties, approached me, asking why I had come to Hooper Bay. I found myself explaining my purpose and, once more, stating that I was not a health worker for the State of Alaska. He seemed interested in my work and without hesitation pointed to some historical photographs tacked to the white plaster wall behind him. The black-and-white images showed some abandoned semisubterranean houses photographed by visitors in the late 1800s or early 1900s. He turned back to me and said, "Have you ever seen the Giant Footprints out there?" as he pointed back in the direction of the stretch of land that leads to the Bering Sea. I smiled and nodded "Yes, I have seen them." He smiled slightly, nodded back, and quietly said, "They're still out there!"

NOTES

Notes to Chapter 1

1. There are many wonderful collections of Yup'ik stories that have been published (see, for example, Orr and Orr 1995; Woodbury 1992). Another, forthcoming in 2017 from the University of Alaska Press, is Ann Fienup-Riordan's *Qanemcit Amllertut—Many Stories to Tell.* This collection of tales, transcribed and translated by Alice Rearden with Marie Meade, includes well-known tales (stories known as *qulirat*) and other less familiar, more recent tales (referred to as *qanemciit*).
2. While the term Inuit is often used as a general term for cultural and linguistic groups across the Arctic, the name "Eskimo" is regularly used in Alaska. For most groups, Inuit means "people" and is a broadly acceptable ethnonym, although each group has specific self-referential terms. For Yupiit, the word for people is not Inuit, but yuut (the word Yupiit means "real yuut"—similarly, their northern neighbors are Inupiat, "real inuit"). For this reason, while Yupiit may accept the term "Inuit" as a collective reference in global contexts such as the Inuit Circumpolar Conference, they do not otherwise tend to use it as a self-reference. Alaskan Yupiit commonly refer to themselves as Eskimos, a term considered derogatory by most, for example, in Canada. The term "Eskimo" is also still commonly used in some phrases such as "the Eskimo language family" where it is arguably more inclusive than saying the "Inuit language family" (by virtue of including peoples who are not self-referentially "Inuit"; e.g., those who are Yup'ik, Cup'ik, Sugpiaq/Alutiiq).
3. The village of Hooper Bay, in a ten-year agreement with Buena Vista (1992), acquired a reel-to-reel version of the film for "exhibition" and "cultural purposes of the Yup'ik Eskimo people."
4. In the Yup'ik tale of the boy who goes to live with the seals, we are told that "when his parents gave *akutaq* to the shaman, the boy received *akutaq* in the seal world" (Fienup-Riordan 1994, 3).
5. Hensel (1996) provides an excellent discussion of "food as an identity marker" in the Yup'ik region. Barbara Bodenhorn (1989) also discusses food and its importance to identity among the Inupiaq Eskimo.
6. Interestingly, the notion of "oral information systems" is now much more widely recognized in South Africa than in the United States. Even within the library system there is an awareness and treatment of oral communication that parallels that of written forms of discourse.

7. This aspect of colonization (privileging the written word over the spoken word) is also well illustrated in James Clifford's work on group identity among Mashpee (Clifford 1988). As previously mentioned, a Native North American land claims trial was quickly transformed into a trial about Indian identity and the privileging of literate forms of knowledge over oral forms of cultural transmission. Again, the "oral" discourse of one group is scrutinized and forced into a "permanent, 'textual' form" by those representing a "literate" tradition (Clifford 1988, 329). Clifford writes:

    > The Mashpee trial was a contest between oral and literate forms of knowledge. In the end the written archive had more value than the evidence of oral tradition, the memories of witnesses, and the intersubjective practice of fieldwork. In the courtroom how could one give value to an undocumented "tribal" life largely invisible (or unheard) in the surviving record? (Clifford 1988, 339)

8. The fluidity of Mabel McKay's narratives, for example, is well illustrated in several tales (e.g., "The Woman Who Loved a Snake" and "What People of Elem Saw").
9. Many authors have discussed differences between spoken and written words, noting that the effect and emotion of the performance is lost when written down. Meanings conveyed through gesture, intonation, pitch, silence, and posture are lost, as well as the dynamics between teller and listener (Bascom 1965, 1977, 1984; Bauman 1986; Ben-Amos and Goldstein 1975; Briggs 1988; Cruikshank 1990; Mather 1995; Odden 1994; Orr and Orr 1995; Ritchie 1995; Tedlock 1983).
10. For those interested in prosody, see Woodbury 1987.
11. Hirsch and O'Hanlon (1997) note that an anthropological perspective on landscape has only recently emerged within the discipline.
12. Central Yup'ik language contains over two dozen distinct bases for "locating things in space." This unique linguistic feature may reflect a relationship to their particular landscape (Jacobson 1984b, 185).

Notes to Chapter 2

1. Keith Basso writes that "ethnographic inquiry into cultural constructions of geographical realities is at best weakly developed" (Basso 1996, 105); however, anthropologists have been taking more interest in these topics while also acknowledging that such attempts may be incomplete and limited endeavors (Marcus and Fisher 1986; Mather 1995; Morrow 1990, 1995; Toelken 1995, 1998).
2. The rate of suicide in the United States was 12.57 suicides per 100,000 people in 2013 (the most recent year available from the Centers for Disease Prevention and Control). That same year, Alaska's rate was 22.3

suicides per 100,000 people. Alaska had 1,525 suicides between 2005 and 2014—an average of 152.5 deaths by suicide per year. In 2014, the rate of Alaska Native males that died by suicide was 50.9 per 100,000, nearly four times the national average (Alaska Department of Health and Social Services, Statewide Suicide Prevention Council 2016).

3. In an attempt to address this serious health issue, the Yukon-Kuskokwim Health Corporation (YKHC) funded a study in the mid-1980s to collect data and examine the issues related to suicide in the Yup'ik region. A Bethel researcher wrote that "compared to Alaska as a whole, or compared to the United States as a whole, the rate of suicide in the YKHC region is very high, and it appears to be increasing in recent years" (Soule 1986, 1).

   The *Elluam Tungiinun* (Toward Wellness) project, funded by the National Center on Minority Health and Health Disparities, uses the culturally based *Qungasvik* (Toolbox) Manual with a focus on "promoting youth sobriety and reasons for living in Yup'ik/Cup'ik communities." The manual contains over thirty cultural and language-based activities that were designed "to build protection from suicide and alcohol abuse in communities, families, and youth" (Alakanuk Community Planning Group, et al. 2009).

Notes to Chapter 3

1. This community-based project was a collaboration between the Hooper Bay Traditional Council, the Naparyarmiut Mikelnguita Commitiat (Parent Organization of the Hooper Bay Head Start Program), and the Sea Lion Corporation of Hooper Bay. This project also involved young people from the Youth Opportunity Center, who conducted several of the oral history interviews with their own elders.
2. Oswalt reported that people in Hooper Bay do "see polar bear once in a great while." There are two words for "bear," but people told her that the "bear doesn't like to be called the first one. Can't say 'it is'" (Oswalt 1951).
3. ANCSA, passed in 1971, extinguished aboriginal title to nine-tenths of Alaska. The cash settlement established village corporations and twelve regional Native corporations in the state of Alaska (Naske and Slotnick 1994; O'Brien 1989).
4. *Alingnarqellriamek* seems to more closely translate as "those being frightening things" or "those who are frightening creatures." The post base *lria-* indicates "one that is V-ing" (action/being; Jacobson 1995, 508), and *Alingnarqe-* translates "to be frightening" (Jacobson 1984a, 57).
5. Jacobson (1984a) says that the Yup'ik Eskimo word for a tunnel entrance is *pugyaraq*. This is also the word for the neck opening on a *qaspeq* (a pullover-style parka).

6. Jacobson defines *ircinrraq* (singular) as a "legendary little person said to inhabit mountain areas" (Jacobson 1984a, 175). English speakers know *ircinrraat* as the "little people," and stories of encounters with these creatures of the spirit world are commonplace, but people at Hooper Bay have told me that they are not always "little" in the sense of their size and may appear in various forms.
7. This spelling reflects a dialect difference between Hooper Bay and the Lower Kuskokwim region.
8. A "smooth mind" is a particular Apache concept, not to be assumed to be the same Yup'ik understandings of "mind" (*umyuaq*) or "awareness" (*ella*).
9. Many ethnographic works reflect this stage-like sense of the land. Dombrowski, for example, reminds readers that "all landscapes are social landscapes; all relations are social relations" (Dombrowski 2001, 21). The author is discussing the "political landscape" of southeast Alaska villages and the impact of the timber industry. In this case, however, the land is cast as a place upon which the actors act, rather than playing an active role itself in response to clear cutting.

Notes to Chapter 4

1. This Hooper Bay elder was a guide for the well-known naturalists Olaus Murie and Herbert Brandt, who studied the flora and fauna of the Yup'ik region in the early 1920s.
2. The people of Nanwalek call themselves Sugpiaq (*suk* "person" plus *-piaq* "real"). The name *Alutiiq* was adopted from a Russian plural form of *Aleut*. Russians used this term to refer to the Native people they encountered from Attu to Kodiak.
3. Closely related to Central Alaskan Yup'ik, the Alutiiq language is divided into the Koniag and the Chugach dialects. Koniag Alutiiq is spoken on the upper part of the Alaska Peninsula and Kodiak Island (and Afognak Island before it was deserted following the 1964 earthquake). Chugach Alutiiq is spoken on the Kenai Peninsula from Nanwalek and Port Graham to Prince William Sound where it meets Eyak (Alaska Native Language Center, University of Alaska Fairbanks 2016).
4. At the neighboring village of Chevak, community members purified and protected their homes during ceremonial festivities by burning Labrador tea (*ayuq*) (Morrow 1984, 119).
5. There are debates over existing ecological constructs of the Native hunter and game (Brightman 1993), but this is certainly an example of hunting restraint in the face of an unusually large number of possible prey.
6. From Nunivak it was said that "of all the seals, the adult bearded seal rated the highest . . . taking the place in religion occupied by whales along the south and north coasts of Alaska" (Lantis 1946, 173).

7. Jacobson lists the Yup'ik words *puga* (singular) and *puget* (plural) for "surfaced seals" (1984a, 297).
8. This same Yup'ik educator, four years earlier, standing before teachers from New York City, had begun his presentation by stating that "to know self, you have to know place." This parallels Gabriel George's statement about place and identity to Thomas Thornton: "These lands are vital not only to our subsistence, but also to our sense of being as Tlingit people" (Thornton 2008, 3).

Notes to Chapter 5

1. Toksook Bay elder Paul John also tells a story about a being who appears as a head (John 2003).
2. *Malirqeraa* translates to "he is chasing it" (Jacobson 1984a, 223).
3. Robert Brightman, in his discussion of Cree lodges of the nineteenth century, notes that "when the structure is sealed, the only visible opening is the smoke hole." Like the smoke-hole opening of traditional Yup'ik sod houses, for Cree this opening has great significance in relation to the spirit world. Brightman says that contemporary stovepipes have replaced the smoke hole in lodges, tents, cabins, and houses. He draws on this connection between the opening and the spirit world (Brightman 1993).

   Brightman also states that "more needs to be known of the symbolism of doorways in boreal Algonquian cultures, but here the doorway is seemingly a transformation of the stovepipe or smoke hole. It is also significant that Rock Crees are careful to avoid physical contact between the doorway and slain animals introduced into a house" (Brightman 1993, 227).

Notes to Chapter 6

1. Oswalt was told by people at Hooper Bay that "if relatives were recognized, they were not attacked" (Oswalt 1951, 8). This statement is in reference to relatives from Mountain Village.
2. The Hooper Bay elder who told the story of the volcano mountains said the children "missed the path that went into the house, but instead went under the path, in those *qasgi* . . . this was during the war."
3. Oswalt was also told that when a bad medicine man (enemy shaman) was killed, people "could tell from his blood that he was really a bad man" (Oswalt 1951, 10).
4. In 1950 it was reported that some Hooper Bay elders "still use wooden urine buckets" (Oswalt 1951, 10).
5. A community member at Hooper Bay said that a "medicine man can make people have very bad dreams, but people don't pay him to do things" (Oswalt 1951, 5).

6. In Yup'ik lore and iconography, an animal may reveal "its person," showing a human face.

Notes to Chapter 7

1. Note that others instruct one to approach a ghost by walking sideways rather than facing it.
2. The dead were similarly pulled through the smoke hole "by means of cords" (Nelson 1983 [1899], 311).

Notes to Chapter 8

1. Note that use of the terms "church" and "the old church" are specific references to the Catholic Church.
2. Phyllis Morrow remarked that the priest's behavior seems uncharacteristic. Given the Catholic Church's concern with proper burial, for example, why was he not bothered by the unburied remains of another clergyman (pers. comm. May 20, 2016)?

Notes to Chapter 10

1. Active resistance on the part of Yupiit is clear in the accounts of Mountain Boy (Fienup-Riordan 1991).
2. Sergei Kan wrote about the Tlingit stating that "the process of missionization often involves a great deal of misunderstanding and miscommunication between missionaries and natives. This is due to cultural and linguistic barriers, the missionaries' ethnocentrism, and native 'impression management,' frequently aimed at protecting the integrity of the indigenous social life, especially practices attacked by missionaries, while simultaneously taking advantage of the missionaries' material and spiritual assistance. The degree to which natives succeed in their efforts depends heavily on the balance of power between the two groups, the amount of change missionaries wish to introduce into native life, and the susceptibility of the specific Christian symbolic forms to being reinterpreted and indigenized" (Kan 1985, 196–97).
3. While I have worked exclusively with the Jesuit archival records, these accounts are sufficient to point out that there were serious and ongoing conflicts between the Catholics and the Protestants. Note that these only represent the Catholic view on those conflicts at Hooper Bay.
4. Oswalt was told that the "dance lasted from 6 p.m. until midnight" in the qasgiq (Oswalt 1951, 5).
5. As I noted in chapter 3, in critical matters such as medical treatment or conflict resolution, people throughout the world turn to combinations

of traditional and officially sanctioned (imposed) remedies, an agentive strategy typical in colonial settings (Janzen 1978).

6. *Naumiki* or *naumi* translates as "I don't know" (Jacobson 1984a, 254).
7. According to Jacobson, *irci* (Nunivak dialect) are defined as a "legendary creature, one side of which is an animal and the other a man" (Jacobson 1984a, 175).

Notes to Chapter 11

1. Contemporary themes, such as finding one's way home through the sea ice with global positioning system, are commonly incorporated into Eskimo dances.

REFERENCES

Archival Sources

AM, Alaska Mission Collection. Hooper Bay Collection, Microfilm Roll 13. Oregon Province Archives of the Society of Jesus. Gonzaga University, Spokane, WA.

AM, Alaska Mission Collection. Hooper Bay Collection, Microfilm Roll 14. Oregon Province Archives of the Society of Jesus. Gonzaga University, Spokane, WA.

AM, Alaska Mission Collection. Pilot Station Collection, Microfilm Roll 23. Oregon Province Archives of the Society of Jesus. Gonzaga University, Spokane, WA.

AM, Alaska Mission Collection. John P. Fox, S.J., Collection, Microfilm Roll 30. Oregon Province Archives of the Society of Jesus. Gonzaga University, Spokane, WA.

AM, Alaska Mission Collection. Martin Lonneux, S.J., Collection, Microfilm Roll 37. Oregon Province Archives of the Society of Jesus. Gonzaga University, Spokane, WA.

APRD, Alaska and Polar Regions Department. Alaska Nurses Association Collection, Box 45 (Folder 30). Elmer E. Rasmuson Library, University of Alaska Fairbanks.

APRD, Alaska and Polar Regions Department. Milotte Collection, Box 31. Elmer E. Rasmuson Library, University of Alaska Fairbanks.

Fox, John P. John P. Fox, S. J., Collection. n.d. the Alaska Mission Collection of the Oregon Province Archives of the Society of Jesus: Gonzaga University. Gale Cengage Learning, *Indigenous Peoples: North America*, online at tinyurl.galegroup.com/. Accessed February 7, 2017.

Hooper Bay Collection, Parts 1 and 2. n.d. MS, the Alaska Mission Collection of the Oregon Province Archives of the Society of Jesus: Gonzaga University. Gale Cengage Learning, *Indigenous Peoples: North America*, online at tinyurl.galegroup.com/. Accessed January 26, 2017.

National Museum of Natural History (NMNH). 1936. Unpublished correspondence of John P. Fox. Archived material. Smithsonian Institution National Museum of Natural History, Washington, DC.

National Museum of Natural History (NMNH). 1927. Unpublished correspondences of Philip Delon, S.J. Archived material. Smithsonian Institution, National Museum of Natural History, Washington, DC.

Other Sources

Abu-Lughod, Lila. 1993. *Writing Women's Worlds: Bedouin Stories*. Berkeley: University of California Press.

Active, John. 2000. "Elders' Help Sought to Locate Pavilla." *Tundra Drums* (Bethel, AK), February 3.

Alakanuk Community Planning Group, et al. 2009. *Qungasvik Toolbox: A Toolbox for Promoting Youth Sobriety and Reasons for Living in Yup'ik/Cup'ik Communities*. Fairbanks: University of Alaska Fairbanks, Center for Alaska Native Health Research.

Alaska Department of Commerce and Economic Development, Community and Regional Affairs. 2016 https://www.commerce.alaska.gov/dcra/DCRAExternal/Community/Details/931e232d-fbe2-4411-aa2b-0c2516e5af1b.

Alaska Department of Community and Economic Development. 2002. Alaska Community Database–Hooper Bay. Juneau: Division of Community Advocacy, Research and Analysis Section.

Alaska Department of Community and Regional Affairs. 1995. Community Profile: Hooper Bay. Juneau: Alaska Department of Community and Regional Affairs, Municipal and Regional Assistance Division.

Alaska Department of Health and Social Services, Statewide Suicide Prevention Council. 2016. Alaska Suicide Facts and Statistics. http://dhss.alaska.gov/SuicidePrevention/Pages/statistics.aspx. Accessed May 15, 2016.

Alaska Native Language Center. 2016. "Languages: Alutiiq/Sugpiaq." 2016. https://www.uaf.edu/anlc/languages/as/. Accessed May 7, 2016.

Arnold, Elizabeth. 2003. "Eskimos Seek Answers to Land Contamination: Yup'iks Suspect Health Woes Are Linked to Past Military Pollution." *All Things Considered*, National Public Radio, November 28.

Austin, Kenneth Frank (Te Sha Kee). 1999. "The Changing Vista of the Northern Northwest Coast Indian Deer Ritual." MA thesis, Department of Anthropology, University of Alaska Fairbanks.

Barber, Russell J., and Frances F. Berdan. 1998. *The Emperor's Mirror: Understanding Cultures through Primary Sources*. Tucson: University of Arizona Press.

Barker, James H. 1993. *Always Getting Ready—Upterrlainarluta: Yup'ik Eskimo Subsistence in Southwest Alaska*. Seattle: University of Washington Press.

Barker, Robin. 1994. "'A Right Mind to Think With': Yup'ik Theory of Human Development." MA thesis, School of Education, University of Alaska Fairbanks.

Bascom, William, ed. 1965. "The Forms of Folklore: Prose Narratives." *Journal of American Folklore* 78:3–20.

———. 1977. *Frontiers of Folklore*. Boulder, CO: Westview Press, for the American Association for the Advancement of Science, Washington, DC.

———. 1984. "The Forms of Folklore: Prose Narratives." In *Sacred Narrative: Readings in the Theory of Myth*, edited by Alan Dundes, 5–29. Berkeley: University of California Press.

Basso, Keith H. 1970. "'To Give Up on Words': Silence in Western Apache Culture." *Southwestern Journal of Anthropology* 26(3):213–30.

———. 1979. *Portraits of "The Whiteman": Linguistic Play and Cultural Symbols among the Western Apache*. Cambridge: Cambridge University Press.

——— 1986. "Stalking with Stories: Names, Places and Moral Narratives among the Western Apache." In *On Nature, Landscape and Natural History*, edited by Daniel Halpern, 95–116. San Francisco: North Point Press.

———. 1988. "'Speaking with Names': Language and Landscape among the Western Apache." *Cultural Anthropology* 3:99–130.

———. 1990. *Western Apache Language and Culture: Essays in Linguistic Anthropology*. Tucson: University of Arizona Press.

———. 1996. *Wisdom Sits in Places: Landscape and Language among the Western Apache*. Albuquerque: University of New Mexico Press.

Bauman, Richard. 1986. *Story, Performance, and Event: Contextual Studies of Oral Narrative*. Cambridge: Cambridge University Press.

Bauman, R., and J. Sherzer, eds. 1989. *Explorations in the Ethnography of Speaking*. New York: Cambridge University Press.

Behar, Ruth. 1993. *Translated Woman: Crossing the Border with Esperanza's Story*. Boston: Beacon Press.

Ben-Amos, Dan. 1972. "Towards a Definition of Folklore in Context." In *Towards New Perspectives in Folklore*, edited by Americo Paredes and Richard Bauman, 3–15. Austin: Publications of the American Folklore Society, University of Texas Press.

———, ed. 1976. *Folklore Genres*. Austin: University of Texas Press.

Ben-Amos, Dan, and Kenneth S. Goldstein, eds. 1975. *Folklore: Performance and Communication*. The Hague: Mouton Press.

Bender, Barbara, ed. 1993. *Landscape: Politics and Perspectives*. Oxford: Berg.

Bingham, Charles. 1996. "Archiving Project 'Repatriates' Photos for Hooper Bay." *Tundra Drums* (Bethel, AK), August 1.

Birket-Smith, Kaj. 1953. *The Chugach Eskimo*. Copenhagen: Nationalmuseets Skrifter, Etnografisk Raekke 6.

Bodenhorn, Barbara. 1989. "'The Animals Come to Me, They Know I Share': Inupiaq Kinship, Changing Economic Relations and Enduring World Views on Alaska's North Slope." PhD diss., Cambridge University.

———. 1993. "Gendered Spaces, Public Places: Public and Private Revisited on the North Slope of Alaska." In *Landscape: Politics and Perspectives*, edited by Barbara Bender, 169–203. Oxford: Berg.

Boraas, Alan S. 2002. "Native Life: One Hundred Centuries of Native Life on the Kenai Peninsula." In *Alaska's Kenai Peninsula: The Road We've Traveled*, edited by Diane Olthuis, 5–18. Hope, AK: Kenai Peninsula Historical Association.

Boraas, Alan S., and Donita Peter. 1996. "The True Believer among the Kenai Peninsula Dena'ina." In *Adventures Through Time: Readings in the Anthropology of Cook Inlet, Alaska*, edited by Nancy Yaw Davis and William E. Davis, 181–96. Anchorage, AK: Cook Inlet Historical Society.

Bourdieu, Pierre, and Hans Haacke. 1995. *Free Exchange*. Stanford, CA: Stanford University Press.

Briggs, Charles L. 1988. *Competence in Performance: The Creativity of Tradition in Mexicano Verbal Art*. Philadelphia: University of Pennsylvania Press.

Brightman, Robert. 1993. *Grateful Prey: Rock Cree Human-Animal Relationships*. Berkeley: University of California Press.

Brody, Hugh. 1982. *Maps and Dreams: Indians and the British Columbia Frontier*. New York: Pantheon Books.

———. 1987. *Living Arctic: Hunters of the Canadian North*. Seattle: University of Washington Press.

Burch, Ernest S., Jr. 1984. "The Central Yupik Eskimos: An Introduction." In *The Central Yupik Eskimos*, edited by Ernest Burch Jr. Supplementary issue of *Etudes/Inuit/Studies* 8:3–20.

———. 1988. *The Eskimos*. Norman: University of Oklahoma Press.

———. 1998. *The Inupiaq Eskimo Nations of Northwest Alaska*. Fairbanks: University of Alaska Press.

Carpenter, Edmund. 1973. *Eskimo Realities*. New York: Holt, Rinehart and Winston.

Carriker, Robert C., Jennifer Ann Boharski, Eleanor R. Carriker, and Clifford A. Carroll, S.J. 1980. *Guide to the Microfilm Edition of the Oregon Province Archives of the Society of Jesus Alaska Mission Collection*. Spokane, WA: Gonzaga University.

Centers for Disease Control and Prevention. 2004. "2003–04 U.S. Influenza Season Summary." Accessed February 7, 2016. http://www.cdc.gov/flu/weekly/weeklyarchives2003-2004/03-04summary.htm.

Clifford, James. 1986. "On Ethnographic Allegory." In *Writing Culture: The Poetics and Politics of Ethnography*, edited by James Clifford and George Marcus, 98–121. Berkeley: University of California Press.

———. 1988. *The Predicament of Culture: Twentieth-Century Ethnography, Literature, and Art*. Cambridge, MA: Harvard University Press.

Cohen, Anthony P. 1987. *Whalsay: Symbol, Segment and Boundary in a Shetland Island Community*. Manchester: Manchester University Press.

Comaroff, Jean. 1985. *Body of Power, Spirit of Resistance: The Culture and History of a South African People*. Chicago: University of Chicago Press.

Connerton, Paul. 1989. *How Societies Remember*. Cambridge: Cambridge University Press.

Cox, James L. 1991. *Studies in the History of Missions*. Vol. 4, *The Impact of Christian Missions on Indigenous Cultures: The 'Real People' and the Unreal Gospel*. Lewiston, NY: Edwin Mellen Press.

Cruikshank, Julie. 1990. *Life Lived Like a Story: Life Stories of Three Yukon Native Elders*. Lincoln: University of Nebraska Press.

———. 1991. *Reading Voices: Dan Dha Ts'edenintth'e: Oral and Written Interpretations of the Yukon Past*. Madeira Park, BC, Canada: Douglas and McIntyre.

———. 1995. "Pete's Song: Establishing Meanings through Story and Song." In *When Our Words Return: Writing, Hearing, and Remembering Oral Traditions of Alaska and the Yukon*, edited by Phyllis Morrow and William Schneider, 53–75. Logan: Utah State University Press.

———. 2005. *Do Glaciers Listen? Local Knowledge, Colonial Encounters, and Social Imagination*. Seattle: University of Washington Press.

Cusack-McVeigh, Holly. 1993. "Anishinaabe Prenatal Observances." MA thesis, Department of Anthropology, Michigan State University, East Lansing.

———. 2015. "The Eskimo of Our Imagination." The Intellectual Property Issues in Cultural Heritage (IPinCH) Appropriation (?) of the Month Blog, October 21. http://www.sfu.ca/ipinch/outputs/blog/appropriation-month-eskimo-our-imagination.

Damas, David, ed. 1984. *Handbook of North American Indians*. Vol. 5, *Arctic*. Washington, DC: Smithsonian Institution Press.

Darnell, Regna. 1974. "Correlates of Cree Narrative Performance." In *Explorations in the Ethnography of Speaking*, edited by Richard Bauman and Joel Scherzer, 315–36. Cambridge: Cambridge University Press.

Delta Discovery. 2014. "A Bigfoot Seen along the Hooper Bay Beach." *Delta Discovery* (Delta Junction, AK), July 23. http://www.deltadiscovery.com/story/2014/07/23/hairy-man/a-bigfoot-seen-along-the-hooper-bay-beach/2303.html.

DeMarban, Alex. 2008. "Historic Hooper Bay Church to Be Torn Down." *Juneau Empire*, August 3. http://juneauempire.com/stories/080308/sta_312976878.shtml#.VtCZz30rLtQ.

Denning-Barnes, Angela. 2001. "Unseen Concern: Military Gives Locals Tour of Polluted Site." *Tundra Drums* (Bethel, AK), October 4.

Dombrowski, Kirk. 2001. *Against Culture: Development, Politics, and Religion in Indian Alaska*. Lincoln: University of Nebraska Press.

Dresch, Paul. 1988. "Segmentation: Its Roots in Arabia and Its Flowering Elsewhere." *Cultural Anthropology* 3(1):50–67.

Drozda, Robert M. 1995. "'They Talked of the Land with Respect': Interethnic Communication in the Documentation of Historical Places and Cemetery Sites." In *When Our Words Return: Writing, Hearing, and Remembering Oral Traditions of Alaska and the Yukon*, edited by Phyllis Morrow and William Schneider, 99–122. Logan: Utah State University Press.

Feld, Steven, and Keith Basso, eds. 1996. *Senses of Place*. Santa Fe, NM: School of American Research Press.

Fienup-Riordan, Ann. 1990. *Eskimo Essays: Yup'ik Lives and How We See Them*. New Brunswick, NJ: Rutgers University Press.

———. 1991. *The Real People and the Children of Thunder: The Yup'ik Eskimo Encounter with Moravian Missionaries John and Edith Kilbuck*. Norman: University of Oklahoma Press.

———. 1994. *Boundaries and Passages: Rule and Ritual in Yup'ik Eskimo Tradition*. Norman: University of Oklahoma Press.

———. 1995. *Freeze Frame: Alaska Eskimos in the Movies*. Seattle: University of Washington Press.

———. 1996. *The Living Tradition of Yup'ik Masks Agayuliyararput: Our Way of Making Prayer*. Seattle: University of Washington Press.

———, ed. Forthcoming. *Qanemcit Amllertut: Many Stories to Tell*. Transcribed and translated by Alice Rearden with Marie Meade. Fairbanks: University of Alaska Press.

Finnegan, Ruth. 1970. *Oral Literature in Africa*. Oxford: Oxford University Press.

———. 1976. *Oral Literature in Africa*. 2d ed. Oxford: Oxford University Press.

———. 1992. *Oral Traditions and the Verbal Arts: A Guide to Research Practices*. London: Routledge.

Fitzhugh, William W., and Susan Kaplan. 1982. *Inua: Spirit World of the Bering Sea Eskimo*. Washington, DC: Smithsonian Institution Press.

Fortuine, Robert. 1992. *Chills and Fever: Health and Disease in the Early History of Alaska*. Fairbanks: University of Alaska Press.

Fox, John P. 1943. "Why That Bell?" Published manuscript. Marquette League. Archived material, Oregon Province Archives of the Society of Jesus Alaska Mission Collection (Frame 425). Gonzaga University, Spokane, WA.

Fox, William A. 1992. "Dragon Sideplates from York Factory: A New Twist on an Old Tail." *Manitoba Archaeological Journal* 2(2):21–35.

Gay, Joel. 2003. "Suicide Strikes Village." *Anchorage Daily News*, February 26, A1.

Gerjevic, Sandi. 2001. "Power of Place: Folklorists Bring Stories from Alaska and the Nation to Anchorage Conference." *Anchorage Daily News*, October 18, D1.

Giddens, Anthony. 1979. *Central Problems in Social Theory: Action, Structure and Contradiction in Social Analysis*. Berkeley: University of California Press.

———. 1984. *The Constitution of Society: Outline of a Theory of Structuration*. Berkeley: University of California Press.

Gillham, Charles E. 1955. *Medicine Men of Hooper Bay: More Tales from the Clapping Mountains of Alaska*. New York: Macmillan.

Goffmann, Erving. 1976. "Replies and Responses." *Language in Society* 5(3):257–313.

Gumperz, John J., and Dell Hymes, eds. 1972. *Directions in Sociolinguistics: The Ethnography of Communication*. New York: Basil Blackwell.

Halbwachs, Maurice. 1925. Les cadres sociaux de la mémoire. Paris: Presses universitaires de France.

Hallowell, Irving A. 1992. *The Ojibwa of Berens River, Manitoba*. Fort Worth, TX: Harcourt Brace Jovanovich College.

Hansen, Susan. 1985. "Yup'ik Eskimo Cultural History and Lore from the Lower Yukon River: Oral Traditions and Their Associations with the Land." Unpublished manuscript on file, Alaska Humanities Forum and the Oral History Project Office, Rasmuson Library, University of Alaska Fairbanks.

Hastrup, Kirsten. 1998. *A Place Apart: An Anthropological Study of the Icelandic World*. Oxford: Clarendon Press.

Hawkes, Ernest William. 1913. *The "Inviting-In" Feast of the Alaskan Eskimo*. Geological Survey Memoir 45, Anthropological Series 3. Ottawa, ON, Canada: Department of Mines, Government Printing Bureau.

Hensel, Chase. 1992. "Where It's Still Possible: Subsistence, Ethnicity and Identity in S.W. Alaska." PhD diss., Department of Anthropology, University of California–Berkeley.

———. 1996. *Telling Our Selves: Ethnicity and Discourse in Southwestern Alaska*. New York: Oxford University Press.

Herzfeld, Michael. 1991. *A Place in History: Social and Monumental Time in a Cretan Town*. Princeton, NJ: Princeton University Press.

Himmelheber, Hans. 1993. *Eskimo Artists (Fieldwork in Alaska, June 1936 until April 1937)*. Fairbanks: University of Alaska Press.

Hirsch, Eric, and Michael O'Hanlon. 1997. *The Anthropology of Landscape: Perspectives on Place and Space*. Oxford: Clarendon Press.

Hofmeyr, Isabel. 1993. *"We Spend Our Years as a Tale That Is Told": Oral Historical Narrative in a South African Chiefdom*. Portsmouth, NH: Heinemann Press.

Hymes, Dell. 1962. "The Ethnography of Speaking." In *Anthropology and Human Behavior*, edited by Thomas Gladwin and William C. Sturtevant, 15–53. Washington, DC: Anthropological Society of Washington.

———. 1971. "Competence and Performance in Linguistic Theory." In *Language Acquisition: Models and Methods*, edited by R. Huxley and E. Ingram, 3–24. New York: Academic Press.

Indian Reorganization Act, June 18, 1934 (Wheeler-Howard Act, 48 Stat. 984, 25 U.S.C. § 461 et seq).

Irwin, Ron. 2000a. "Bethel Man Dead of Exposure." *Tundra Drums* (Bethel, AK), January 6.

———. 2000b. "Troopers Suspend Search for Snowmachiner." *Tundra Drums* (Bethel, AK), January 20.

Ives, Edward D. 1988. *George Magoun and the Down East Game War: History, Folklore, and the Law*. Urbana: University of Illinois Press.

Jacobson, Steven A. 1984a. *Yup'ik Eskimo Dictionary*. Fairbanks: Alaska Native Language Center, University of Alaska Fairbanks.

———. 1984b. "Semantics and Morphology of Demonstratives in Central Yup'ik Eskimo." In *The Central Yupik Eskimos*, supplementary issue *Etudes/Inuit/Studies*, vol. 8, edited by Ernest S. Burch Jr. Quebec: University of Laval.

———. 1995. *A Practical Grammar of the Central Alaskan Yup'ik Eskimo Language*. Fairbanks: Alaska Native Language Center, University of Alaska Fairbanks.

Janzen, John M. 1978. *The Quest for Therapy: Medical Pluralism in Lower Zaire*. Berkeley: University of California Press.

Jernigan, Kevin, ed. 2014. "A Guide to the Ethnobotany of the Yukon-Kuskokwim Region." Accessed May 6, 2016. https://www.uaf.edu/anlc/resources/yk_ethnobotany/.

John, Paul. 2003. *Stories for Future Generations: The Oratory of Yup'ik Eskimo Elder Paul John*. Seattle: University of Washington Press.

Johnson, Leslie Main, and Eugene S. Hunn, eds. 2010. *Landscape Ethnoecology: Concepts of Biotic and Physical Space*. Oxford: Berghahn Books.

Jolles, Carol Zane. 1989. "Salvation on St. Lawrence Island: Protestant Conversion among the Sivuqaghhmiit." *Arctic Anthropology* 26(2):12–27.

———. 1994. "Cutting Meat, Sewing Skins, Telling Tales: Women's Stories in Gambell, Alaska." *Arctic Anthropology* 31(1):86–102.

———. 2002. *Faith, Food, and Family in a Yup'ik Whaling Community*. Seattle: University of Washington Press.

Kan, Sergei. 1985. "Russian Orthodox Brotherhoods among the Tlingit: Missionary Goals and Native Response." *Ethnohistory* 32(3):196–223.

———. 1987. "Native Cultures and Christianity in Northern North America." *Arctic Anthropology* 24:1–66.

———. 1991. "Shamanism and Christianity: Modern-Day Tlingit Elders Look at the Past." *Ethnohistory* 38(4):363–87.

Kamerling, Leonard, and Sarah Elder. 1989. *Uksuum Cauyai: The Drums of Winter*. Alaska Native Heritage Film Project. Fairbanks, Alaska.

Kawagley, Oscar. 1995. *A Yupiaq Worldview: A Pathway to Ecology and Spirit*. Prospect Heights, IL: Waveland Press.

Küchler, Susanne. 1993. "Landscape as Memory: The Mapping of Process and Its Representation in a Melanesian Society." In *Landscape: Politics and Perspectives*, edited by Barbara Bender, 85–106. Oxford: Berg.

Lantis, Margaret. 1946. "The Social Culture of the Nunivak Eskimo." *Transactions of the American Philosophical Society* N.S. 35(3). Philadelphia, PA.

———. 1947. *Alaskan Eskimo Ceremonialism*. Seattle: University of Washington Press.

———. 1960. *Eskimo Childhood and Interpersonal Relationships: Nunivak Biographies and Genealogies*. Seattle: University of Washington Press.

Lee, Molly C., ed. 1999. *Not Just A Pretty Face: Dolls and Human Figurines in Alaska Native Cultures*. Fairbanks: University of Alaska Museum of the North.

Lee, Nella. 2000. "Crime and Culture in Yup'ik Villages: An Exploration Study." *Criminology Studies* 10. Lewiston, NY: Edwin Mellen Press.

Levinson, Stephen A. 1983. *Pragmatics*. Cambridge: Cambridge University Press.

Llorente, Segundo. 1990. *Memoirs of a Yukon Priest*. Washington, DC: Georgetown University Press.

Lovejoy, Arthur O. 1964. *The Great Chain of Being: A Study of the History of an Idea*. Cambridge: Harvard University Press.

Lowenstein, Tom. 1992. *The Things That Were Said of Them: Shaman Stories and Oral Histories of the Tikigaq People*. Berkeley: University of California Press.

Malinowski, Bronislaw, and Robert Redfield. 1922. *Argonauts of the Western Pacific: An Account of Native Enterprise and Adventure in the Archipelagos*. New York: Dutton Press.

———. 1954. *Magic, Science and Religion*. Garden City, NY: Doubleday/Anchor Books.

Marcus, George E., and Michael M. J. Fisher. 1986. *Anthropology as Cultural Critique: An Experimental Moment in the Human Sciences*. Chicago: University of Chicago Press.

Marsh, Ken, ed. 1997. "Hold That Pose: Unknown Village Photos Turn Up." *Alaska Magazine*, March 63(2).

Mather, Elsie. 1985. *Cauyarnariuq: A Time for Drumming*. Anchorage: Alaska Humanities Forum, University of Washington Press.

———. 1995. "With a Vision beyond Our Immediate Needs: Oral Traditions in an Age of Literacy." In *When Our Words Return: Writing, Hearing, and Remembering Oral Traditions of Alaska and the Yukon*, edited by Phyllis Morrow and William Schneider, 13–26. Logan: Utah State University Press.

Meade, Marie. 1996. *Agayuliyararput—Our Way of Making Prayer: Yup'ik Masks and the Stories They Tell*. Seattle: University of Washington Press and the Anchorage Museum of History and Art.

Menager, Francis M., S.J. 1962. *The Kingdom of the Seal*. Chicago: Loyola University Press.

Michael, Henry N. 1967. *Lieutenant Zagoskin's Travels in Russian America 1842–1844: The First Ethnographic and Geographic Investigations in the Yukon and Kuskokwim Valleys of Alaska*. Toronto, ON, Canada: University of Toronto Press.

Miller, Doug, ed. 1982. *"Qigeckalleq Pellullermeng"—A Glimpse of the Past: A Collection of Short Stories by the Hooper Bay Upward Bound Students*. Fairbanks, AK: Spirit Mountain Press.

Montgomery, Robert Lynn. 1996. *Register to the Papers of Aleš Hrdlička: Finding Aids to the National Anthropological Archives*. Washington, DC: National Anthropological Archives.

Morrow, Phyllis. 1984. "It Is Time for Drumming: A Summary of Recent Research on Yupik Eskimo Ceremonialism." In *The Central Yupik Eskimos*, supplementary issue *Etudes/Inuit/Studies*, vol. 8, edited by Ernest S. Burch Jr. Quebec: University of Laval.

———. 1990. "Symbolic Actions, Indirect Expressions: Limits to Interpretation of Yupik Society." *Etudes/Inuit/Studies* 14(1–2):141–58.

———. 1991. "The One True Faith?: Certainty and Possibility in Yupik and Euroamerican Categorizations of Reality." Paper presented at the annual meeting for the Alaska Anthropological Association, Anchorage, March 22.

———. 1992. "What Drives the Birds? Molting Ducks, Freshman Essays, and Cultural Logic." In *The Naked Anthropologist: Tales from Around the World*, edited by Philip R. DeVita, 119–30. Belmont, CA: Wadsworth.

———. 1995. "On Shaky Ground: Folklore, Collaboration, and Problematic Outcomes." In *When Our Words Return: Writing, Hearing, and Remembering Oral Traditions of Alaska and the Yukon*, edited by Phyllis Morrow and William Schneider, 27–51. Logan: Utah State University Press.

———. 1996. "Yup'ik Eskimo Agents and American Legal Agencies: Perspectives on Compliance and Resistance." *Journal of Royal Anthropology Inst.* N.S. 2:405–23.

———. 2002. "A Woman's Vapor: Yup'ik Bodily Powers in Southwest Alaska." *Ethnology* 41(4):335–48.

Morrow, Phyllis, and Chase Hensel. 1992. "Hidden Dissension: Minority-Majority Relationships and the Use of Contested Terminology." *Arctic Anthropology* 29(1):38–53.

Morrow, Phyllis, and William Schneider, eds. 1995. *When Our Words Return: Writing, Hearing, and Remembering Oral Traditions of Alaska and the Yukon*. Logan: Utah State University Press.

Morrow, Phyllis, and Toby Alice Volkman. 1975. "The Loon with the Ivory Eyes: A Study in Symbolic Anthropology." *Journal of American Folklore* 88(348):143–50.

Moses, George, Sr. 1988. Taped interview transcript. Robert Drozda, interviewer; Vernon Chimegalrea, interpreter. Akiachak, Alaska. 23 August. Translated and transcribed by Lucy Coolidge Daniels, Irene Reed, and Sophie Manutuli Shield. Edited by Robert Drozda. Tape and transcript 88CAL160. U.S. Bureau of Indian Affairs, ANCSA Office, Anchorage and AHP CPSU and ANCSA Collection, University of Alaska, Rasmuson Library, Alaska and Polar Regions Department, Fairbanks.

Moses, John. 1977. Taped interview transcript. S. Fox, interviewer. Akiachak, Alaska. February 22. Tape and transcript 77CAL013. U.S. Bureau of Indian Affairs, ANCSA Office, Anchorage and AHP CPSU and ANCSA,

University of Alaska, Rasmuson Library, Alaska and Polar Regions Department, Fairbanks.
Mullins, Paul R. 2014. The Archaeology of Absence: Displacement, Effacement and Conflicted Heritage. Paper presented at the Wenner-Gren Workshop *Archaeologies of the Present: Critical Engagements with Post-Industrial Urban Transformations*, Detroit, Michigan. August.
Musqueam: A Living Culture. 2016. Musqueam. http://www.musqueam.bc.ca/. Accessed May 11, 2016.
Napoleon, Harold. 1991. *Yuuyaraq: The Way of the Human Being*. Fairbanks: Center for Cross-Cultural Studies, College of Rural Alaska, University of Alaska Fairbanks.
Narayan, Kirin. 1989. *Storytellers, Saints and Scoundrels: Folk Narrative in Hindu Religious Teaching*. Philadelphia: University of Pennsylvania Press.
Naske, Claus-M., and Herman E. Slotnick. 1994. *Alaska: A History of the 49th State*. Norman: University of Oklahoma Press.
Nelson, Edward W. 1983 [1899]. *The Eskimo about Bering Strait*. Washington, DC: Smithsonian Institution Press.
Nelson, Richard K. 1983. *Make Prayers to the Raven: A Koyukon View of the Northern Forest*. Chicago: University of Chicago Press.
O'Brien, Sharon. 1989. *American Indian Tribal Governments*. Norman: University of Oklahoma Press.
Odden, Mary. 1994. *Oral Tradition: Folklore and Oral History. A Course Book for the Center for Distance Education and Independent Learning*. Fairbanks: University of Alaska Fairbanks.
Olwig, Kenneth Robert. 1993. "Sexual Cosmology: Nation and Landscape at the Conceptual Interstices of Nature and Culture; or, What Does Landscape Really Mean?" In *Landscape: Politics and Perspectives*, edited by Barbara Bender, 307–43. Oxford: Berg.
Ong, Aihwa. 1987. *Spirits of Resistance and Capitalist Discipline: Factory Women in Malaysia*. Albany: State University of New York Press.
Orr, Eliza Cingarkaq, and Ben Orr, eds. 1995. *Qanemcikarluni Tekitnarqelartuq—One Must Arrive with a Story to Tell: Traditional Narratives by the Elders of Tununak, Alaska*. Fairbanks: Lower Kuskokwim School District and the Alaska Native Language Center.
Oswalt, Helen. 1951. "Ethnological Notes from Hooper Bay." Unpublished manuscript, Alaska and Polar Regions Department, University of Alaska Fairbanks.
Oswalt, Wendell H. 1952. "The Archaeology of Hooper Bay Village, Alaska." *Anthropological Papers of the University of Alaska* 1(1):47–91.
———. 1990. *Bashful No Longer: An Alaskan Eskimo Ethnohistory, 1778–1988*. Norman: University of Oklahoma Press.
Paredes, Americo, and Richard Bauman, eds. 1972. *Toward New Perspectives in Folklore*. Austin: University of Texas Press.

Partnow, Patricia. 1993. "Alutiiq Ethnicity." PhD diss., Department of Anthropology, University of Alaska Fairbanks.

———. 1995. "The Days of Yore: Alutiiq Mythical Time." In *When Our Words Return: Writing, Hearing, and Remembering Oral Traditions of Alaska and the Yukon*, edited by Phyllis Morrow and William Schneider, 139–83. Logan: Utah State University Press.

Philips, Susan U. 1972. "Participant Structures and Communicative Competence: Warm Springs Children in Community Classrooms." In *Functions of Language in the Classroom*, edited by Courtney B. Cazden, Vera P. John, and Dell Hymes, 370–93. New York: Teachers College Press.

———. 1974. "Warm Springs, 'Indian Time': How Regulation of Participation Affects the Progression of Events." In *Explorations in the Ethnography of Speaking*, edited by Richard Bauman and Joel Sherzer, 92–109. New York: Cambridge University Press.

———. 1983. *The Invisible Culture: Communication in Classroom and Community on the Warm Springs Indian Reservation*. New York: Longman Press.

Povinelli, Elizabeth A. 1993. *Labor's Lot: The Power, History, and Culture of Aboriginal Action*. Chicago: University of Chicago Press.

Pratt, Kenneth L. 1984. "Classification of Eskimo Groupings in the Yukon-Kuskokwim Region: A Critical Analysis." In *The Central Yupik Eskimos*, supplementary issue *Etudes/Inuit/Studies*, vol. 8, edited by E. S. Burch Jr. Quebec: University of Laval.

Pullar, Gordon L. 1992. "Ethnic Identity, Cultural Pride, and Generations of Baggage: A Personal Experience." *Arctic Anthropology* 29(2):182–91.

Ray, Dorothy Jean. 1975. *The Eskimos of Bering Strait, 1650–1898*. Seattle: University of Washington Press.

Renner, Louis L., S.J., and Patty Walter. 2003. "Our Lady of the Snows Parish, Hooper Bay, Alaska: 1928–2003." *Alaskan Shepherd* 41(5).

Ritchie, Donald A. 1995. *Doing Oral History*. New York: Twayne Publishers.

Rosaldo, Michelle Z. 1980. *Knowledge and Passion: Ilongot Notions of Self and Social Life*. Cambridge: Cambridge University Press.

Ross, Rupert. 1992. "Dancing with a Ghost: Exploring Indian Reality." *Canadian Journal of Native Studies* 12(2):343–49.

Sarris, Greg. 1991. "'The Woman Who Loved A Snake' and 'What People of Elem Saw': Orality in Mabel McKay's Stories." *American Indian Quarterly* Spring, 15(2):171.

———. 1993. *Keeping Slug Woman Alive: A Holistic Approach*. Berkeley: University of California Press.

———. 1994. *Mabel McKay: Weaving the Dream*. Berkeley: University of California Press.

Scheper-Hughes, Nancy. 1979. *Saints, Scholars, and Schizophrenics: Mental Illness in Rural Ireland*. Berkeley: University of California Press.

———. 1992. *Death without Weeping: The Violence of Everyday Life in Brazil.* Berkeley: University of California Press.

Schneider, William. 1992. "Writing Life Histories from the Field." *Journal of Narrative and Life History* 2(1):61–74.

———. 1995. "Lessons from Alaska Natives about Oral Tradition and Recordings." In *When Our Words Return: Writing, Hearing, and Remembering Oral Traditions of Alaska and the Yukon*, edited by Phyllis Morrow and William Schneider, 185–204. Logan: Utah State University Press.

———. 2002. *So They Understand . . . Cultural Issues in Oral History: Documentation, Representation, Preservation, and Interpretation Illustrated with Stories from South Africa, Alaska, and the Yukon*. Logan: Utah State University Press.

Scollon, Ronald, and Suzanne B. K. Scollon. 1979. *Linguistic Convergence: An Ethnography of Speaking at Fort Chipewyan, Alberta*. New York: Academic Press.

Seremetakis, Nadia C. 1991. *The Last Word: Women, Death, and Divination in Inner Mani*. Chicago: University of Chicago Press.

Sherzer, Joel. 1983. *Kuna Ways of Speaking: An Ethnographic Perspective.* Austin: University of Texas Press.

Shinkwin, Anne D., and Mary C. Pete. 1982. "Alaskan Villagers' Views on Problem Drinking: 'Those Who Forget.'" *Human Organization* 41(4):315–22.

Simon-Sakurai, Katrin Annemarie. 2013. "Never Alone: Narratives of Spirits in an Alaskan Yup'ik Community." MA thesis, Department of Anthropology, University of Alaska Fairbanks.

Soboleff, Walter. 1991. "Yuuyaraq: A Commentary." In *Yuuyaraq: The Way of the Human Being*, by Harold Napoleon. Fairbanks: Center for Cross-Cultural Studies, College of Rural Alaska, University of Alaska Fairbanks.

Soule, Susan. 1986. *Finding Our Way: Ideas and Programs for the Prevention of Suicide*. Bethel, AK: Yukon-Kuskokwim Health Corporation.

Stockburger, Mike. 2000. "Hooper Bay: Famous Basket Maker's Home." Unpublished manuscript, accreditation report: A Description of Hooper Bay Village and School.

Swann, Brian, ed. 1994. *Coming to Light: Contemporary Translations of the Native Literatures of North America*. New York: Random House.

Tedlock, Dennis. 1983. *The Spoken Word and the Work of Interpretation.* Philadelphia: University of Pennsylvania Press.

Tennant, Edward A., and Joseph N. Bitar. 1981. *Yuut Qanemciit Yup'ik Lore: Oral Traditions of an Eskimo People*. Bethel, AK: Lower Kuskokwim School District.

Thomas, Julian. 1993. "The Politics of Vision and the Archaeologies of Landscape." In *Landscape: Politics and Perspectives*, edited by Barbara Bender, 19–48. Oxford: Berg.

Thomas, Nicholas, and Caroline Humphrey. 1994. *Shamanism, History, and the State*. Ann Arbor: University of Michigan Press.

Thornton, Thomas F. 2008. *Being and Place among the Tlingit*. Seattle: University of Washington Press.

Tilley, Christopher. 1994. *A Phenomenology of Landscape: Places, Paths and Monuments*. Oxford: Berg.

Toelken, Barre. 1979. *The Dynamics of Folklore*. Boston: Houghton Mifflin.

———. 1995. "Fieldwork Enlightenment: Are We the Beneficiaries of Other People's Traditions?" *Parabola* 20(2):28.

———. 1998. "The Yellowman Tapes 1966–1997." *Journal of American Folklore* 111(442):381–92.

Tuan, Yi-Fu. 1980. *Landscapes of Fear*. Oxford: Basil Blackwell.

Vogel, Steve, and Fredrick Kunkle. 2002. "Day of Remembrance, Recommitment." *Washington Post*, September 12.

Wiget, Andrew, ed. 1994. *Dictionary of Native American Literature*. New York: Garland.

Williams, Jack U., Sr. 1986. Taped interview transcript. Robert Drozda and Miriam Stark, interviewers. Mekoryuk, Alaska. 2 July. Transcribed by Robert Drozda. Conducted in English.

Wolfe, Robert J. 1982. "Alaska's Great Sickness, 1900: An Epidemic of Measles and Influenza in a Virgin Soil Population." *Proceedings of the American Philosophical Society* 126(2).

Woodbury, Anthony C. 1987. "Meaningful Phonological Processes: A Consideration of Central Alaskan Yupik Eskimo Prosody." *Language* (December) 63(4):685–740.

———. 1992. *Cev'armiut Qanemciit Qulirait: Eskimo Narratives and Tales from Chevak, Alaska*. Fairbanks: Alaska Native Language Center, University of Alaska Press.

Wyatt, Victoria. 1987. "Alaskan Indian Wage Earners in the 19th Century." *Pacific Northwest Quarterly* 78(1–2):43–49.

Znamenski, Andrei A., ed. 2003. *Through Orthodox Eyes: Russian Missionary Narratives of Travels to the Dena'ina and Ahtna, 1850s–1930s*. Fairbanks: University of Alaska Press.

APPENDIX

Excerpt from an interview with George Moses Sr. about Qemirrluar, 1988

Vernon: Mm-hm. Taumi, tuani Qemirrluarmi, waten-wa pilaqait, iciw' irr'inarqellriamek-gguq-qaa tuani Qemirrluarmi qalamcirtangqertuq-qaa taum Qemirrluam tungiinun? Tuavet-gguq- qaa taukurmiut-gguq-qaa Qemirrluarmiullret irr'inarqellriamek tuani qaill' pillruut avani, wall'u-qaa qalamcimek wall' camek tua-i irr'inarqellria tuani pillermek.

Yes. At that Qemirrluar, you know, is there, they ask, what they call an unusual event there at Qemirrluar, is there a story concerning that Qemirrluar? [He asks if the former inhabitants of Qemirrluar did anything unusual in the past, or is there a story or anything unusual that happened there?]

George: Tua-i-w' irr- . . . nallukeka tua-i tauna irr'inarqellria, taugaam una uitallra, cali-llu kan'a iciw' waniw' keluani nanevpagtangqertuq.

I don't know about the unusual event part, but its site here, and that down there, has a huge lake above it.

Vernon: Mm-hm.

George: Una wani nanevpak tauna irr'inaqluni pitulliniuq. Yuk wani, iciw' qaillun ayuqaqan, ilii-llu wall' piarkaukun, tua-i- ll' tauna qeraquniu anuq'vangararulluku. Tauna tua-i pitulliniluni, keluani waniw' manuqliqluku nanevpak. Tua-i-ll' cali tauna Qemirrluar, tangellra tua-i, tangllemteni, anuq'vatuciqluni, iciw' quyiami.

This huge lake here acts in unusual ways, so I discovered. If a person, you know, is a certain way, or if something is to happen to his/her kin, then when he crosses that one, a fierce wind will come up on him. That's how that one would do, here above it, the huge lake, in its front. And then that Qemirrluar, when we see it, its appearance is that of a place of high winds, you know, because it's high.

George: Tua-i tauna tuaten ayuqelliniluni. Cali amna amatii kelulirnera tuaten pilriani anuq'vagluni cali, amta-ll' pikna qulvaq anuqetaunani. Tua-i taun' irr'inarqellria.

That, I discovered, is like that. Also, the part beyond it, the part behind it, will also be very windy just like down there; however, there will be no wind in the part way up above. That is an unusual occurrence.

Vernon: Mm-hm.

George: Tua tuaten ayuqelliniluni. Cali-llu tauna yuut waten tumyarauluni, tevyarauluni tua-i waten, tevyaraulun' nutem. Yugnun tamalkuitnun pavavet pitulrianun aturyugtainun, tevyarauluni nutem. Piuluni tua-i. Tua arulairluteng tev'tuluteng.

That's how it is, I discovered. That, also, the people, it's a trail, a portaging place, a portaging place from the beginning. It's a portaging place from the beginning for all people who need it to travel back there. So it is. Stopping there they would portage.

Vernon: Mm-hm.

George: Cali-ll' neqsullerviuluni. Neqet amlleqapiarluteng avatiini ayuqenrilnguut. Neqet tua-i amllerluteng. Unguvavikluku ellaita tauna, tuan' taukut ciuliamta, aanamta ataitgun. Unguvavikluku tauna cali.

It also is a former place for catching fish. There were plenty of different kinds of fish in its surrounding areas. Plenty of fish. It was their place of survival, those ancestors of ours, through our mothers' fathers. That one was also their place of survival.

Robert: In an instance like that where a storm or something would arise that would signify that something bad is going to happen, were there any rules for behavior, was there anything that they could do to um . . .

George: Mm-hm. <Yes.>

Vernon: Anuqengaruskani [anuqengararuskani] nallunriciiquq yuk tuquqatarniluni. Tamatum-gguq-qaa wangkuta-gguq-qaa qaill' piciryarangqellruukut tamana tuaten pillerkaa avitengnaqluku?

When a windstorm comes up, a person will know that he is going to die. Did we, he asks, have any ritual or way to try to keep that from happening?

George: Mm-hm. Tauna wani, waten ciuliamta taumun nani, pitulit amllertut, tamakut tuaten ayuqelriit. Qanruyucetangqerrluni taum tungiinun. Waten-llu cali, taum tungiinun ilavut pikan, nakmiin ilaput.

Yes. Now that one, this is how our ancestors . . . toward that anywhere, such things are many, those things that are like that. And there's a saying concerning that. And this, also, concerning this, should such a thing [i.e., windstorm] happen to one of our kin . . .

Vernon: Mm-hm.

George: . . . pikan, tua-i pissuusqumavkenata alingnarqellriamek, taum wani uitasngaitelliniakut, tuaten ayuqluta pissuqumta, pingnaqkumteggu taum alingnarqellriim uitasngaitelliniluta, caumakciqliniluta.

. . . if it happens to him/her, they discourage us from hunting fearsome animals, because that one would not leave us alone, if we hunt in that condition, if we try to get it, that fearsome animal would not leave us alone, not leaving us alone, it would confront us persistently.

Vernon: Mm-hm.

George: Tua-i tuaten ayuqellinian qanruyucetarluni, tauna nanvaq, qerararkauvkenaku tuaten ayuqelriim, avitengnaqerkauluku taugaam naugg'un tayim', wall'u nunakun, ilai, tungell- . . . ilai- w' tua-i qeraqataqata tevyarturluteng. Tauna wani maaggun nunakun, nanvamun ekenrilnge'rmi, tauna nunakuarluni avitengna- qerkauluku tamana ilani taukut pitekluki, tauna atuqataatgu. Cali-llu aug'ucetun tauna alingnarqellria pissuqataqatgu taukunun ilausngaunani, taukut-wa tua-i piqataatgu tauna neqkaseng alingnarqengraan. Taukunun ilauskuni taum caulineqciqngani, taukut taugaam tua-i allat pivkarluki, tua-i ellii avilluni. Tungelquni-llu ukut, ilangqerquni, avilluku tauna, pimallerkani, taukunun taum canun pivkarluku tua-i allanun taukunun. Taugaam alerquucetarluni cali qanruyutemtenek ciuliamtenek: Tauna-gguq alingnarqellria pistekarput piqataqumteggu, waniw' tua-i kiiqapiaramta, iciw', ilaunata allamek, nutaan ullagarkaugaput tauna alingnarqengraan piarkaullininggraakut-llu ilangqerqumta. Taugaam-gguq ilaunata kiiqapiaramta nutaan ullagarkauluku, tauna wani nutaan tuqutarkauluku cavkenata tua-i tuaten kiirramta. Tuaten alerquuterluni tamana.

So because it is so, there is a saying that a person in that condition is not to cross that lake, but is to try to avoid it by any means, that is, by land, if his/her kin are about to cross over in order to portage. If the family is going to portage by way of the lake that one is to try to avoid that for the sake of the family by not using the lake but to go by way of the land. And also, similar to what I mentioned, if they are about to hunt that fearsome animal, he is not to join them, because they are about to go after that food source of theirs even though it's fearsome. Because if he joins them, that fearsome one would not leave him alone, but letting others do it, thereby allowing himself to escape. And if he has siblings, if he has family, he allows the relatives to hunt for it and in that way avoid that what is supposed to happen to him. But there is a command, also a saying from our ancestors: If we are going to go after that fearsome animal, they say, the one that is to harm us, here all by ourselves, you know, with no other companion, then we are to go to that fearsome animal, even though he is to harm us when we have companions. But, they say, with no companion, all by ourselves, we are to then go to it, we are to kill it then without being harmed in that condition—all alone. That is the command for that.

Vernon: Mm.

George: Tauna-llu tayima ayuqaa. Nanvaq tauna anuqenga'artetuli pikuni, tauna wani atuqataquniu taum kiirrarmi, cali augucetun alingnarqellriacetun tauna aturyuuumanganaku ayuqucingqertuq. Tua-i kiirrarmi pillerkaani. Tuaten taun' augna umyuaqura'arqamku taringela'arqa augna alingnarqellria uitatesciigalucia tuaten ilalliqelria. Tua-i-ll' tamana cali kiimi piyugngallini- luku, kiiqapiarmi taugaam.

Aa, augna pitekluku cali angukara'urluum ciulirnem qanrutellruanga. Tangrraanga qukartuqerlua, nutaan waten qanertuq: maa-i-gguq yuut kassaurcaaqut—iciw' Qaneryaraq-llu iciw' augkunek picingssagnek pinrirluni. Iciw' waten elliurluku augarluki picingssiit augkut, anuqenga'artetulit-llu tamakut.

Picingssiit ukveqevkenaki. Tamakut waten piyaaqai. Waten piyaaqluki ava-i.

And that one must be similar to it. If one were to apply it to that lake that has wind storms, if that one were about to go through that one all alone, it appears that he can go through it, like the fearsome animal case that was mentioned. In the event that he is all alone. That's so. When I contemplate on what was mentioned about how it is impossible for him to ignore that fearsome animal [when he is alone] I get the understanding that he is also allowed to do that [cross the lake] by himself, but all alone.

More about what was just mentioned, that an old man, an elder, told me. He looked at me directly, then he said this: Nowadays, he said, the people [Yup'iks] have turned into white men—you know, the Bible also . . . you know, no longer dealing with the past superstitions. You know, by doing such and such, by doing away with past superstitions, including those things that have windstorms. Not believing the superstitions. It did thus with them. Thus, it did so to them.

Vernon: Mm-hm.

George: Qaneryaram. Taugaam angukara'urluum taum, ciulirnem, tang'errlua elluarrlua qanrutaanga waten: man'a-gguq ciuliamtenek ayagluku, ayagluni ak'aki avaken yaaqvaneg ayagluni piciryararkaq wangkutnun qanrutkumalria inerquusngalria-llu, tamana-gguq tuqunrituq, tuqungaituq-gguq watqapik, taugaam-gguq unguvaarkauguq, wangkutnun.

Arnaq-llu ava-i, apqemtenek eyagluni-gguq, tamakut qanrutkelallratnek. Eyanrilkuni-gguq ellminek piarkauluni apqucirkaminek tayima. Usgunri yuuluteng wall' usgunerminek... usgunri anluteng, iciw', assiirulluteng. Tuaten piarkauluni arnaq maligtaqutenrilnguq, iciw' eyallerkaminek tamakut picirya- raitnek. Tuaten-llu cali, tua-i angun- . . . arnaq arcaqerlun' qanrutkumalria tamatum tungiinun, eyallerkaa.

Tua-i-llu taum tua-i angukara'urluum qanrutellrani qanrutaanga tua-i tuaten: unguvaniluku tamana qanrutkumalria avaken yaaqvaneg ayaglun' ciuliamtenek, unguvaluni tuqungaunani-llu-gguq. Tuaten tua-i qanrullua.

The Word. But that old man, the elder, looking straight at me, said this to me: that this code of conduct which was told to us and that is forbidden, which started with our ancestors, which started in the distant past, it did not die, that it will not die whatsoever, but that it will be alive for us.

INDEX

Numbers in *italics* indicate photographs.